# THE Chinese Food Lover's GUIDE

# THE Chinese Food Lover's
## ·GUIDE·

GINGER CHANG AND STEPHEN NATHANSON

Random House
*Toronto*

TX
641
.C533
1987

Copyright©1988 by Ginger Chang and Stephen Nathanson

All rights reserved under International and Pan-American Copyright Conventions

Published in Canada in 1987 by Random House of Canada Limited.

Canadian Cataloguing in Publication Data

Chang, Ginger, 1949-
  The Chinese food lover's guide

ISBN 0-394-22003-X

1. Cookery, Chinese. 2. Gastronomy. 3. Chinese - Food. I. Nathanson, Stephen, 1948- . II. Title.

TX641.C44 1987     642'.5     C86-094597-9


DESIGN: Brant Cowie/Artplus Limited
COVER PHOTOGRAPH: Peter Paterson
Chinese characters typeset by Chip Yick Typesetting & Printing Co., Hong Kong

Printed in Canada by Gagné Printing

*To the unsung hero of the Chinese culinary world, the Chinese restaurant cook.*

# TABLE OF CONTENTS

**Chapter 1**
    **Introduction to Chinese Food**    1
        Food and Culture    1
        Chinese-American and
           Authentic Chinese Food    4

**Chapter 2**
    **Chinese Restaurant Cooking**    7
        Cooking Methods    9

**Chapter 3**
    **The Chinese Restaurant**    12
        Choosing a Chinese
           Restaurant    12
        Types of Restaurants    14
        Tipping    16
        Ordering    17
        Sample Orders for Complete
           Meals    19
        Eating Chinese Style    25
        Drinks    26

**Chapter 4**
    **How to Use the Book**    28
        Using the Regional Menus    29
        Using the Cantonese Dim
           Sum Menu    30
        A Note on Chinese
           Pronunciation    32

## Chapter 5

### A Canton Menu — 33

- Appetizers — 39
- Soups — 43
- Main Dishes
  - Bean Curds — 48
  - Beef — 50
  - Casseroles or Hot Pots — 55
  - Chicken — 59
  - Ducks and Other Birds — 70
  - Exotic Ingredients — 75
  - Fish — 81
  - Lamb — 85
  - Pork — 86
  - Shellfish — 91
  - Vegetables — 104
- Side Dishes — 106
  - Congee — 106
  - Fried Noodles — 108
  - Lo Mein or Tossed Noodles — 111
  - Noodles in Broth — 113
  - Rice Dishes — 115
  - Snacks or Miscellaneous Dishes — 119
  - Desserts — 121

## Chapter 6

### A Peking Menu — 124

- Appetizers — 127
- Soups — 134
- Main Dishes
  - Bean Curds — 135
  - Beef — 137
  - Chicken — 138

| | |
|---|---|
| Duck | 146 |
| Exotic Ingredients | 152 |
| Fish | 159 |
| Lamb | 166 |
| Pork | 172 |
| Shellfish | 180 |
| Vegetables | 186 |
| Snacks or Side Dishes | 191 |
| Desserts | 196 |

**Chapter 7**

| | |
|---|---|
| **A Shanghai Menu** | **200** |
| Appetizers | 203 |
| Soups | 209 |
| Main Dishes | |
|    Bean Curd | 213 |
|    Beef | 215 |
|    Casseroles | 216 |
|    Chicken and Eggs | 218 |
|    Duck and Quail | 223 |
|    Exotic Ingredients | 225 |
|    Fish | 227 |
|    Pork | 232 |
|    Shellfish | 238 |
|    Vegetables | 243 |
| Snacks or Side Dishes | 248 |
| Desserts | 257 |

**Chapter 8**

| | |
|---|---|
| **A Szechwan Menu** | **260** |
| Appetizers | 263 |
| Soups | 265 |
| Main Dishes | |
|    Bean Curds | 268 |

| | |
|---|---|
| Beef | 270 |
| Casseroles | 271 |
| Chicken and Eggs | 273 |
| Duck | 278 |
| Exotic Ingredients | 279 |
| Fish | 282 |
| Pork | 285 |
| Shellfish | 290 |
| Vegetables | 293 |
| Snacks or Side Dishes | 296 |
| Desserts | 298 |

**Chapter 9**

| | |
|---|---|
| **A Cantonese Dim Sum Menu** | **299** |
| Trolleys | |
| Steamer | 301 |
| Pan-Fried | 310 |
| Baked Dishes | 312 |
| Sautéed Dishes | 313 |
| Deep-Fried Dishes | 314 |
| Rice Casseroles | 317 |
| Stuffed Rice Rolls | 318 |
| Blanched Dishes | 319 |
| Stewed Dishes | 321 |
| Desserts | 323 |

**Glossary**    **330**

# CHAPTER ONE

# Introduction to Chinese Food

## FOOD AND CULTURE

Few cultures have been as food-oriented as the Chinese. To the Chinese, food is more than sustenance: for centuries, it has been used as a way to communicate. The Chinese speak to their ancestors through offerings of food. They use food to add solemnity to religious and folk rituals. Food is used to express feelings such as joy, grief and sadness. Intellectuals and poets write about fine food as seriously as fine art. The great scholar Ch'u Yuan, in the third century BC, talked himself out of suicide by thinking of the foods that made his life worth living:

> O Soul come back to joys beyond all telling! . . .
> Where pies are cooked of millet and bearded maize.
> Guests watch the steaming bowls
> And sniff the pungency of peppered herbs.
> The cunning cook adds slices of bird-flesh,

Pigeon and yellow-heron and black crane.
They taste the badger-stew.
O Soul come back to feed on foods you love!

The Chinese exaltation of food dates as far back as the Shang dynasty (eighteenth to twelfth century BC). The founder of the dynasty, King T'ang, made I Yin, a cook, his prime minister after sampling some of his dishes. Four thousand people worked in King T'ang's palace; more than half of them worked in the kitchen. There were a hundred chefs who cooked daily meals; another hundred made only banquets. There were twenty-four turtle and shellfish specialists, three hundred fish specialists, sixty-two game specialists and sixty-two pickle-and-salt specialists.

The fundamental character of Chinese cooking has remained unchanged in three thousand years. Confucius, a philosopher who lived in the Chou dynasty (twelfth to third century BC), described in his *Analects* the basic conditions of good cooking: "For him [a gentleman] the rice could never be white enough and minced meat could never be chopped fine enough. When it was not cooked right, he would not eat. When the food was not in season he would not eat. When the meat was not cut correctly, he would not eat. When the food was not served with its proper sauce, he would not eat." These basic conditions remain unchanged: rice must be washed, meat sliced, vegetables served in season, and ingredients and flavors blended to complement each other in taste, texture and shape.

Another Chou-dynasty concept that has survived is the duality of energy as expressed in the principles of yin and yang. The ancient Chinese believed that all food contained either yin (female or cold energy) or yang (male or hot energy). To be healthy, a person had to have a balance of both. Yin is present in all grains, shellfish, bean curd and green ingredients, such as mung beans and most vegetables. Yang is found in red meats, hot spices and some nuts, such as peanuts. Chinese people today may not be conscious of balancing yin and yang, but the concept remains entrenched in their recipes and eating customs. At a Chinese meal, for example, it is common to see rice, vegetables, bean curd and seafood served with nuts or red meat.

In feudal times, a Chinese gentleman was expected to display literary skills and a knowledge about food and wine. Food aesthetics became a serious pursuit in the Sung dynasty (960-1279 AD). Su Tung Po, a well-known Sung poet, wrote: "I would rather forgo meat than bamboo [shoots]. Without meat, one grows thin; without bamboo, one becomes vulgar. There is a cure for thinness but none for vulgarity." Li Liweng, a poet who lived in the seventeenth century, advocated the virtue of simple refinement, such as using fresh garden vegetables, unusual ingredients such as shark's fin and dried bird's saliva (or bird's nest). He frowned on pungent ingredients such as garlic and onions, and ate only the tips of chives, which were milder than the stalks. About rice, Li was particular in the extreme. Every morning at dawn, his wife was sent to collect dew drops from flower petals, which Li would sprinkle over his steamed rice at dinner. And not just any dew drops. He preferred those from wild roses and the flowers of cassia and citron trees. The dew drops from garden roses he dismissed as being too perfumy and common.

Many rites of passage are ritualized with food. During a woman's pregnancy, she is fortified with a sweet stew made of fatty pork, ginger, hard-boiled eggs and sweet dark vinegar. After the birth of a child, this stew and red-dyed hard-boiled eggs are given to friends as symbols of fertility. At the end of a wedding banquet, guests are served a sweet bland soup cooked with lotus seeds, because the words for "lotus seeds" (*leen tse*) sound the same as the words for "having many sons." After the wedding night, to proclaim that the groom found his wife a virgin, his family sends to the bride's family a whole roasted suckling pig to be distributed to friends. At a funeral or the anniversary of a death, family members offer plates of oranges, apples, roast pig and poached chicken at the grave or family altar. At funeral banquets as a gesture of mercy toward all living beings, the food served is usually vegetarian.

## CHINESE-AMERICAN AND AUTHENTIC CHINESE FOOD

Most non-Chinese people who live outside of Asia are probably more familiar with Chinese-American food than with authentic Chinese food. Chinese-American food is a collection of dishes invented by Chinese pioneers who went to North America to build the railroad in the mid-nineteenth century. These people were unskilled cooks, and their meager knowledge was undermined by the lack of Chinese ingredients and utensils. Egg rolls, chop suey and eggs *foo yung* are familiar examples of Chinese-American cooking. Chinese-American meat and seafood dishes are usually dipped in a batter, deep-fried and served with a syrupy sweet-and-sour sauce.

Chinese-American food bears scant resemblance to authentic Chinese cooking which, with its many regional styles, is one of the world's greatest and most wide-ranging cuisines. Because of the immense scope of the cuisine, many people, Chinese included, are at a loss when ordering food in a Chinese restaurant. They may not know what to order, or which dishes belong to which region. A good way to start learning about Chinese food is to become familiar with the best-known of the regional cuisines. The four most notable are the south (including Canton), Shanghai, Szechwan and Peking.

Cantonese food, one of China's most diverse cuisines, is characterized by fresh ingredients, light, transparent sauces and quick cooking methods, such as sautéeing and fast steaming. Blessed with a lush, subtropical climate, Canton (Kwangchow or Guangzhou) and the surrounding southern provinces provide a wide variety of vegetables and fruits year round. A variety of domestic animals are raised, and the long uninterrupted coastline ensures a steady supply of seafood. Cantonese cooking also includes some lesser-known cuisines, such as Hakka and Chiu Chow. Hakka cooks are known for their use of Chinese ginger powder; they make texturally interesting dishes, such as smooth bone marrow and crunchy beef balls. Chiu Chow food is similar to Cantonese though it is more pungent and full of bold spices: raw garlic, lemon grass, fresh or dried lemons, Szechwan peppercorns and Chiu Chow chili sauce.

Shanghai is between Canton and Peking, and was once the largest seaport in Asia. People brought the best ingredients and cooking ideas from all over China, so the food of Shanghai is eclectic. Shanghai and its neighboring provinces are rich in agriculture, and Shanghai cooks have a wide variety of vegetables, as well as seafood and domestic animals. Shanghai food is characterized by the generous use of dark and light soy sauces and by rock sugar, which is used to offset the saltiness of the soy. The food tends to be rich, slightly sweet in taste and dark brown in color.

Szechwan, in southwestern China, is surrounded by mountains. The Szechwanese season many of their dishes with strong spices such as hot chilies, ginger, garlic, star anise and tingling red peppercorns. Szechwan cooks also like to emphasize the textures of certain foods. They braise some meats until they are chewy but full of juicy flavors. To create a Szechwan-style crumbly texture, they steam meat and fish with long-grain rice that has been roasted and pulverized with spices.

The Chinese capital, Peking, is located in the north, and

has a temperate climate. The cuisine has been variously called Peking, Mandarin and northern. The northern Chinese have a simple hearty cuisine that is full-flavored and satisfying. Limited access to fresh greens and seafood has led the northerners to cook with a small repertoire of ingredients: garlic, leeks, Chinese cabbage, poultry and red meats such as pork and lamb. They eat noodles, bread and dumplings as staples instead of rice.

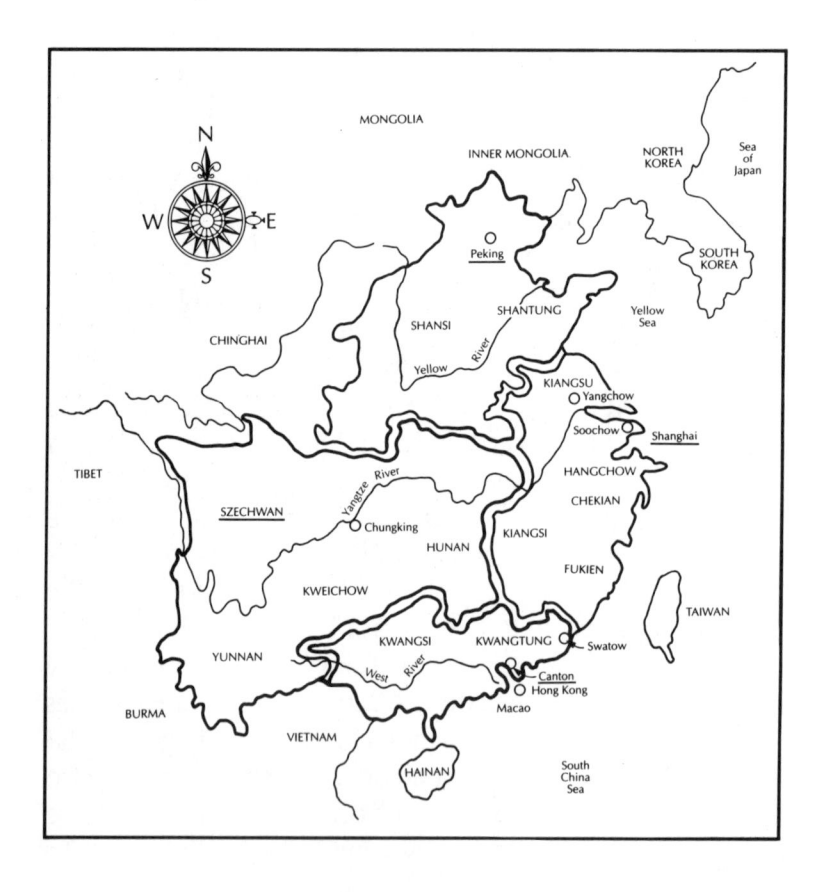

*Map of China*

# CHAPTER TWO

# Chinese Restaurant Cooking

A Chinese-restaurant kitchen needs superb teamwork and organization to produce good food. Because most Chinese food is sautéed, fried or steamed, it loses its taste and appearance quickly. Most dishes are prepared from scratch right before they are served. Chinese food also requires much more preparatory work than other cuisines. Before a dish is cooked, the ingredients must be assembled. Then they are cut, sliced or minced. The meat and seafood are marinated; various seasonings are combined for the sauce. Anyone who knows Chinese food will agree that it is labor-intensive and difficult to prepare. To be successful, a Chinese restaurant must have excellent equipment and a professional staff that works well together.

The person who pulls the kitchen together is the head cook, the indisputable boss of the kitchen. He is in charge of personnel, purchasing, menu planning and food traffic. And—unlike a European chef, who mainly supervises—the Chinese head cook spends most of his working hours cooking or "tossing" at a wok. The restaurant wok is four to five times the size of the domestic version and is fueled by powerful gas burners. To be a head cook, an individual must be strong enough to lift the wok and toss its contents.

He must be agile and alert as he is working with high temperatures, hot metals and hot oils. He must have split-second timing, and know when to turn the burners up or down and when to add ingredients that require different cooking times. He must be creative with new ingredients or cooking trends. And he must be unflappable.

Next to the head cook is the assistant cook. He works at the wok but usually makes less complicated dishes. At busy times, however, the assistant cook works close to the head cook, often making the same dishes. He also prepares certain specialties, such as poached or barbecued meats, and takes over when the head cook is not around.

Next in rank is the cutter-assembler, who must know a great deal about Chinese dishes and ingredients. All orders come into the kitchen through him. He sets the pace for the head cook by assembling ingredients for the next dish that has to be made. The cutter-assembler also puts together cold appetizers, which require no cooking, and he makes garnishes during his spare time.

The jack of all trades in the kitchen is the kitchen assistant. In a large restaurant, there may be half a dozen of them. These people clean and scale fish, open oysters and crabs, slice meat and vegetables, marinate meat, operate fryers and steamers and mix ingredients for dips and sauces.

At the bottom of the hierarchy is the washer. The washer cleans everything in the kitchen—vegetables, dishes, appliances, floors, walls—and does whatever odd jobs come along.

On a busy night in a Chinese restaurant, the kitchen is like a garrison under seige. But seldom do things get out of control. The authority of the head cook is unquestioned—everyone pitches in, and even the restaurant owner stays out of the kitchen. The people who work in Chinese restaurant kitchens are a special breed. Dedicated, hard-working and often underpaid, they are truly the unsung heroes of the culinary world.

# COOKING METHODS

Some cooking methods are universal; some are unique to Chinese cooking.

*Marinating*: Marinating is an essential step in Chinese cooking. The Chinese believe that marinating tenderizes the ingredients and ensures that the seasonings are well distributed. Meats such as beef or pork are cut first, then marinated in soy sauce, vegetable oil, eggs, wine and cornstarch. Seafood is usually marinated in a lightly flavored marinade with salt and pepper. Unless otherwise specified, monosodium glutamate is always added to marinades.

*Sautéing*: Sometimes called stir-frying, this method involves tossing food with a bit of vegetable oil in a hot wok. Usually safflower oil (sometimes called rapeseed oil) is used, although some restaurants use peanut oil, which has more flavor. Sautéing requires a great deal of skill. If a hot wok is tossed the wrong way, the food can easily fall apart or become charred at the edges.

*Dry-sautéing*: Food is fried first, drained, then tossed in a hot, dry wok with salt, pepper and sometimes minced hot peppers.

*Frying*: Shallow-frying requires half a wok of oil; deep-frying requires three-quarters. Food that is going to be fried is usually marinated first, then dredged in flour or coated with a batter.

*Braising*: Ingredients are sautéed or fried first. Then a liquid, usually broth, is added, and the food is cooked, bubbling, over medium or low heat. Some dishes are braised in an open wok; others are braised covered.

*Steaming*: Food is elevated above boiling water and cooked

by hot steam for a short time (seafood such as rock cod) or for a long time (meats and poultry).

*Stewing*: Meat is fried or parboiled first; sautéed with seasonings such as brown bean sauce, garlic, ginger and wine; then cooked in liquid in a pot over low heat until it is tender. Red-cooking is a stewing method used in Shanghai. Meat is cooked tender over low heat with soy sauce, rock sugar and water.

*Pan-frying*: Ingredients are fried on one side, then the other in a wok or on a flat grill with a bit of oil over medium-high heat until they are browned on both sides. No sautéing is involved in this method.

*Barbecuing*: Poultry or meats are rubbed with seasonings, basted, skewered or hung on hooks and roasted in barrel-sized ovens. In Cantonese cooking, some poultry, usually goose or duck, is skewered and trussed whole and barbecued the traditional way—rotated by hand over an open coal fire. This time-consuming method, however, is quickly disappearing.

*Poaching*: Meat or seafood is gently cooked in hot water or seasoned liquid (a master sauce or marinade) over medium-low heat.

*Smoking*: Ingredients are steamed or fried first, then placed on an oiled rack over wood chips or tea leaves in a wok. The wok is then heated and the ingredients are smoked for ten to twenty minutes.

*Casserole Cooking*: Sometimes called hot-pot cooking, this method uses a Chinese casserole, made of clay or carbon steel, which can be heated on the stove top. Meat or fish is sautéed or stewed first, then poured into the casserole and cooked, covered, over high heat until it bubbles. The casserole is carried to the table where the waiter removes the lid.

*Cold-mixing*: Ingredients are parboiled or salted first, drained, then tossed with a dressing of sesame oil, salt, pepper and sugar. Cold-mixed dishes are served chilled or at room temperature.

*Pickling with wine:* The Shanghainese "cook" raw seafood by pickling it in coarse salt and wine, a technique similar to that used to make ceviche, a South American seafood dish.

*Pickling:* Vegetables such as Chinese cabbage or radish are pickled with salt and vinegar and sugar, and served chilled, usually as appetizers.

# CHAPTER THREE

# The Chinese Restaurant

## CHOOSING A CHINESE RESTAURANT

What do you look for when you choose a Chinese restaurant? The signs of quality are a little different from those of a Western restaurant. Polished service, a good wine list, a special ambience are not what you should look for in your quest for good Chinese food, because these things are not on the list of priorities of most Chinese restaurateurs. They value the best cooks, the freshest ingredients and special equipment for wok cooking. Most Chinese restaurants are humbly decorated: Arborite tables, folding metal chairs and fluorescent lights are standard features. (A few exquisitely decorated Chinese restaurants with superb food and service do exist, particularly in Asia.) When evaluating Chinese restaurants, start with the menu.

The menu can give you many clues to food quality. If you see mostly chop suey, eggs *foo yung*, sweet-and-sour dishes and combination plates, to order anything more unusual may be asking too much of the cook. Avoid restaurants that claim to serve all four regional cuisines; no cook is that capable. On the other hand, in many cities, Peking, Shanghai and Szechwan cuisines are grouped together in one restaurant where a limited selection of each cuisine is served. This is not a bad sign. But Cantonese cuisine, because of its wide-ranging menu, should stand on its own and not be combined with other cuisines. As well, avoid restaurants that advertise "Chinese Canadian" or "Chinese American" food. It is never promising to find hamburgers and omelets on a menu with chow mein and beef and broccoli.

Next, look at the plates of food emerging from the kitchen. The food should be attractively arranged, not heaped on the plate. The portions should be neither skimpy nor overflowing, but generous. Ingredients in the dishes should be uniform in size, whether minced, shredded or diced. They should appear to complement each other in taste, texture and color; they should not be burned or charred at the edges. Sauces should look light and smooth, not gluey, curdled or runny. Except for cold salads or appetizers, Chinese food should be served piping hot, and should smell good. An expert cook tossing food in a well-heated wok creates this aroma, called *wok hay*.

Although service is not a major factor in gauging food quality in a Chinese restaurant, it should be taken into account. Friendly, smiling service is not usually a characteristic of Chinese restaurants, but the waiter should be able to explain the dishes, advise you on what is fresh and good, and serve the dishes in a logical sequence (appetizers and soup, then main dishes with rice).

Hygiene is important, and reflects the overall attitude of the restaurateur. The restaurant does not have to be fancy, but it must be clean. Take a few deep breaths and glance around. If the restaurant smells or looks dirty, you should leave.

There are other valuable indicators of quality: for example live fish swimming in tanks in restaurants that claim to specialize in fresh seafood. Though it is a well-worn observation, seeing Chinese patrons eating in the restaurant is also a good indicator, simply because most Chinese know where to get good Chinese food. It is not encouraging to come upon a restaurant that sets its tables only with knives and forks. This suggests that the restaurateur is not expecting anyone who can handle chopsticks to eat in the restaurant.

## TYPES OF RESTAURANTS

The most common type of Chinese restaurant belongs to a category we call the "dinner restaurant." The dinner restaurant specializes in multicourse meals, which may include a soup, several main dishes, a staple or two, side dishes and perhaps a dessert. These restaurants tend to be large; some have liquor licenses, and they pay some attention to decor and service. There are dinner restaurants specializing in all the major regional cuisines. In some cities, dinner restaurants specialize in lesser-known regional cuisines such as Hakka, Chiu Chow (or Swatow) and Hunan, which is similar to Szechwan. In large cities, dinner restaurants tend to do a brisk business, particularly on weekends. For this reason, you should always call ahead to reserve a table.

The dim sum restaurant exists only in the daytime; in the evening it usually becomes a dinner restaurant. A dim sum restaurant may be open from as early as 7:30 AM to as late as 2:30 PM and no reservations are taken. *Dim sum*, literally translated, means "to touch the heart," but the phrase refers to a dainty appetizer or snack. Dim sum snacks vary from region to culinary region in taste and appearance. A dim sum item from Peking, for example, may be a hefty wedge of green-onion cake, while a typical Cantonese item is a delicate shrimp dumpling. Most people know dim sum in its Cantonese form; outside Asia, it is certainly the most popular. Some Asian cities also have restaurants that serve Peking and Shanghai dim sum, though the menus are not as varied. The Cantonese have what seems like an inexhaustible variety of dim sum. In dim sum restaurants, most of the items are displayed on trolleys pushed by waitresses who holler out the dish names in Cantonese. To order, all you have to do is point. Some dishes can be ordered through the waiter; they include "one-dish meals" such as fried noodles, noodles in soup or plates of rice with toppings.

For those who want to eat Chinese food on the run, Cantonese fast-food won ton houses are ideal. They have low prices, spare decor, and brusque but speedy service; on a busy day you are expected to share your table and leave as soon as you have finished your meal. These restaurants specialize in simple one-dish meals, such as plates or bowls of noodles or steamed rice served with a variety of toppings, such as stewed beef brisket, barbecued meat or sautéed meat and vegetables. One-dish meals are often prepared by cooks working at the front windows of the won ton house. In one window there may be a barbecue cook in charge of basting and cutting barbecued meats. In another window, there may be a *congee* (rice porridge) cook ladling porridge for the breakfast patrons; in still another, a noodle cook may be busy cooking bundles of noodles, ladling soups and stews, and blanching vegetables. In some won ton houses, you can also order main dishes, which are prepared in a kitchen in the back; with these you can have bowls of rice on the side.

A smaller, humbler version of the dinner restaurant is the

family-style restaurant sometimes known in Cantonese as *siu sic* or small eats. It usually offers home-cooked multi-course Chinese meals which are simpler and less expensive than those served in a dinner restaurant. In cities where a great variety of Chinese restaurants exists, you might find different specialty restaurants: for example, Chinese Moslem food, in which no pork is used; Mongolian hot pot, in which lamb is the main feature; or vegetarian food, in which bean curds, processed gluten and vegetables are the primary ingredients.

## TIPPING

Tipping practices in Chinese restaurants vary from country to country, but a few general principles apply. The percentage of gratuity is based on the total price of food; alcohol is not included in the calculation. In some Asian cities, for example Hong Kong, a ten-percent service charge is often tacked on to your bill, particularly in dinner restaurants. If this has been done, you may add a small additional tip to round out the total on the bill. Here are recommended tips:

| | |
|---|---|
| dinner restaurant: | 10 – 15% |
| dim sum restaurant: | 8 – 10% |
| fast-food won ton house: | 8 – 10% |
| family-style restaurant or "small eats": | 8 – 12% |
| specialty restaurants: | 8 – 15% |

# ORDERING

## In a Dinner Restaurant

How much food to order depends on how many there are in your party and how hungry you are. For a group with average appetites, calculate one main dish per person, then add a soup and perhaps also an appetizer. For large parties (more than eight people), the rules are a little different. You may want to reduce the total number of main dishes by one or two and double the portions of some dishes so that there is enough of each dish to go around.

Chinese soups are usually made with a chicken or pork-based broth. The broth is cooked and served with shredded meat and vegetables or thickened with cornstarch and made into a thick soup. Both types of soup are good as starters; thick soups such as Hot and Sour Soup are more filling and ideal for cold, wintry nights.

Chinese appetizers are served hot or cold. Hot appetizers, usually of Cantonese origin, include scallops, clams or oysters steamed in the shell and served with a sauce. Cold appetizers, called cold plates, frequently include more than one item. In most of the regional menus, you can select one, two or more items from the "Appetizers" category and have them put on a combination cold plate. For example, the Shanghai appetizers—Sautéed Shrimp, Saucy Duck and Drunken Chicken—can be ordered together on a combination cold plate, or they can be ordered separately. Some excellent one-item appetizers in the Peking menu include Shredded Chicken and Tientsin Bean Sheet Salad, and Five Spices Beef. Smoked Fish and Cucumber Salad are well-known

Shanghai starters and a spicy and delicious Szechwan appetizer is Bong Bong Chicken.

With main dishes, try to order a variety of meat, poultry and seafood dishes (seafood is usually best in a Cantonese restaurant). For variation, select main dishes with different cooking methods—sautéed, steamed, braised, fried, poached, roasted or cooked in a casserole.

With a complete meal, order a traditional staple. With Cantonese food, it is invariably steamed rice. The delicate nature of Cantonese food calls for the lightness that steamed rice provides. It can be ordered individually by the bowl or communally in a large container. With the cuisines of Shanghai, Peking and Szechwan, you can order steamed rice or northern staples such as steamed bread, noodles and pancakes, which provide a robust balance for dishes that are heavily seasoned. Chow mein and fried rice, eaten as one-dish meals for lunch or served at the end of elaborate banquets, are not ordinarily ordered as staples at regular meals.

In a Chinese meal, desserts are seldom given as much importance as the main dishes. Unless it is a special occasion, Chinese people do not usually eat dessert. Because they lack dairy products, Chinese cooks have invented sweet and often unusually textured desserts. These desserts are not always appealing to the Western palate. There are some exceptions, however, and they can often be found in Peking restaurants, for example Apple or Banana Fritters or Red Bean Fried Crepe. If you are not too keen on Chinese desserts, you can always ask your waiter to put together a fresh-fruit platter. (This may be available only in better restaurants.)

Here are some sample menus for complete meals for groups of two, four, five, six and eight people.

# SAMPLE ORDERS FOR COMPLETE MEALS

*For 2 People*

Saucy Duck and Smoked Fish Appetizers
(#10 and #17 Shanghai Menu)
Twice Cooked Pork (#93 Szechwan Menu)
Fried Chicken with
Sweet-Vinegar Sauce (#40 Szechwan Menu)
Silver Thread Bread (#334 Peking Menu)

*For 2 People*

Diced Winter Melon Soup (#21 Canton Menu)
Oyster Beef (#61 Canton Menu)
Singing Chicken Casserole (#90 Canton Menu)
Sautéed Chinese Greens (#343 Canton Menu)
Steamed Rice

*For 4 People*

Steamed Oysters Appetizer (#16 Canton Menu)
Fried Crispy Chicken
(a half portion) (#114 Canton Menu)
Steamed Fish Steaks (#217 Canton Menu)
Beef with Ginger and
Onions Casserole (#88 Canton Menu)
Buddha's Feast (#348 Canton Menu)
Steamed Rice

*For 4 People*

| | |
|---|---|
| Bong Bong Chicken Appetizer | (#1 Szechwan Menu) |
| Fragrant Crispy Duck (a half portion) | (#61 Szechwan Menu) |
| Fish-Fragrant Pork | (#92 Szechwan Menu) |
| Sautéed Shrimp | (#181 Shanghai Menu) |
| Vegetarian Ten Mix | (#206 Shanghai Menu) |
| Steamed Rice or Flower Bread | (#335 Peking Menu) |

*For 5 People (A Chiu Chow Sample Menu)*

| | |
|---|---|
| Fried Shrimp Balls and Crab Balls Combination Appetizer | (#18 and #19 Canton Menu) |
| Lemon Duck Soup | (#41 Canton Menu) |
| Beef in *Sar Char* or Satay Sauce | (#70 Canton Menu) |
| Szechwan Peppercorn Chicken or Chicken with *Chin Jew* | (#129 Canton Menu) |
| Stuffed Cabbage Rolls | (#153 Canton Menu) |
| Smoked Pomfret | (#231 Canton Menu) |
| Steamed Rice | |

*For 5 People (A Hakka Sample Menu)*

| | |
|---|---|
| Stuffed Bean Curd Casserole | (#91 Canton Menu) |
| Beef Balls Sautéed with Chinese Vegetables | (#81 Canton Menu) |
| Salt Baked Chicken | (#118 Canton Menu) |
| *Mui Choy* or Preserved Salty Vegetables and Pork | (#255 Canton Menu) |

Sautéed Snow Pea Shoots  (#351 Canton Menu)
Beef Bone Marrow
with Three Ingredients  (#84 Canton Menu)
Steamed Rice

*For 6 People*

Shredded Pork and
Snow Cabbage Soup  (#33 Shanghai Menu)
Shrimp over Sizzling Rice  (#118 Szechwan Menu)
Smoked Chicken in Sauce  (#57 Peking Menu)
Wine Residue Braised Fish  (#156 Peking Menu)
Teppan Lamb  (#210 Peking Menu)
Minced Pork with
Preserved Kohlrabi  (#225 Peking Menu)
Peking *Shaobing*
(double portion)  (#333 Peking Menu)
Sautéed *Bok Choy* or
*Tarp Qwar Choy*  (#201 and #220 Shanghai Menu)
Dipped Glutinous Rice
Dumplings  (#278 Shanghai Menu)

*For 6 People*

White Chicken, Poached Pork
Hock and Poached
Octopus Appetizers  (#110, #4 and #8 Canton Menu)
Beef Lettuce Wraps
(double portion)  (#73 Canton Menu)
Peppery Salt Shrimp  (#270 Canton Menu)
Bean Curds with
Assorted Meats  (#53 Canton Menu)
Prawns with *Gai Lan*  (#269 Canton Menu)
Deep-Fried Duck with Taro
Root (a half portion)  (#170 Canton Menu)

Steamed Rice
Fruit Platter (#433 Canton Menu)

*For 8 People*

Eggs and Beef Thick Soup (#29 Canton Menu)
Chicken in a Bird's Nest (#122 Canton Menu)
Crab in White
Sauce (large) (#296 Canton Menu)
Shredded Pork,
Beansprouts and
Black Mushrooms (#252 Canton Menu)
Barbecued Duck (#167 Canton Menu)
Fish Steamed
with Black Beans (#229 Canton Menu)
Teppan Beef Slices
(double portion) (#78 Canton Menu)
Steamed Rice
Almond Jelly (#436 Canton Menu)

*For 8 People*

Shredded Chicken
and Tientsin Bean
Sheets Salad (#20 Peking Menu)
Braised Duck with Leeks (#96 Peking Menu)
Szechwan Peppercorn
Chicken (double portion) (#45 Szechwan Menu)
*Mooshu Roo* with
Mandarin Pancakes
(double portion) (#223 Peking Menu)
Chungking Beef
(double portion) (#32 Szechwan Menu)

Fish-Fragrant Fish Slices    (#88 Szechwan Menu)
*Ma Po* Tofu                 (#24 Szechwan Menu)
Red Bean Fried Crepe         (#346 Peking Menu)

## In A Dim Sum Restaurant

Cantonese dim sum is a complicated cuisine to order for a first-time patron. The selection seems never-ending, the restaurant is noisy and crowded, and the dim sum waitresses may not speak English. If it's your first time, we suggest that you go with someone who has been to dim sum before.

We recommend that you choose dim sum snacks that are steamed (shrimp dumplings, stuffed rice rolls, chicken and black mushrooms over rice) or poached (blanched *choy sum*) rather than deep-fried dishes (spring rolls, taro-root dumplings, shrimp toasts). Deep-fried dishes tend to be greasy and may lead to indigestion. Aside from a few exotic items—chicken feet, duck-feet bundles, coagulated chicken or pig's blood, stewed tripe and organ meats—most dim sum dishes are made with conventional ingredients and are quite delicious. Dumplings and rolls are usually stuffed with a mixture of ground shrimp and pork or beef, or with a variety of minced vegetables such as bamboo shoots and black mushrooms.

If you get hungry while waiting for the dim sum trolleys to come around, order a fried noodle dish, such as Shredded Chicken Chow Mein, or try Fried Rice Noodles with Beef.

Sweets can be eaten throughout a dim sum lunch, to clean your palate and to counterbalance the savory items. Because dim sum is rich and sometimes oily, hot tea is the ideal beverage to drink. For more information on ordering dim sum, read "Using the Cantonese Dim Sum Menu" in Chapter 4, and Chapter 9, *A Cantonese Dim Sum Menu*.

## In a Fast-Food Won Ton House

One-dish meals are the specialty of the fast-food won ton house. One-dish meals are plates or bowls of rice or noodles with various toppings. You can order them by the bowl or plate (the plate is larger). By the bowl you get rice topped with barbecued or poached meats, for example barbecued pork or duck or white poached chicken. The plate comes with a greater variety of toppings: barbecued meat, stewed beef brisket, or sautéed meat and vegetables.

You can also order a one-dish meal of noodles. There are three categories to choose from: chow mein noodles, won ton noodles or rice noodles.

Chow mein noodles are thin egg noodles which are fried until crispy, then topped with sautéed meat or seafood with vegetables.

Won ton noodles are firm and chewy and come in two sizes, thin (like vermicelli) and thick (like fettucine). They are boiled and served in a bowl of broth with won tons, shrimp dumplings, beef stew or barbecued meats; or they are boiled, drained and served on a plate with various toppings, such as ginger and green onions, stewed beef brisket or barbecued meats, and called *lo mein*. With *lo mein* a bowl of broth is served on the side.

Rice noodles (or *fun*) are available in three sizes: vermicelli-size, spaghetti-size and fettucine-size. These noodles tend to be softer and more slippery than the won ton noodles. They also have a strong rice flavor. Rice noodles are served in broth with toppings or sautéed with sliced meat and vegetables and made into fried rice noodles, called *chow fun*.

A light one-dish meal is *congee* (*joke*), a smooth savory rice porridge. It is served plain or with shredded meat or seafood. Tasty and nutritious, *congee* is a favorite breakfast and late-night item with the Chinese.

Ordering at a won ton house is easy: select a one-dish meal and some extra plates of sautéed or blanched vegetables (*gai lan* or *choy sum*), chow mein, barbecued meat combinations or, if you want something hot and soothing, a bowl of plain *congee*.

## EATING CHINESE STYLE

On a traditional Chinese table, at each place setting, you will find a rice bowl, a small serving plate, a small sauce plate, a spoon and pair of chopsticks.

The Chinese observe fewer rules of eating etiquette than Westerners. For example, it is not considered rude to slurp when drinking soup or to talk and eat at the same time. But, as the Chinese have a communal style of eating, they do observe some rules to facilitate the process.

Most dishes are served communally in the middle of the table; reach over and help yourself. It is considered poor form to pile large amounts of food on your plate. You should take and eat small portions, a bit at a time. Take food from the communal dish and place it on your small serving plate or, better still, in your rice bowl. To eat rice, combine it with some food with chopsticks, bring the bowl close to your mouth and shovel the mixture in with chopsticks.

When selecting food to put in your bowl, there are some clear rules to follow. Once your chopsticks touch a piece of food, you are obliged to take it. If you don't care for it, take it anyway and leave it on your small serving plate. Leave anything you don't want, such as skin or bones, on your serving plate, not on the communal dish. Never rummage through a communal dish. Look carefully and make a mental choice before reaching for a piece of food. If a serving spoon or fork is available, use it.

Use chopsticks to shovel rice into your mouth and also to carry or cut food. If you want to serve food from the communal dish to the other diners and no serving spoon is available, you can turn your chopsticks around and use the other end. Then wipe them clean, turn them around and resume eating. Do not use your chopsticks as drumsticks or toothpicks. Spoons are used for drinking soup and also to transport food from the communal dish; they should not be licked.

If you are not adept with chopsticks, don't be shy: ask for a fork.

## DRINKS

The most popular beverage consumed with Chinese food is tea. The Chinese believe that tea gets rid of the richness inherent in restaurant food. Most restaurants serve four kinds of Chinese tea: *bo lay*, a strong, bitter, dark-brown tea; *heung peen* or jasmine, a light brown tea that is fragrant and mild; *teak quon yum* or "iron goddess of mercy," a fragrant and refreshing green tea; and *lung jang* or "dragon well," a light, slightly bitter green tea.

Lightly flavored beer is another popular drink with Chinese food. With the spicy cuisine of Szechwan, few drinks can rival a cold beer. Brews that complement Chinese food nicely include Heineken, Coors, Tsing Tao, Carlsberg and most light beers.

Many people, particularly the Chinese, prefer to drink hard liquor with Chinese food. Though this may seem odd, many people believe that Chinese food is so full-flavored that little taste would be lost by drinking hard liquor with it. Favorite liquors include whiskey, brandy and cognac, consumed straight or with water.

As for wine, we find white goes better with Chinese food than red. Red wine, which is often dryer and more subtle in taste, tends to turn sour or go flat with Chinese food. For white wine, we recommend a medium-dry, fruity or spicy variety. Reisling, Chardonnay, Leibfraumilch and Gewurztraminer are all good. For special occasions and to complement the less spicy Chinese dishes, we recommend medium-dry champagne.

# CHAPTER FOUR

# How to Use the Book

For many English-speaking people, the Chinese-restaurant menu is a baffling enigma. Often unnecessarily long, overly ambitious and written in poor English, most Chinese-restaurant menus do a sorry job of communicating what the house has to offer. For example, on any given menu, there may be three dishes named "Braised Fish in Pieces"; without the assistance of a waiter well-versed in Chinese cuisine *and* the English language, it is impossible for most people to tell these and many other dishes apart and to make sensible choices. Also, a uniform system for naming dishes in English does not exist. The English name of a dish may bear no resemblance to the Chinese name, or the dish may be called by completely different names in other restaurants, thus making it nearly impossible for the patron to find the dish again. Thus, ordering Chinese food is all too often a hit-and-miss affair. In addition, most people are unfamiliar with the many regional styles of Chinese cuisine. With this book, we have tried to remove some of the mystery surrounding authentic Chinese food. Designed as a pocket menu and handy reference, *The Chinese Food Lover's Guide* will help food lovers order in Chinese restaurants.

The book includes five comprehensive menus. Four are regional menus; one is a Cantonese dim sum menu. In each regional menu, dishes are categorized by course; main dishes are subdivided by primary ingredient.

Readers should note that China's regional cuisines are not clearly defined. Some dishes can be found in more than one regional menu, because more than one region has claimed them or because they have traveled well from one region to another.

## USING THE REGIONAL MENUS

The brief introduction to each regional menu gives you background information on the characteristics and specialties of that cuisine. You can look up the dishes by course—soups, appetizers, side dishes—or, for main dishes, by primary ingredient—pork, chicken or fish. If you are in a Szechwan restaurant and want a spicy pork main dish, you refer to Chapter Eight, A Szechwan Menu, and to the category entitled "Main Dishes—Pork." Look up the descriptions of the pork dishes listed. For easy selection, the most common and popular dishes, such as Fish-Fragrant Pork or Twice Cooked Pork, are listed first; the more unusual or hard-to-get dishes, such as Hot and Tingling Kidneys or Sautéed Pig's Liver, are listed last. The descriptions will give you a general impression of how certain dishes are made and how they might taste. Make a list of initial choices.

Then ask the waiter whether the dishes on your list are prepared in more or less the same way as described in the book. If they are, you will know what to expect when they arrive. Keep in mind that our descriptions are not the last word on how the dishes should be made; allow for minor variations. All kitchens are different.

Chinese restaurant food, prepared one dish at a time, may sometimes suffer from small inconsistencies. For example, a particular dish may have button mushrooms one time and straw mushrooms the next; or it may be spicier the first time than the second. These inconsistencies are minor and should be overlooked.

However, you should not overlook the substitution of ingredients in a dish so that its authentic taste is lost. Some restaurants use canned bean sprouts in place of seasonal Chinese vegetables; they use an excess of sugar or monosodium glutamate (MSG) instead of fresh, naturally good-tasting ingredients; they season Szechwan food with ketchup rather than hot bean sauce. These are examples of excessive deviation from the traditional methods and are indications that the restaurant is unconcerned about the quality of its food.

## USING THE CANTONESE DIM SUM MENU

Chapter Nine, A Cantonese Dim Sum Menu, is organized differently from the regional menus. Dim sum is particularly difficult for non-Chinese speakers to order because, in most dim sum restaurants, the dishes are not ordered by menu through a waiter but chosen by the patrons from tea trolleys pushed by waitresses who occasionally call out the dish names in Cantonese. These waitresses are often not proficient in English and may not be able to explain what the dishes are. Patrons usually have to rely on their own resources when ordering dim sum.

So that you can recognize the dim sum dishes quickly, we have categorized the dishes not by course or ingredient, but by the types of trolley on which the dishes are displayed: steamer trolley, pan-fried dishes trolley, baked dishes trolley, sautéed dishes trolley, deep-fried dishes trolley, rice casserole trolley, stuffed rice rolls trolley, blanched dishes trolley, stewed dishes trolley and dessert trolley. So you can recognize what the waitresses are calling out, we have included the physical descriptions of the snacks and their names in phonetic Cantonese. With these pointers, you should be able to identify most of the dishes, then look them up in the menu to find out what they are.

In all five menus, we describe how dishes are made, what ingredients are in them and, in some instances, how they should taste. These descriptions come from a number of sources: interviews with food experts; research into authentic menus and food books; the commercial kitchen experience of one of the authors; and observations of practices in Chinese restaurants in North America, China and Hong Kong.

The names of dishes in the menus are written in both Chinese and English. The English names are from two derivations: the authors' translation of dish names, and common restaurant usage (with grammatical corrections). Some dishes, therefore, have two or more English names. The Chinese names are names of dishes taken from menus and cookbooks. They are widely used by the Chinese and familiar to restaurant staff. It is usually easier to order by referring to the Chinese names, because these have remained the same through time, from country to country, restaurant to restaurant. To communicate your requests clearly, point out the Chinese names in the book to your waiter.

The alphabetical glossary, at the back of the book, explains all unfamiliar ingredients, regions and cooking terms.

While the menus are intended to be a comprehensive listing of Chinese dishes, they are by no means exhaustive. Chinese cuisine is so vast that we could not include everything. Similarly, it would not be reasonable to expect any one restaurant to serve every dish listed in any one of the menus. In preparing the menus, we tended to select the most popular dishes; we left out those that were obscure or difficult to make and therefore not readily available in most restaurants. We did include a few rare dishes for people who are interested in exotica.

## A NOTE ON CHINESE PRONUNCIATION

To describe some of the ingredients and dishes, we have included their names in phonetic Cantonese. Cantonese was chosen because it is the most widely used Chinese dialect in Chinese communities outside of China.

# CHAPTER FIVE

# A Canton Menu

At the mouth of the Pearl River in South China, the city of Canton (Guangzhou) has, for hundreds of years, been the gateway to the Pacific. It was from Canton and the surrounding area that most Chinese emigrated. The people from South China have spread far and wide and, as a result, Cantonese culture and cuisine are known in every corner of the globe. The Cantonese influence became so strongly identified with Chinese culture that, for a long time, most non-Chinese thought the Cantonese were the only Chinese, and Cantonese food the only kind of Chinese food. They were mistaken—but they were not mistaken about the pleasure that Cantonese food gave them. With its delicacy, variety and freshness, it may well be the best of China's regional cuisines.

The Canton culinary region embraces the southern provinces of Kwangtung and Kwangsi and the British colony of Hong Kong. Lush and fertile, the land yields three plantings annually, and an astounding twelve for certain crops. It has a subtropical climate, and spring and summer merge into one long, hot and humid season. The winter is brief and mild. The varied landscape is blessed with plenty of rain brought by the monsoon winds. Farmers grow a great variety of crops—rice, vegetables, sugar cane and tropical fruits such as bananas, lychees and papayas. Cantonese farmers have also adopted and cultivated crops from every major region of the world: white and sweet potatoes, corn, tomatoes, peppers and carrots have been growing in southern China for so long they have been incorporated into the cuisine and used in authentic Cantonese dishes. Fish, too, forms an important part of the diet, and the uninterrupted coastline provides access to a great variety of fish and shellfish. Cantonese fishermen are highly skilled and very much at home on the water; many of them live their entire lives on boats with their families and are called "water people." There are also domesticated fresh-water fish, such as carp, which are reared in ponds and flooded rice fields and prized for their rich, tender meat. The many ponds and waterways of South China also create an ideal environment for raising ducks and geese. Together with chicken, they figure prominently on the Cantonese menu.

An ancient Chinese saying lays down the four rules for living an ideal life: "To be born in Suzhou, to eat in Guangzhou, to dress in Hangzhou and to die in Liuzhou." Suzhou is physically beautiful, Hangzhou has the finest silks, Liuzhou is known for its wood from which coffins are made. But Guangzhou (Canton) is the place to be if you really want to eat well. The excellence of Cantonese food is based on a few sound cooking principles: use subtle, not powerful, seasonings; cook with fast, efficient methods to preserve the natural flavors and textures of food; and work with fresh ingredients.

For subtle seasonings, the Cantonese prefer light soy sauce, sugar, salt and white-pepper powder. The most pungent spices they use are garlic and ginger. The Cantonese also use two indigenous seasonings to give dishes their distinctive southern flavor: oyster sauce and fermented black beans. Oyster sauce, made from ground-up dried oysters, has no oyster flavor at all; like soy sauce, it is a versatile salty seasoning. Fermented black beans are dried salty preserved soybeans, which have a powerful aroma and a pleasing taste. They are used in sautéing meat and in seafood sauces.

Two of the commonest cooking methods used in the Cantonese kitchen are sautéing and steaming. In sautéing (also called stir-frying), a fine art perfected by the Cantonese, meat, seafood and vegetables are tossed for a few seconds in a piping-hot wok with a bit of oil. The high temperature of the wok sears the outer surface of the food to form a crust, which seals in the juices. Meat cooked this way remains tender and juicy; vegetables stay crisp and bright green. In sautéing, timing is all important; the cook has to move fast to prevent the food from charring. The Cantonese cook usually slices and marinates his seafood or meat and cuts and blanches his vegetables. He then fries the meat or seafood briefly in hot oil (a procedure called "pulling through oil"), drains the ingredients and sautées them with a bit of oil, minced ginger and garlic. Vegetables are added, then a cornstarch paste. The food is tossed until a sheen appears on the ingredients. This kind of high-temperature sautéing is designed to create an effect the Cantonese call *wok hay*, the energy and aroma created by a well-heated wok. In a Cantonese restaurant, sautéed meat dishes are usually very good, especially beef. The meat is thinly sliced and tenderized in a flavorful marinade before it is quick-fried and sautéed. Meat sautéed for such a short time remains soft, tasty and succulent.

Another favorite Cantonese cooking method is steaming. Steamed food tends to retain its original shape and natural juices. Delicate food such as fresh fish is steamed for brief periods and served with a subtle-tasting soy-based sauce.

Methods such as sautéing and steaming tend to highlight the natural flavors and textures of food, so the ingredients must be of the highest quality. To the Cantonese, quality means freshness; the Cantonese obsession with freshness probably dates back to a time when there was no refrigeration and food deteriorated quickly in the hot climate. In the markets of Hong Kong, vendors take great pride in the freshness of their produce, and shoppers have high standards.

Vegetables must be young and fresh, fruits shiny and firm. Live poultry and fish abound, for the Cantonese like to keep their dinner fresh until the very last moment.

The Cantonese are acknowledged masters of fish and seafood cooking. In many good Cantonese dinner restaurants, the seafood is kept alive in huge aquariums. When an order comes in, a fish is netted, put in a bucket and brought to the table for inspection before it is taken into the kitchen. The whole fish (usually a fresh snapper or rock cod) is steamed for just the right length of time, drizzled with a soy-green-onion sauce and served steaming hot.

The Cantonese love of freshness is the subject of comment among other Chinese. They like to joke that the Cantonese will eat anything that moves. The joke refers not only to the Cantonese love of freshness, but also to an adventurous streak in their culinary tastes. The Cantonese have been known to eat a great variety of animals not usually associated with the dinner table: cat, dog, beetle, raccoon, and owl, to mention just a few.

The Cantonese also believe that certain foods have medicinal value. Snake meat, for example, is thought to warm one's blood, and for this reason the Cantonese eat lots of it during autumn and winter, particularly in soup, served with chrysanthemum petals and lemon leaves. Other exotic ingredients, such as shark's fins, bird's nest (or bird's saliva), fish maw (fish bladder), sparrow, frog fat, chicken testicles and deer ligaments are also prized by the Cantonese. Some of these dishes are featured in the exotic ingredients section of this menu.

The Cantonese like most of their dishes served piping hot. The Chinese hot pot, casserole, or *bo* is a popular menu choice in a Cantonese restaurant. Though other regional cuisines also have casseroles, the Cantonese have the greatest variety. Made of clay or carbon steel, the casserole is presented with the food bubbling; steamy aromas rise from the pot. Some popular *bo* include Singing Chicken

Casserole, chicken pieces sautéed in a slightly sweet brown sauce, and Oysters with Ginger and Green Onions Casserole, succulent shelled oysters sautéed with ginger and green onions.

One specialty the Cantonese are known for around the world is their barbecued and poached meats. Barbecued pork and barbecued duck are as popular in Canton as they are in Toronto and New York, and prepared in the same way. Strips of marbled pork are marinated in a well-seasoned sauce, roasted until the edges are crusty, and then basted with honey. The duck is stuffed with aromatic spices, basted and roasted to a crispy reddish brown. Chicken, duck, quail and even octopus are poached in master sauces, or seasoned liquids, which usually contain soy sauce, green onions, ginger and spices such as star anise, licorice root and cassia bark. Barbecued and poached meats are served in fast-food won ton restaurants. These establishments specialize in one-dish meals, such as won tons in broth, noodles topped with barbecued meats or rice topped with sautéed meat and vegetables. Won ton houses provide fast, nutritious and delicious meals at low prices. In this menu, most fast-food won ton house dishes can be found in the section called Side Dishes.

Also included in the Cantonese menu are some Chiu Chow dishes. The Chiu Chow are a seafaring people who live in and around Swatow (Shantou), a seaport located about 170 miles east of Canton. Chiu Chow food is light and delicate, like Cantonese cuisine, but it tends to be more seasoned and spicier. Chiu Chow cooks like to use a spicy flavorful sauce called *sar char*. They are also partial to dried lemons and Szechwan peppercorns. Lemon Duck Soup and Beef Sautéed with *Chin Jew* (Szechwan peppercorns) are both Chiu Chow favorites. A sample order of Chiu Chow dishes is provided in the section called "Sample Orders For Complete Meals" in Chapter Three.

Another unique cooking style included in this Cantonese

menu is Hakka food. The Hakkas are displaced northerners who migrated to South China in the twelfth and thirteenth centuries when the north was overrun by invaders. The work *Hakka* means "guest families." Through the ages the Hakka have become largely assimilated among their Southern hosts, but they have preserved certain characteristics of their cuisine. The best-known Hakka specialty is probably Salt Baked Chicken. The chicken is stuffed with spices, wrapped, covered and baked in coarse salt. Other well-known Hakka dishes include Stuffed Bean Curds, which are hollowed out and steamed with a delicate fish stuffing and served with a pungent soy-based sauce; Beef Balls Sautéed with Chinese Vegetables; and Beef Bone Marrow with Three Ingredients, soft and silky bone marrow strips sautéed with mushrooms and meat slices. A sample order of Hakka dishes is provided in Chapter Three in the section called "Sample Orders For Complete Meals."

The Cantonese have a magnificent dim sum for which they are famous. To do it justice, we have given Cantonese dim sum its own menu in Chapter Nine.

With its subtle flavors, fresh ingredients and seemingly endless variety, Cantonese food will always be popular. Good Cantonese food can be found in most cities. With the information provided in this chapter, you should be able to tackle the Cantonese menu with knowledge and confidence—and ultimately with great pleasure.

# A CANTON MENU

## APPETIZERS

Some of these appetizers can be ordered on a combination plate. Ask the waiter which ones can be combined.

春 卷
### 1. Spring Rolls:
*Crispy long rolls are stuffed with shredded pork and vegetables, then deep-fried. Worcestershire sauce is served as a dip.*

海 蜇
### 2. Tossed Jellyfish:
*Shredded jellyfish, with a crunchy and rubbery texture, is tossed with salt and sesame oil and served at room temperature. Jellyfish is prized for its unusual texture.*

海 蜇 芝 麻 鷄
### 3. Jellyfish and Shredded Chicken:
*Shredded jellyfish is tossed with sautéed shredded chicken and served topped with toasted sesame seeds.*

燻 蹄
### 4. Poached Pork Hock:
*Pork hock is boned whole, stuffed with meat, trussed, then poached in a seasoned liquid. It is sliced paper-thin and served cold.*

蒜子蜜汁骨

**5. Honey and Garlic Ribs:**
*Small pieces of pork ribs are marinated, fried and braised in a minced garlic-honey sauce.*

沙爹串燒牛肉

**6. Satay Beef:**
*Marinated beef cubes are skewered, then roasted or fried and served with a peanut sauce. This dish is of Southeast Asian origin.*

鹵水鷄翼

**7. Poached Chicken Wings:**
*Chicken wings are poached in a soy-based liquid, drained and served lukewarm.*

鹵墨魚

**8. Poached Octopus:**
*Octopus is poached in an orange-colored seasoned liquid until tender, then drained, sliced and served cold. Octopus meat is firm and supple.*

金錢蟹盒

**9. Fried Crab Meat Toasts:**
*A crab meat or shrimp meat paste is smeared on tiny pieces of bread and deep-fried until golden brown.*

明蝦大沙律

**10. Prawn Salad:**
*This is an elaborate dish of poached, shelled prawns served over a potato-fruit salad. A mayonnaise-based dressing is*

*drizzled over the salad. The waiter usually mixes the salad with the dressing before serving.*

## 龍 蝦 沙 律
### 11. Lobster Salad:
*This is the same as the prawn salad above except that poached fresh shelled lobster meat is used.*

## 白 灼 蝦
### 12. Poached Shrimp:
*Small to medium shrimp are poached or steamed, drained and served with a soy-chili dip. To eat, remove shell and head with fingers; dip meat in the sauce.*

## 白 灼 蜆
### 13. Poached Clams:
*Clams in the shell are poached or steamed, then served with a soy-chili or black bean dip.*

## 白 灼 帶 子
### 14. Poached Pink Scallops:
*Pink scallops in the shell are poached or steamed, then served with a soy-chili dip or a black-bean dip.*

## 白 灼 象 拔 蚌
### 15. Poached Geoduck:
*Pronounced "gooey duck," these giant meaty clams are available on the west coast of North America. Shelled, cleaned and sliced, geoduck are poached and served with a soy and green-onion dip.*

蒸 蠔

**16. Steamed Oysters:**
*Oysters in the shell are steamed and served with a black-bean sauce.*

鹵 鴨 或 鵝

**17. Poached Duck or Goose:**
*Goose or duck is poached in a seasoned liquid, drained, then cut into small pieces. This dish is only available in Chiu Chow restaurants.*

炸 蝦 棗

**18. Fried Shrimp Balls:**
*Shrimp meat, fat pork and water chestnuts are minced, mixed together and formed into balls, deep-fried until golden brown and served with a molasses-based sauce. This dish is only available in Chiu Chow restaurants.*

炸 蟹 棗

**19. Fried Crab Balls:**
*Crab meat, fat pork and water chestnuts are minced, mixed together and formed into balls, deep-fried and served with a molasses-based sauce.*

鹵 水 珍 肝

**20. Poached Livers and Giblets:**
*Chicken livers and giblets are poached in a seasoned liquid, then sliced and served at room temperature.*

## SOUPS

There are basically two types of Chinese soups. Both are served with sundry ingredients. One is made with broth, the other is made with broth thickened with cornstarch.

## 八寶冬瓜粒湯

**21. Diced Winter Melon Soup:**
Diced chicken, black mushroom and squash-like winter melon, crab meat and shrimp are served in a broth.

## 冬瓜湯

**22. Whole Winter Melon Soup:**
This is an elaborate soup served at banquets; advance notice is required. A whole or half a winter melon is seeded, filled with broth and a diced assortment of ham, dried scallops, crab meat, shrimp and black mushrooms. It is then steamed. The melon with its contents is served on a melon holder. The waiter ladles out equal portions of soft winter melon, broth and diced meats into small soup bowls. For special occasions, the cook will carve the sides of the melon with ornate decorations.

## 八珍豆腐羹

**23. Assorted Meat, Bean Curd and Vegetable Thick Soup:**
Diced pork, bamboo shoots, black mushrooms and bean curds are served in a thickened soup.

## 西洋菜湯
**24. Watercress Soup:**
Watercress is cooked until wilted in a broth with giblets or pork bones.

## 時菜肉片湯
**25. Pork and Vegetables Soup:**
Sliced pork is cooked in a broth with seasonal Chinese greens.

## 火鴨芥菜湯
**26. Duck and Mustard Greens Soup:**
Barbecued duck pieces and mustard greens are cooked in a broth.

## 鷄茸粟米湯
**27. Chicken and Creamed Corn Thick Soup:**
Minced chicken is served in a thickened soup with canned creamed corn. This soup is filling.

## 例湯
**28. House Soup:**
This soup is available in most low- to medium-priced restaurants. The house soup is usually pork and a vegetable (watercress or bok choy) cooked in a broth. Though not listed in most menus, it is available on request for a nominal charge.

## 西湖牛肉羹
**29. Eggs and Beef Thick Soup; or Beef, Egg-Swirl Thick Soup with Chinese Parsley:**
Minced or sliced beef is served in a thickened soup with beaten eggs and Chinese parsley.

# 清蝦丸湯
**30. Shrimp Balls Soup:**
Ground shrimp and pork are formed into balls, poached and served in a broth with vegetables.

# 上湯魚丸
**31. Fish Balls Soup:**
White fish balls are served in a broth with black mushrooms, bamboo shoots and vegetables.

# 清燉鳳足冬菇湯
**32. Chicken Feet and Black Mushroom Soup:**
Black mushrooms, chicken feet, ginger and green onions are steamed in a casserole of broth until tender. The soup is served in small bowls. Dip the mushrooms and chicken feet in soy sauce before eating.

# 豆腐海鮮湯
**33. Seafood Bean-Curd Soup:**
Bean-curd cubes, shrimp and squid are served in a broth.

# 蝦丸豆腐湯
**34. Shrimp Balls Bean-Curd Soup:**
Bean-curd cubes and shrimp balls are served in a broth.

# 青豆蛋花湯
**35. Peas and Egg Soup:**
Beaten eggs and peas are served in a broth.

# 蘑菇蛋花湯
**36. Mushroom and Egg Soup:**
Sliced mushrooms and beaten eggs are served in a broth.

## 雙丸湯
**37. Fish and Beef Balls Soup:**
*White fish balls and beef balls are served in a broth.*

## 蕃茄牛肉湯
**38. Beef and Tomato Soup:**
*Sliced beef and tomatoes are served in a broth.*

## 紫菜湯
**39. Seaweed Soup:**
*Seaweed or nori sheets are served in a broth with sliced vegetables. Some restaurants add beaten eggs to this soup.*

## 清燉冬菇
**40. Steamed Black Mushrooms:**
*Black mushrooms are steamed in a casserole filled with broth.*

## 檸檬鴨湯
**41. Lemon Duck Soup:**
*Duck is cooked tender in a broth with dried lemons. This soup is tangy and flavorful. It is only available in Chiu Chow restaurants.*

## 蟹肉會冬茸羹
**42. Crab Meat and Mushroom Thick Soup:**
*Crab meat is served in a thickened soup with diced black mushrooms.*

## 花膠會鴨絲羹
**43. Duck and Fish Maw or Bladder Thick Soup:**
*Shredded barbecued duck meat is served in a thickened soup*

with sliced fish bladder, which is prized for its soft, spongy texture.

## 芙蓉瑤柱羹
**44. Dried Scallop Thick Soup:**
*Shredded dried scallops are served in a thickened soup with bamboo shoots, black mushrooms and beaten eggs.*

## 八寶瑤柱羹
**45. Assorted Dried Scallop Thick Soup:**
*Shredded dried scallops are served in a thickened soup with black mushrooms, bamboo shoots, pork and dried shrimp.*

## 韭黃瑤柱羹
**46. Dried Scallop and Chives Thick Soup:**
*Shredded dried scallops are served in a thickened soup with yellow chives.*

## 蟹肉魚肚羹
**47. Crab Meat and Fish Maw (Bladder) Thick Soup:**
*Shredded fish bladder, cooked until soft and spongy, is served in a thickened soup with crab meat.*

## 鷄茸魚肚羹
**48. Minced Chicken and Fish Bladder Thick Soup:**
*Minced chicken is served in a thickened soup with soft and spongy sliced fish bladder.*

## 香茜猪紅湯
**49. Pig's Blood Soup:**
*Coagulated pig's blood, steamed and cubed, is served in a broth with Chinese parsley.*

## MAIN DISHES—BEAN CURDS

### 東江釀豆腐
**50. Stuffed Bean Curds:**
*Of Hakka origin, this dish consists of pieces of bean curd that have been hollowed out, stuffed with ground pork and fish meat, then steamed and served with soy-based sauce.*

### 紅燒釀豆腐
**51. Red-Cooked Stuffed Bean Curds:**
*Pieces of bean curd are hollowed out, stuffed with ground pork and fish meat, deep-fried, and braised in a soy-based sauce. Some restaurants serve the bean curds with shredded pork and Chinese greens. This dish is of Hakka origin.*

### 北菇扒豆腐
**52. Black Mushrooms and Bean Curds:**
*Black mushrooms are braised in a brown soy-based sauce with tender pieces of bean curd.*

### 八珍扒豆腐
**53. Bean Curds with Assorted Meats:**
*Fried bean-curd pieces are braised in a brown sauce with mushrooms, bamboo shoots, barbecued pork and seafood.*

### 蠔油豆腐
**54. Bean Curds with Oyster Sauce:**
*Bean-curd cubes are braised in oyster sauce with bamboo shoots, mushrooms and Chinese greens. Some restaurants slice and pan-fry the bean curds before braising them.*

蝦 仁 滑 豆 腐

**55. Shrimp and Bean Curds:**
*Bean-curd cubes are braised in a sauce with small shrimp.*

蟹 肉 扒 豆 腐

**56. Crab Meat and Bean Curds:**
*Bean-curd cubes are braised and served with crab meat.*

叉 燒 豆 腐

**57. Barbecued Pork and Bean Curds:**
*Sliced barbecued pork is braised in a sauce with bean-curd cubes.*

蠔 油 菜 膽 扒 豆 腐

**58. Bean Curds with Mushrooms and Vegetables:**
*Fried bean-curd squares are braised in a brown sauce with black mushrooms and oyster sauce. They are served garnished with blanched lettuce or Chinese greens.*

金 錢 豆 腐 盒

**59. Stuffed Bean-Curd Rounds:**
*Round pieces of bean curd are layered with ground shrimp meat, steamed, then braised in a sauce with a shredded mixture of pork, black mushrooms and dried shrimp.*

煎 琵 琶 豆 腐

**60. Fried *Pei Pa* (Chinese Mandolin) Tofu:**
*Mashed bean curds are mixed with minced ham and chicken and molded into Chinese spoons. They are then steamed, and deep-fried until golden brown. This dish is seldom available because of the elaborate preparation required.*

## MAIN DISHES — BEEF

### 蠔油牛肉
**61. Oyster Beef or Beef in Oyster Sauce:**
*Marinated, thinly sliced beef is quick-fried, then sautéed with minced garlic, ginger, sliced carrot, and oyster sauce.*

### 時菜牛肉
**62. Beef Sautéed with Seasonal Vegetables:**
*Sliced, marinated beef is quick-fried, then sautéed with Chinese vegetables such as* bok choy *or* choy sum.

### 百家利牛肉
**63. Beef Sautéed with Broccoli:**
*Sliced, marinated beef is quick-fried, then sautéed with blanched broccoli.*

### 豉椒牛肉
**64. Beef in Black-Bean Sauce:**
*Sliced, marinated beef is quick-fried, then sautéed with onions, peppers and pungent black beans.*

### 雪荳牛肉
**65. Beef Sautéed with Snow Pea Pods:**
*Sliced, marinated beef is quick-fried, then sautéed with snow pea pods and sliced mushrooms.*

薑 葱 牛 肉

66. Beef Sautéed with Ginger and Green Onions:
*Sliced, marinated beef is quick-fried, then sautéed with shredded ginger and green onions.*

西 芹 牛 肉

67. Beef Sautéed with Celery:
*Sliced, marinated beef is quick-fried, then sautéed with sliced celery.*

芥 蘭 牛 肉

68. Beef Sautéed with *Gai Lan:*
*Sliced, marinated beef is quick-fried, then sautéed with blanched* gai lan.

蕃 茄 牛 肉

69. Beef Sautéed with Tomatoes:
*Sliced, marinated beef is quick-fried, then sautéed with sliced tomatoes. This dish is slightly tangy in flavor.*

沙 茶 牛 肉

70. Beef in *Sar Char,* or Satay Sauce:
*Sliced, marinated beef is quick-fried, then sautéed in a sauce that has a faint curry flavor. The beef is usually garnished with sautéed vegetables such as* bok choy *or* gai lan. *This dish is only available in Chiu Chow restaurants.*

川 椒 牛 肉

71. Beef Sautéed with *Chin Jew* or Szechwan Peppercorns:
*Sliced, marinated beef is quick-fried, then sautéed with crushed chilies and Szechwan peppercorns. This dish is of Chiu Chow origin.*

## 龍馬牛肉
**72. Beef Sautéed with Fried Doughnut Slices:**
*Sliced, marinated beef is quick-fried, then sautéed with crunchy slices of fried Chinese doughnuts.*

## 牛肉鬆
**73. Beef Lettuce Wraps:**
*Minced beef is marinated and sautéed with an assortment of minced vegetables, such as bamboo shoots, black mushrooms and carrots. It is then served over crunchy rice vermicelli with large lettuce leaves and* hoi sin *sauce on the side. To eat, smear* hoi sin *sauce in the hollow of a leaf, fill with a couple of tablespoons of sautéed beef, roll tightly and eat with fingers.*

## 雀巢牛柳絲
**74. Beef in a Bird's Nest:**
*Shredded marinated beef is sautéed with a variety of vegetables and served in a deep-fried shoestring-potato or taro-root basket. To eat, break up the nest with a spoon and take equal portions of filling and nest.*

## 炆牛腩
**75. Beef Stew:**
*Beef brisket chunks are slow-cooked until tender in a soy-based brown sauce with onions and ginger.*

## 金錢牛排
**76. Beef Filets with Sweet-and-Sour Sauce:**
*Medallion-sized pieces of marinated beef are fried and served with a sweet-and-sour sauce with deep-fried shoestring potatoes.*

中式牛排

77. Chinese Filets of Beef:
*Medallion-sized pieces of beef are marinated, fried and served with tomato and pineapple slices.*

鐵板牛肉

78. Teppan Beef Slices:
*Marinated beef slices are sautéed with sliced ginger and green onions, then served sizzling on a hot teppan plate.*

鐵板洋葱牛肉

79. Teppan Onion and Beef Filet:
*Sliced marinated beef and sliced white onions are sautéed and served sizzling on a hot teppan plate.*

鐵板沙爹牛肉

80. Teppan Satay Beef:
*Marinated beef skewers are served sizzling on a hot teppan plate with a pungent sauce.*

菜扒牛肉丸

81. Beef Balls Sautéed with Chinese Vegetables:
*Beef slices are ground up and pounded to a fine paste, shaped into small balls, poached, cut open in a crisscross pattern and sautéed with Chinese greens. This dish is only available in Hakka restaurants. Hakka beef balls have a bouncy texture.*

菜遠炒雙丸

82. Beef and Fish Balls with Chinese Vegetables:
*Beef balls and white fish balls are sautéed with Chinese greens.*

## 涼瓜炒牛肉
**83. Bitter Melon Sautéed with Beef Slices:**
*Marinated slices of beef are quick-fried and sautéed with bitter melon slices, minced garlic and black beans. This dish emphasizes the bitter flavor of the melon and the pungency of the garlic and black beans.*

## 牛骨髓會三鮮
**84. Beef Bone Marrow with Three Ingredients:**
*Soft and slippery strips of bone marrow are sautéed in a brown sauce with a variety of ingredients such as canned abalone, boned duck feet, baby corn, sliced pork or chicken and black mushrooms. This dish is of Hakka origin.*

## 白灼牛栢葉
**85. Poached Tripe or Omasun:**
*White layered beef tripe or omasun, the cow's third stomach, is used for this dish. It is sliced, poached and served with a black-bean dip. The tripe is chewy.*

## 豉椒牛栢葉
**86. Tripe with Black Beans or Omasun:**
*White layered tripe is sliced and sautéed with hot peppers and pungent black beans.*

## 咸酸菜牛栢葉
**87. Tripe with Pickled Mustard or Omasun:**
*White layered tripe is sliced and sautéed with sour and crunchy pickled mustard greens.*

## MAIN DISHES — CASSEROLES OR HOT POTS

The Cantonese call their casseroles, which are always served bubbling at the table, *bo*. Casseroles are very popular in Cantonese restaurants, particularly in the winter.

## 薑葱牛肉煲
88. Beef with Ginger and Onions Casserole:
*Marinated beef slices are quick-fried, then sautéed with ginger and green onions and served in a Chinese casserole.*

## 柱候牛腩煲
89. Beef Brisket Casserole:
*Chunks of beef brisket are slow-cooked until tender in a flavorful brown sauce, then served in a casserole with lettuce at the bottom.*

## 啫啫鷄煲
90. Singing Chicken Casserole:
*Marinated chicken chunks, still on the bone, are fried and sautéed in a slightly sweet sauce, then served bubbling vigorously (hence singing) in a casserole.*

## 東江豆腐煲
91. Stuffed Bean Curd Casserole:
*Bean-curd pieces are hollowed out and stuffed with fishmeat and served bubbling in a casserole of broth with Chinese vegetables. This dish is of Hakka origin.*

薑葱牛展煲
92. Beef Shanks with Ginger and Onions Casserole:
*Sliced beef shanks are marinated, quick-fried, then sautéed with ginger and green onions and served bubbling in a casserole.*

八珍豆腐煲
93. Bean Curd with Assorted Meats Casserole:
*Fried bean-curd chunks are braised with seafood, barbecued pork and mushrooms and served with lettuce in a casserole.*

打邊爐
94. Cantonese Mongolian Hot Pot:
*This is a Chinese fondue cooked at the table. The broth-filled fondue pot is placed in the middle of the table. Around the fondue are plates of raw seafood and meat, bean thread noodles, bean curds and vegetables. To cook: dip ingredients in the broth and retrieve when cooked. Pour some soy sauce into your bowl to use as a dip. At the end of the hot pot meal, some restaurants serve a casserole of rice steamed with Chinese sausages and cured duck. Some restaurants now offer a Chiu Chow Hot Pot. The ingredients are the same but the bubbling broth is flavored with* sar char *sauce.*

粉絲蟹煲
95. Crab and Bean Thread Noodles Casserole:
*Fried crab pieces, still in the shell, are served in a bubbling casserole with soft and slippery bean thread noodles.*

蘿白根腩煲
96. Beef Stew and Radish Casserole:
*Beef brisket chunks and pungent Chinese white radish are*

slow-cooked until tender in a flavorful brown sauce and served in a casserole.

班腩豆腐煲
97. Cod and Bean Curd Casserole:
Fried pieces of cod are braised with fried bean-curd squares and served in a casserole. Make sure to tell your waiter if you want the fish boned.

紅炆班腩
98. Red-Cooked Cod Casserole:
Fried pieces of cod are braised in a brown soy-based sauce and served in a casserole. Make sure to tell your waiter if you want the fish boned.

八珍蠔煲
99. Oyster and Assorted Meats Casserole:
Shelled fried oysters are served bubbling in a casserole with mushrooms, fried bean curds, bamboo shoots and barbecued pork.

羗葱生蠔煲
100. Oysters with Ginger and Green Onion Casserole:
Shelled oysters are sautéed with ginger and green onions and served in a casserole.

東江什錦煲
101. Hakka Assorted Casserole:
An assortment of ingredients such as beef balls, fish balls, black mushrooms, chicken livers, sliced pork and cuttlefish are cooked in a bubbling casserole of broth with sliced pig's livers and kidney. This dish is of Hakka origin and may not be available in every Cantonese restaurant.

## 枝竹羊腩煲
**102. Mutton Casserole:**
*Lamb or mutton chunks are slow-cooked until tender with sticks of bean curd skin, then served in a casserole.*

## 香芋油鷄煲
**103. Chicken and Taro Casserole:**
*Chicken pieces, still on the bone, are fried and braised in a casserole with chunks of taro root.*

## 香芋油鴨煲
**104. Duck and Taro Casserole:**
*This dish is prepared the same as the chicken casserole above, except pieces of duck are used.*

## 砂窩焗鷄
**105. Braised Chicken Casserole:**
*Marinated chicken pieces, still on the bone, are sautéed with ginger and green onions, then slow-cooked and served in a casserole with black mushrooms.*

## 蝦球豆腐煲
**106. Shrimp Balls and Bean Curd Casserole:**
*Ground shrimp and pork are shaped into balls and served in a casserole of broth with bean-curd squares.*

## 鮑魚鵝掌煲
**107. Abalone and Goose Feet Casserole:**
*Canned abalone slices are served bubbling in a casserole with boned whole goose feet, which have a chewy consistency. This dish is of Chiu Chow origin.*

柱候牛什煲

**108. Beef Organs Casserole:**
*A variety of beef organs such as tripe, stomach, lung and spleen is cooked until tender in a flavorful sauce and served in a casserole.*

蒜子大鱔

**109. Eel Casserole:**
*Chunks of eel are sautéed with garlic and served in a casserole.*

---

## MAIN DISHES—CHICKEN

---

Most Chinese chicken dishes, unless otherwise specified by the restaurant, are served still on the bone. Most unboned chicken dishes, such as White Chicken or Fried Crispy Chicken, can be ordered whole or in halves.

白切鷄

**110. White Chicken:**
*Chicken is poached in a seasoned liquid, drained, cut up into small pieces and served with a flavorful minced-ginger and green-onion dip. Also served as an appetizer.*

豉油鷄

**111. Soy Sauce Chicken:**
*Chicken is poached in a dark brown seasoned liquid, drained and cut into small pieces.*

## 時菜鷄球
**112. Chicken with Vegetables:**
*Marinated chicken pieces, still on the bone, are fried and sautéed with garlic, carrot slices and seasonal Chinese greens.*

## 羗葱油淋鷄
**113. Steamed Chicken with Ginger and Green Onions:**
*A marinated chicken is steamed, cut up, sprinkled with shredded ginger and green onions and then drizzled with hot oil.*

## 炸子鷄
**114. Fried Crispy Chicken:**
*Marinated chicken is fried until golden brown, cut into small pieces and served with crunchy shrimp chips (they are like potato chips) and a peppery salt dip. To eat, sprinkle a pinch of salt over the chicken.*

## 芥蘭鷄球
**115. *Gai Lan* and Chicken:**
*Marinated chicken pieces, still on the bone, are quick-fried and sautéed with* gai lan.

## 清蒸滑鷄
**116. Steamed Chicken:**
*Boned bite-sized pieces of chicken meat are marinated, topped with ginger and black mushrooms, steamed and sprinkled with sesame oil.*

## 豆豉燜鷄
**117. Braised Chicken with Black Beans:**
*Chicken pieces are marinated, quick-fried, sautéed with*

garlic, ginger, chili flakes and pungent black beans, then covered and braised until tender.

## 東江鹽焗鷄

**118. Salt Baked Chicken:**
This dish is of Hakka origin. Chicken is marinated, wrapped in muslin, covered with coarse salt and baked. The chicken is served cut into small pieces, with a Chinese ginger-powder dip. Most restaurants take a short cut with this dish by using poached chicken and flavoring it with salt and Chinese ginger powder; it is less flavorful.

## 椰汁葡國鷄

**119. Macao Chicken:**
Also called Portuguese Chicken, this is a curried chicken casserole. Small pieces of chicken, still on the bone, are marinated, fried with onions, carrots and potatoes, and baked in a curried coconut-flavored sauce. Eat this casserole with lots of steamed rice.

## 生炒鷄片

**120. Sautéed Chicken Slices:**
Marinated chicken slices are quick-fried, then sautéed with sliced black mushrooms and water chestnuts. Some restaurants put sautéed seasonal Chinese greens around the chicken.

## 金華玉樹鷄

**121. Chicken with Ham and Chinese Greens:**
Small pieces of boned chicken meat are steamed on a plate with cooked Chinese ham. They are served with a transparent sauce and garnished with long stalks of sautéed gai lan. This is an elaborate dish suitable for four or more people.

## 彩鳳還巢
**122. Chicken in a Bird's Nest:**
*Shredded, marinated chicken meat is sautéed with a variety of vegetables such as snow pea pods and mushrooms and served in a deep-fried shoestring potato or taro root basket. To eat, use a spoon to break up the basket and take equal portions of filling and nest.*

## 北菇蒸滑鷄
**123. Chicken Steamed with Black Mushrooms:**
*Marinated chicken pieces, still on the bone, are steamed with black mushrooms.*

## 炒鷄鬆
**124. Chicken Lettuce Wraps:**
*Minced chicken is sautéed with a minced assortment of bamboo shoots, snow pea pods, carrots and black mushrooms, served over deep-fried crunchy rice vermicelli, with large lettuce leaves and* hoi sin *sauce on the side. To eat, smear the hollow of a lettuce leaf with* hoi sin *sauce, add a spoonful of filling, wrap tightly and eat with fingers.*

## 香芒炒鷄片
**125. Chicken with Mango Slices:**
*Marinated chicken slices are sautéed with sweet slices of mango.*

## 紙包鷄
**126. Paper-Wrapped Chicken:**
*Bite-sized pieces of marinated chicken meat are layered with bamboo shoots and green onions, and wrapped either in small pieces of parchment paper or in edible wafers. The*

packages are deep-fried to a golden brown. The edible wafer is crunchy and light. If parchment paper is used, unwrap before eating.

## 雙菰炒鷄片

**127. Chicken and Two Kinds of Mushrooms:**
Boned, marinated chicken slices are quick-fried and sautéed with button and straw mushrooms.

## 三菰鷄片

**128. Chicken and Three Kinds of Mushrooms:**
Boned, marinated chicken slices are quick-fried and sautéed with button, straw and black mushrooms.

## 川椒鷄

**129. Szechwan Peppercorn Chicken, or Chicken with *Chin Jew*:**
Marinated chicken cubes are quick-fried and sautéed with crushed Szechwan peppercorns and chilies. The chicken is garnished with crunchy deep-fried spinach leaves. This dish is only available in Chiu Chow restaurants.

## 梅菜鷄

**130. Chicken with *Mui Choy*, or Preserved Vegetables:**
Chicken is boned whole, stuffed with a mixture of mui choy, bamboo shoots, black mushrooms, pork and ham, sewn up, steamed, then deep-fried. It is served drizzled with its own juice.

## 香露鷄

**131. Fragrant Chicken:**
Chicken is poached in a fragrant seasoned liquid, drained, cut into small pieces, topped with ginger and green onions and drizzled with a mixture of hot vegetable and sesame oils.

## 蠔油手撕鷄

**132. Shredded Chicken:**
*Poached chicken is boned, shredded and tossed with an oyster-flavored sauce.*

## 腰果鷄丁

**133. Cashew Chicken:**
*Boned chicken meat is cubed, marinated, quick-fried and sautéed with cashew nuts and peppers.*

## 核桃鷄卷

**134. Walnut Chicken Rolls:**
*Boned chicken slices are stuffed and rolled with ham and walnuts, dipped in a batter, deep-fried, then braised in a sauce with mushroom slices.*

## 菜膽上湯鷄

**135. Chicken with Vegetable Hearts:**
*Poached white chicken is boned and served with sautéed hearts of* bok choy *in a transparent sauce.*

## 蠔油北菇煀鷄

**136. Braised Chicken and Black Mushrooms:**
*Marinated chicken pieces, still on the bone, are sautéed and braised with oyster sauce and black mushrooms.*

## 沙茶鷄絲

**137. Shredded Chicken in** Sar Char **Sauce or Shredded Chicken Sautéed with Peppers and Satay Sauce:**
*Boned chicken meat is shredded, marinated and sautéed in a piquant sauce with green peppers.*

## 豉 汁 鷄 礫
**138. Chicken Balls with Black-Bean Sauce:**
*Marinated chicken pieces, still on the bone, are fried and sautéed with hot peppers and pungent black beans.*

## 奶 油 椰 子 鷄
**139. Coconut Cream Chicken:**
*Marinated chicken pieces, still on the bone, are fried and baked in a casserole with a creamy coconut sauce.*

## 金 鐘 凍 鷄
**140. Jellied Chicken:**
*Steamed, boned chicken meat is diced, then chilled to form an aspic with cooked sliced egg whites, ham, bamboo shoots and Chinese parsley.*

## 乾 煎 鷄 甫
**141. Pan-Fried Chicken Breast:**
*A boned piece of chicken breast is marinated, pan-fried, sliced and served with a mixture of sautéed vegetables.*

## 臘 腸 蒸 鷄
**142. Steamed Chicken with Sausages:**
*Marinated chicken pieces, still on the bone, are steamed with Chinese sausages and black mushrooms.*

## 鷄 茸 燴 豆 苗
**143. Snow Pea Shoots and Minced Chicken:**
*Minced, marinated chicken is sautéed and served over sautéed tender shoots of the snow pea.*

蜜糖子薑雞球

**144. Honeyed Ginger Chicken:**
*Chicken pieces, still on the bone, are marinated, fried and sautéed with pickled pink ginger, garlic and honey.*

芙蓉炒雞柳

**145. Chicken Sautéed with Egg Whites:**
*Shredded, marinated chicken meat is sautéed with milk and beaten egg whites.*

原盅椰子燉雞

**146. Coconut Chicken:**
*Chicken meat, ginger, green onions and broth are steamed and served in a coconut shell.*

乾炸童子雞

**147. Crispy Half-Grown Chicken:**
*A small half-grown chicken is marinated and fried until golden brown.*

雞柳扒菜膽

**148. Shredded Chicken and Vegetable Hearts:**
*Shredded, marinated chicken meat is sautéed and served over sautéed hearts of bok choy.*

油煎子雞

**149. Fried Chicken:**
*Chicken pieces are marinated, fried, then braised in broth and glutinous rice wine.*

雙 喜 如 意 鷄

**150. Stuffed Chicken:**
A chicken is deboned into one large sheet, stuffed with julienned ham and celery, rolled up, then steamed and fried until golden brown. It is served sliced, with a sauce studded with black mushrooms and bamboo shoots.

珊 瑚 玉 樹 鷄

**151. Chicken, Ham and Greens with a Crab Meat Sauce:**
Marinated chicken slices are layered and steamed with Chinese ham, surrounded with sautéed Chinese greens and topped with a white crab meat sauce.

脆 皮 糯 米 鷄

**152. Crispy Stuffed Chicken:**
Chicken is boned whole, stuffed with a glutinous rice mixture, sewn up, steamed, then fried until golden brown.

繡 球 白 菜 包

**153. Stuffed Cabbage Rolls:**
Chinese cabbage leaves are softened, stuffed and rolled with minced chicken, ham and black mushrooms, then slow-cooked in broth, drained and served with straw mushrooms and a transparent sauce. This dish is only available in Chiu Chow restaurants.

太 爺 鷄

**154. Smoked Chicken:**
Chicken is poached in a seasoned liquid, smoked over tea leaves, then cut into bite-sized pieces.

## 釀七星鷄

**155. Chicken Stuffed with Shrimp Meat:**
*Boned chicken slices are marinated, smeared with a ground shrimp-meat mixture, topped with minced ham, Chinese parsley and black mushrooms, steamed and served with a transparent sauce.*

## 八珍屈鷄

**156. Chicken with an Assortment:**
*Marinated chicken is slow-cooked in a casserole with ham, fried onions, shredded dried scallops, straw and black mushrooms, gingko nuts, chicken giblets and livers. When tender, the chicken is cut into small pieces and served with the other ingredients.*

## 奶油八寶鷄

**157. Eight Precious Chicken:**
*Chicken is boned whole, stuffed with a mixture of lotus seeds, dried scallops, black mushrooms, giblets, livers, ham and bamboo shoots. Then it is sewn up, steamed until tender and served with its own juice.*

## 五彩鳳肝

**158. Braised Chicken Livers:**
*Marinated slices of chicken liver are fried, then braised with peas, peppers, fried walnuts and bamboo shoots.*

## 針菜鬱鷄

**159. Chicken with Golden Needles:**
*Chicken pieces, still on the bone, are slow-cooked with pungent golden needles (gum jum).*

## 百花雞

**160. Chicken with Shrimp Meat:**
*A large piece of chicken meat, with the skin, is spread with a paste made of ground chicken and shrimp meat. It is then topped with ham and crab meat, steamed, fried and served sliced. This dish requires advance notice.*

## 鐵板豆豉雞

**161. Teppan Black-Bean Chicken:**
*Marinated chicken pieces, still on the bone, are sautéed with onions and black beans, then served sizzling on a hot teppan dish.*

## 鳳凰彩雞

**162. Braised Chicken Meat:**
*Deboned sliced chicken is marinated, dipped in a batter, fried, then braised with Chinese ham, sautéed black mushrooms, bamboo shoots and topped with a transparent sauce.*

## 鳳肝金華雞

**163. Chicken and Giblets:**
*Chicken meat and giblets are sliced and steamed with ham, garnished with Chinese greens and a transparent sauce.*

## 網油鳳肝卷

**164. Liver Roll:**
*Poached chicken livers are chopped, mixed with ham and bamboo shoots, wrapped in caul, then deep-fried to a golden brown. The fried roll is served sliced.*

荔 枝 鷄 球

**165. Chicken and Lychees:**
*In this Chinese-American dish, boned marinated chicken pieces are fried in a batter and braised in a syrupy sweet-and-sour sauce with peppers and canned lychees.*

檸 檬 鷄

**166. Lemon Chicken:**
*In this Chinese-American dish, a piece of chicken breast is boned, marinated, dipped in a batter, deep-fried, sliced and served with a yellow sweet-and-sour sauce.*

## MAIN DISHES — DUCKS AND OTHER BIRDS

Some duck dishes can be ordered whole, in halves or quarters. The more elaborate duck dishes need advance notice because they take time to prepare.

掛 爐 鴨 或 火 鴨

**167. Barbecued Duck:**
*Duck is stuffed with seasonings, sewn up, basted with a honey-vinegar solution, hang-dried, then roasted until it is reddish brown. It is served on the bone, cut into small pieces.*

琵 琶 鷄

**168. *Pei Pa* Duck:**
*Duck is split open along the backbone, marinated with special seasonings, then roasted until reddish brown. It is served on the bone, cut into small pieces.*

鴨 肉 炒 鬆

**169. Duck Lettuce Wraps:**
*Minced duck meat is sautéed with minced carrot, black mushrooms and bamboo shoots, then served over deep-fried rice vermicelli with large lettuce leaves and* hoi sin *sauce on the side. To eat, smear the hollow of a lettuce leaf with* hoi sin *sauce, add a spoonful of filling, roll tightly and eat with fingers.*

芋 茸 香 酥 鴨

**170. Deep-Fried Duck with Taro Root:**
*Half a deboned poached duck is filled with a seasoned taro-root mixture, dipped in a batter and deep-fried until golden brown. It is served cut into small pieces over shredded lettuce leaves.*

八 珍 扒 肥 鴨

**171. Braised Duck with an Assortment:**
*Duck is split open along the backbone, fried, then slow-cooked until tender with ginger and green onions. It is served with its own juice and braised sea cucumbers, abalone, black mushrooms, bamboo shoots, dried scallops and shrimp. Some restaurants also garnish this dish with Chinese cabbage or Chinese greens.*

霸 王 鴨

**172. Great Warrior's Duck:**
*Duck is stuffed with glutinous rice, chestnuts and salty duck egg yolk. It is then sewn up, fried and served with a sauce. Advance notice is required for this dish.*

## 時菜扒大鴨

**173. Duck and Seasonal Vegetables:**
*Duck is slow-cooked until tender in a soy-based sauce and served over Chinese cabbage or greens.*

## 北菰扒大鴨

**174. Duck and Black Mushrooms:**
*Duck is slow-cooked until tender in a soy-based sauce and served with supple black mushrooms.*

## 羅漢扒大鴨

**175. Duck with Buddha's Feast:**
*Duck is slow-cooked until tender and served with braised gluten, bamboo shoots, black moss, black mushrooms and Chinese vegetables.*

## 陳皮燉全鴨

**176. Duck Steamed with Tangerine Peels:**
*Duck pieces are steamed in a covered casserole with broth and dried tangerine peels.*

## 蠔油出骨鴨

**177. Boned Duck in Oyster Sauce:**
*Duck is slow-cooked until tender with oyster sauce and green onions, boned, fried and served with sautéed vegetables and its own juice.*

## 鴨絲銀芽

**178. Shredded Duck and Bean Sprouts:**
*Cooked shredded duck meat is sautéed with crunchy silver sprouts (bean sprouts with the heads and roots removed).*

鐵板西檸煎嫩鴨

**179. Teppan Lemon Duck:**
Slices of duck meat are marinated, pan-fried, then served sizzling on a teppan cast-iron plate with a lemon sauce.

蠔油鴨掌

**180. Stewed Duck Feet in Oyster Sauce:**
Duck feet are boned whole and cooked tender in spices and oyster sauce.

鮑魚鴨掌

**181. Duck's Feet and Abalone:**
Boned duck's feet are stewed until tender and served with thin slivers of canned abalone.

脆皮鵪鶉

**182. Crispy Quail:**
Quail is poached in a seasoned liquid, basted, then fried until golden brown. It is usually served quartered.

鵪鶉鬆

**183. Quail Lettuce Wraps:**
Minced quail meat is sautéed with a variety of minced vegetables such as carrot, black mushrooms and bamboo shoots, and served over rice vermicelli with lettuce leaves and hoi sin sauce on the side. To eat, smear the hollow of a leaf with hoi sin sauce, fill with a spoonful of the quail mixture, roll tightly and eat with fingers.

琥皮鵪鶉蛋

**184. Braised Quail Eggs:**
Hard-boiled quail eggs are shelled, marinated, fried and

braised with oyster sauce, bamboo shoots, ham, shrimp and Chinese greens.

## 迎春接福

**185. Steamed Quail Eggs:**
*Tiny quail eggs are broken and poured into black mushroom caps, garnished with minced ham and Chinese parsley, then steamed. They are served with sautéed Chinese greens and juice from the mushrooms.*

## 鹵水乳鴿

**186. Poached Pigeon:**
*Whole pigeon is poached in a seasoned liquid with spices such as star anise, fennel seeds and Szechwan peppercorns. It is drained, basted and cut into small pieces.*

## 脆皮乳鴿

**187. Crispy Pigeon:**
*Pigeon is poached in a seasoned liquid, basted and fried until golden brown. It is cut into small pieces and served with crunchy shrimp chips or a peppery salt dip.*

## 瓦罉魚露鴿

**188. Pigeon with Fish Sauce:**
*Pigeon is slow-cooked until tender in a clay casserole with fish sauce.*

## 鐵板黑椒乳鴿

**189. Teppan Pigeon with Black Peppers:**
*Pigeon is poached, fried, cut and served sizzling on a hot teppan plate with ginger, onion and crushed black peppers.*

燒 鵝

**190. Roasted Goose:**
*A marinated goose is roasted until reddish brown and served cut into bite-sized pieces.*

---
## MAIN DISHES — EXOTIC INGREDIENTS
---

The Cantonese eat a great variety of exotic ingredients. Several are highly prized for their alleged medicinal value. Some ingredients, such as shark's fins and bird's nest (or dried bird's saliva), come in dehydrated form. They are expensive and require elaborate preparation. Because of their relative obscurity, only the most popular of these exotic dishes are included here. Most of the dishes listed here are main dishes; there are a few soups.

紅 扒 大 羣 翅

**191. Braised Whole Shark's Fin:**
*A whole shark's fin is used for this dish. It is slow-cooked until soft and gelatinous, then steamed with pork and chicken pieces. The fin is then drained, braised and served over sautéed bean sprouts and garnished with shredded ham and a flavorful sauce.*

紅 燒 鷄 包 翅

**192. Chicken and Shark's Fin:**
*A shark's fin is slow-cooked with a chicken until soft and gelatinous, then served in a thickened soup with boned*

chicken meat. Shark's fins are also made into thickened soups with minced chicken or crab meat.

## 蟹肉燴燕窩
### 193. Crab Meat and Bird's Nest Soup:
*Bird's nest is cooked until soft and gelatinous and served in a thickened soup with crab meat and beaten egg whites.*

## 鷄絲燴燕窩
### 194. Shredded Chicken and Bird's Nest Soup:
*Shredded, marinated chicken meat is served in a thickened soup with soft and gelatinous bird's nest and beaten egg whites.*

## 嶺南椰子盅
### 195. Bird's Nest in a Coconut:
*A coconut with the top sliced off is filled with chicken meat, dried abalone, black mushrooms, ham, cooked bird's nest and broth. It is then steamed; the soup is served in the shell.*

## 髮菜扣蠔豉
### 196. Dried Oysters with Black Moss:
*Chewy and somewhat fishy-tasting dried oysters are braised with pork and black moss. In Cantonese, black moss is fat choy, which sounds the same as "make a fortune." This dish is eaten for good luck at Chinese New Year.*

## 三蛇羹
### 197. Three Types of Snake Soup:
*Only available in countries where snake is an acceptable culinary ingredient, this is a thickened soup with three different types of snake meat, black mushrooms and bamboo shoots. The snake meat is subtle-tasting and resembles*

chicken meat. Chrysanthemum petals, Chinese parsley leaves, fried crackers and shredded lemon leaves are served on the side. To eat: sprinkle a bit of each of the accompaniments over your bowl of soup. The Cantonese like to have snake meat in the fall and winter because they believe it keeps the chill away. Poisonous snakes such as cobra or krait are particularly prized. Some restaurants serve Five Types of Snake Soup. Snake meat is also served sautéed.

## 花膠會鴨絲
**198. Shredded Duck and Fish Maw or Bladder Soup:**
Shredded fish bladder, cooked until soft and spongy, is served in a thickened soup with shredded duck meat, bamboo shoots and black mushrooms.

## 清湯魚肚
**199. Fish Maw or Bladder Soup:**
Shredded fish bladder is cooked until soft and spongy and served in a seasoned broth.

## 桂花魚肚
**200. Braised Fish Bladder:**
Sliced fish bladder is cooked until soft and spongy and served in a thickened soup with beaten egg yolks.

## 鳳絲魚唇
**201. Fish Lips and Chicken Soup:**
Dried fish lips are cooked until soft and gelatinous, and served in a thickened soup with shredded bamboo shoots, black mushrooms, chicken meat, dried scallops and canned abalone.

## 蠔油排魚唇
**202. Fish Lips in Oyster Sauce:**
Dried fish lips, cooked until soft and gelatinous, are braised in oyster sauce. Sautéed Chinese greens are sometimes used as garnishes.

## 八珍烏石參
**203. Steamed Sea Cucumbers:**
Sea cucumbers are steamed with diced chicken, ham, black mushrooms, giblets and bamboo shoots, and served in a large soup bowl with a seasoned broth.

## 海參鵝掌
**204. Sea Cucumbers and Goose Feet:**
Goose feet, boned and stewed, are braised until soft with spongy sea cucumbers and oyster sauce. This dish is only available in Chiu Chow restaurants.

## 冬瓜乾貝燉田鷄
**205. Steamed Frog Legs:**
Frog legs, cubes of winter melon and dried scallops are put into a casserole with broth, then covered and steamed. This dish is prized for its tasty broth.

## 豉椒田鷄腿
**206. Frog Legs with Black Beans:**
Marinated frog legs are quick-fried and sautéed with hot peppers, garlic and black beans.

## 西芹田鷄球
**207. Celery and Frog Legs:**
Marinated frog legs are quick-fried and sautéed with garlic, celery and black mushrooms.

油泡田鷄

**208. Sautéed Frog Legs:**
*Marinated frog legs are quick-fried and sautéed with garlic, bamboo shoots and black mushrooms. Sautéed* gai lan *is served around the frog legs.*

百花釀田鷄

**209. Stuffed Frog Legs:**
*Frog legs are wrapped with a seasoned ground shrimp paste, coated with bread crumbs and fried until golden brown.*

珊瑚藏雪蛤

**210. Frog Fat and Crab Meat:**
*Kernels of frog fat, supposedly extracted from a hibernating frog and believed to have a rejuvenating effect, are cooked in broth until gelatin-like. They are then drained and served with broccoli and a white crab-meat sauce.*

紅燒大水魚

**211. Red-Cooked Turtle:**
*Turtle is cut into small pieces, sautéed with garlic, then braised until tender with black mushrooms and bamboo shoots.*

鳳足燉鹿筋

**212. Chicken Feet and Deer Ligaments:**
*Chicken feet and chunks of deer ligaments are steamed in a container with broth. This dish is prized for the broth and the soft texture of the ligaments.*

焗禾花雀

**213. Braised Sparrow:**
*Tiny sparrows are marinated, fried and braised in a sweet-and-sour sauce.*

鷄腰排鴿蛋

**214. Chicken Testicles and Pigeon Eggs:**
*Chicken testicles and fried pigeon eggs are braised in oyster sauce with ham and mushrooms, then garnished with sautéed snow-pea shoots.*

蝦子金錢菇

**215. Shrimp Eggs Braised with Mushrooms:**
*Black and fresh mushrooms are braised in a brown sauce with shrimp eggs. This dish is garnished with sautéed mustard green hearts.*

御品佛跳牆

**216. Buddha Will Jump over the Wall:**
*This is a casserole made up of a variety of precious, exotic ingredients. It is allegedly so delicious that Buddha will jump over the wall for it. This dish has an imperial origin and is expensive. Shark's fin, deer ligaments, abalone, black mushrooms, dried scallops, goose feet, Chinese herbs and a silkie (a chicken with black meat and black bones, prized for its nutritious value) are slow-cooked and served in a broth.*

## MAIN DISHES — FISH

If the Cantonese are particular about all their ingredients, they are positively fastidious about their seafood. Fish must be the freshest available and live fish is preferred, though it is more expensive. Recipes are designed to enhance the natural flavors of seafood with the emphasis on light sauces, subtle seasonings and brief cooking times. When ordering Cantonese seafood, you should get the waiter's assurance that the fish used by the restaurant is not frozen.

清蒸石班或其他魚
### 217. Steamed Rock Cod or Other Fish:
*A whole fish is steamed and served with ginger, green onions and a soy-based sauce. Bream, snapper, pickerel, sole, flounder and the inimitable rock cod can all be prepared this way. Sometimes restaurants will also cook fresh fish steaks, such as salmon and black cod, in the same way with excellent results.*

油泡石班球
### 218. Sautéed Rock Cod Fillets:
*Boned, marinated pieces of cod are quick-fried and sautéed with vegetables.*

五柳石班
### 219. Rock Cod with Sweet-and-Sour Sauce:
*A whole rock cod is dipped in a light batter, fried until crispy and served with a sweet-and-sour sauce.*

## 生炒魚片
**220. Sautéed Fish Slices:**
*Boned, marinated fish slices are quick-fried and sautéed with mushrooms and* choy sum *or* gai lan.

## 白汁班塊
**221. Rock Cod with White Sauce:**
*Boned, marinated pieces of rock cod are dipped in a light batter, fried, then braised in a creamy white sauce.*

## 珍珠石班塊
**222. Rock Cod Slices with Creamed Corn Sauce:**
*Boned, marinated cod pieces are dipped in a light batter, fried and braised in a sauce made from canned creamed corn.*

## 鐵板龍利球
**223. Teppan Sole or Flounder:**
*Boned, marinated sole or flounder slices are quick-fried, sautéed with ginger and green onions, then served sizzling on a hot cast-iron teppan plate.*

## 七彩魚塊
**224. Fish Slices in a Sweet-and-Sour Sauce:**
*Boned, marinated fish slices are dipped in a batter, fried and served with a garlicky sweet-and-sour sauce.*

## 玉蘭班塊
**225. Fish Slices and *Gai Lan*:**
*Boned, marinated cod pieces are quick-fried and sautéed with* gai lan.

## 沙魚炒芥蘭

**226. Sautéed Sturgeon:**
*Boned, marinated sturgeon slices are quick-fried and sautéed with* gai lan. *Sturgeon tastes like halibut.*

## 三鮮麒麟魚

**227. Steamed Fish Slices with Ham and Black Mushrooms:**
*Boned, marinated fish slices are layered with slices of ham and black mushroom, steamed and served with their own juice, which has been thickened. This is an elaborate dish usually served at a banquet.*

## 玉樹麒麟班

**228. Steamed Fish Slices with Ham, Black Mushrooms and Gai Lan:**
*This dish is the same as above except that sautéed* gai lan *is arranged around the fish.*

## 豉椒蒸魚

**229. Fish Steamed with Black Beans:**
*A whole fish is steamed and served with a pungent garlic and black-bean sauce.*

## 乾煎鮮龍利

**230. Pan-Fried Flounder:**
*Flounder is marinated and pan-fried to a golden brown.*

## 煙鯧魚

**231. Smoked Pomfret:**
*Pomfret is marinated, pan-fried and smoked over tea leaves. This dish is of Chiu Chow origin. Most restaurants don't smoke the fish, but serve it with a slightly sweet sauce that has a smoky flavor.*

## 骨香龍利球
**232. Sautéed Flounder with Crunchy Bones:**
A whole flounder is deboned. The backbone, still attached to the head and tail, is dusted with cornstarch and fried until crispy. The fish meat is sliced, marinated, sautéed with vegetables and served over the fried backbone. This dish emphasizes the contrast of textures, the softness of the fish meat and the crunchiness of the fried bones.

## 東江魚丸
**233. Hakka Fish Balls:**
A white fish such as ling cod or snapper is ground up, seasoned, shaped into small balls, poached and drained. Fish balls can be served in soups or casseroles, or sautéed with vegetables. This dish is of Hakka origin.

## 紅燒班腩
**234. Red-Cooked Cod:**
Chunks of rock cod, still on the bone, are dusted with flour, fried, braised in a soy-based sauce with shredded pork and black mushrooms, and served over blanched lettuce. This dish is also served bubbling in a Chinese casserole. Tell the waiter if you want the fish boned.

## 豉椒蒸魚雲
**235. Fish Head and Black Beans:**
A large meaty fish head is cut up, marinated and steamed with hot peppers and pungent black beans.

## 蒜子燜白鱔
**236. Garlic Eel:**
Chunks of white eel are quick-fried, sautéed, then braised with chi hau sauce, roasted pork, black mushrooms, garlic

and dried tangerine peels. *This is a special dish available only in some restaurants.*

椒鹽白鱔球

**237. Peppery Salt White Eel:**
*Chunks of white eel are marinated, fried and tossed in a hot dry wok with salt and pepper.*

五柳鱔條

**238. Sautéed Yellow Eel:**
*Boned, shredded yellow eel is sautéed with shredded black mushrooms, barbecued pork, ham, ginger, yellow chives and dried tangerine peels. It is served over crunchy deep-fried rice vermicelli, drizzled with hot garlic oil and sprinkled with white pepper powder.*

---

## MAIN DISHES — LAMB

---

燉羊肉

**239. Steamed Lamb or Mutton:**
*Lamb or mutton is boiled, drained, sautéed, then steamed in a container with Chinese herbs.*

燜羊肉

**240. Lamb or Mutton Stew:**
*Lamb or mutton is cubed, sautéed, then slow-cooked until tender with garlic, onions and bean sauce. This dish is often served bubbling in a Chinese casserole.*

炒 綿 羊 絲

**241. Sautéed Shredded Lamb:**
Lamb is shredded, marinated and sautéed with shredded ginger, black mushrooms and bamboo shoots.

酥 炸 羊 腩

**242. Fried Lamb or Mutton:**
A slab of lamb or mutton is steamed, dipped in batter and fried until golden brown. It is served sliced with hoi sin sauce or a peppery salt dip.

## MAIN DISHES — PORK

叉 燒

**243. Barbecued Pork:**
Strips of pork are marinated in five spices, soy and hoi sin sauces. The pork is then roasted, basted with honey and sliced.

燒 排 骨

**244. Barbecued Spareribs:**
Spareribs are marinated in five spices, soy and hoi sin sauces. The ribs are roasted, basted with honey, then cut up.

燒 肉

**245. Roasted Pork:**
A whole pig is marinated, roasted until the skin is crispy, and served in small portions. The meat is usually salty and layered with fat. This dish is prized for its crunchy skin.

# 烤乳猪

**246. Roast Suckling Pig:**
A suckling pig is marinated, then roasted until the skin is crispy. It is cut into bite-sized pieces and served with hoi sin sauce. This dish is known for its delicious lean meat (albeit layered with fat) and its crunchy skin.

# 京都排骨

**247. Capital Pork Chops or Sweet-and-Sour Pork Chops:**
Marinated strips of pork chops are fried, then braised in a sweet-and-sour sauce.

# 時菜肉片

**248. Chinese Vegetables and Pork Slices:**
Marinated thinly sliced pork is quick-fried, then sautéed with blanched seasonal Chinese vegetables.

# 咕嚕肉

**249. Sweet-and-Sour Pork:**
Pieces of pork are marinated in a batter, fried, then braised in a sticky sweet-and-sour sauce with red and green peppers and pineapple chunks.

# 生菜包

**250. Pork Lettuce Wraps:**
Minced pork is sautéed with a combination of minced vegetables, such as carrot, snow pea pods and bamboo shoots, and served with large lettuce leaves and hoi sin sauce on the side. To eat, smear the hollow of a leaf with hoi sin sauce, add a spoonful of filling, roll tightly and eat with fingers.

## 生炒排骨

**251. Sweet-and-Sour Spareribs:**
*Pieces of sparerib are marinated, fried, then braised in a sweet-and-sour sauce with peppers and pineapple chunks.*

## 北菰芽菜肉絲

**252. Shredded Pork, Bean Sprouts and Black Mushrooms:**
*Shredded, marinated pork is sautéed with bean sprouts and shredded black mushrooms.*

## 豉椒炒排骨

**253. Spareribs with Black Beans:**
*Marinated rib pieces are quick-fried, then sautéed with sliced peppers and pungent black beans.*

## 雀巢猪肉絲

**254. Shredded Pork in Bird's Nest:**
*Shredded pork and vegetables are sautéed and served in a deep-fried shoestring potato basket. To eat: break up the nest with a spoon and take equal portions of filling and nest.*

## 梅菜扣肉

**255. Mui Choy or Preserved Salty Vegetables and Pork:**
*Mui choy, a pungent preserved vegetable, is chopped and steamed with thick slices of pork belly that have been poached, marinated and fried. This dish is prized for the pungent taste of the mui choy and its contrasting textures—chewy lean meat marbled with soft and spongy fat pork. This dish is of Hakka origin.*

# 南乳猪手

**256. Stewed Pig's Feet:**
*Chunks of pig's feet are slow-cooked until tender in soy sauce and sweet red preserved bean curds.*

# 梅子蒸肉排

**257. Sour Plums and Spareribs:**
*Small pieces of spareribs are marinated in preserved sour plums, ginger, garlic and soy sauce, then steamed until tender.*

# 南乳扣肉

**258. Pork Belly and Red Preserved Bean Curds:**
*Marbled pork belly is fried, sautéed with minced garlic and red preserved bean curds, layered with taro root slices, steamed, then served with its own juice. Seasonal Chinese greens are sometimes placed around the meat and taro root.*

# 咸鱼蒸肉饼

**259. Salted Fish Steamed with Minced Pork:**
*Salted fish is mashed and mixed in a plate with seasoned ground pork. The mixture is then steamed. This plain dish is usually available in small restaurants that specialize in home-cooked meals.*

# 咸蛋蒸肉饼

**260. Salty Duck Eggs Steamed with Minced Pork:**
*Salty duck eggs are cracked over and steamed with seasoned ground pork.*

## 東坡肉
**261. Tung Po Pork:**
Marbled pork belly is stewed, fried, dipped in cold water, then slow-cooked until almost melting in soy sauce with green onions. Sautéed Chinese greens are served around the pork. This dish is rarely available in restaurants.

## 酸甜佛手排骨
**262. Stuffed Spareribs:**
Long pork ribs are marinated, wrapped with seasoned ground pork, dipped in batter and deep-fried. They are served with a sweet-and-sour sauce.

## 大良野鷄捲
**263. Stuffed Pork Rolls:**
Large pork slices are marinated, rolled with julienned ham, dipped in batter, then fried to a golden brown. The rolls are served with a peppery salt dip.

## 生炒腰花
**264. Sautéed Kidneys:**
Kidney slices are sautéed with ginger, garlic, black mushrooms and bamboo shoots.

## 生炒肝片
**265. Sautéed Liver:**
Liver slices are quick-fried, then sautéed with black mushrooms and bamboo shoots.

## 八寶釀涼瓜

**266. Stuffed Bitter Melons:**
*Chunks of bitter melon are hollowed out, stuffed with a seasoned pork and glutinous rice mixture, steamed, then fried, and served with oyster sauce.*

## 東江炸肥腸

**267. Fried Intestine:**
*Pig's intestine is stuffed with seasonings such as malt syrup and vinegar, tied, fried, sliced and served with a peppery salt dip.*

## 脆炒肚尖

**268. Sautéed Stomach:**
*Slices of pig's stomach are marinated, fried and sautéed with bamboo shoots and black mushrooms.*

---

MAIN DISHES — SHELLFISH

---

## 菜薳蝦球

**269. Prawns with *Gai Lan*:**
*Shelled, marinated prawns are sautéed until pink with gai lan.*

## 椒鹽蝦

**270. Peppery Salt Shrimp:**
*Large shrimp, in the shell, are fried, then tossed in a hot, dry wok with salt and pepper.*

## 玻璃蝦球
**271. Sautéed Crystal Prawns:**
*Shelled, marinated prawns are sautéed with minced garlic and ginger. This dish is prized for the crunchy texture of the prawns.*

## 雙菇蝦球
**272. Sautéed Prawns with Two Mushrooms:**
*Shelled, marinated prawns are sautéed with button and straw mushrooms.*

## 蝴蝶蝦
**273. Butterfly Prawns:**
*Shelled, marinated medium shrimp are sliced open, layered with bacon, dipped in batter and pan-fried until golden brown. They are served plain or with a curry-flavored sauce.*

## 酥炸蝦球
**274. Fried Shrimp Balls:**
*Ground pork and shrimp are seasoned, shaped into balls, dipped in bread crumbs and fried until golden brown.*

## 豆豉蝦球
**275. Prawns with Black Beans:**
*Shelled, marinated prawns are sautéed with ginger, garlic, hot chilies and pungent black beans.*

## 吉列蝦球
**276. Shrimp Cutlets with Sweet-and-Sour Sauce:**
*Shelled medium shrimp are marinated, dredged in bread crumbs and fried. They are served with a sweet-and-sour sauce. Instead of bread crumbs, some restaurants dip the shrimp in a batter.*

## 腰果炒蝦仁

**277. Shrimp and Cashews:**
Shelled, marinated shrimp are sautéed with crunchy cashew nuts.

## 時菜炒蝦球

**278. Sautéed Prawns and Vegetables:**
Shelled, marinated prawns are sautéed with blanched seasonal Chinese greens.

## 金錢明蝦

**279. Fried Layered Shrimp:**
Shelled, marinated shrimp are sliced open, layered with fatty pork and ham, and pan-fried until golden brown.

## 茄汁明蝦球

**280. Prawns in Tomato Sauce:**
Shelled, marinated prawns are sautéed in a tangy, sweet tomato sauce.

## 豉汁蒸明蝦

**281. Shrimp Steamed with Black-Bean Sauce:**
Shelled large shrimp are steamed with a pungent, spicy black-bean sauce.

## 醉翁蝦

**282. Drunken Shrimp:**
Live medium shrimp are served in a glass casserole at the table. They are drenched in Chinese glutinous rice wine (far dew) which causes them to jump up and down in the casserole. The far dew is ignited with a match and the shrimp are sautéed by a waiter, who adds broth, seasonings, and

minced garlic, ginger and chilies to the shrimp. This dish is only available in specialty seafood restaurants.

## 金錢蝦餅
**283. Fried Shrimp Toasts:**
A paste of ground shrimp and pork is smeared onto small round pieces of bread and fried until golden brown. They are served with a peppery salt or ketchup dip.

## 滑蛋炒蝦仁
**284. Scrambled Eggs with Shrimp:**
Shelled, marinated shrimp are sautéed with beaten eggs.

## 煎百花釀青椒
**285. Pan-Fried Stuffed Peppers:**
Green peppers are cut in half, stuffed with a ground shrimp paste and pan-fried.

## 百花釀青瓜
**286. Stuffed Cucumbers:**
Chunks of cucumber are hollowed out, stuffed with a ground shrimp paste, then steamed. The dish is served with mushrooms and the juice from the steamed cucumbers.

## 釀冬菇
**287. Stuffed Black Mushrooms:**
Black mushroom caps are stuffed with a ground shrimp paste, steamed and served with their own juice.

## 脆奶拼蝦仁
**288. Sautéed Shrimp and Crispy Milk Curds:**
Curds made of milk are deep-fried until golden brown and served next to sautéed shrimp.

油泡帶子蝦球

**289. Sautéed Prawns and Scallops:**
*Shelled, marinated prawns and scallops are quick-fried, then sautéed with minced ginger and garlic.*

鐵板蝦球

**290. Teppan Prawns:**
*Shelled, marinated prawns are sautéed with ginger and green onions, then served sizzling on a hot cast-iron teppan plate.*

蟹肉扒雙菰

**291. Crab Meat over Mushrooms:**
*A white sauce made with crab meat is served over two types of mushrooms, such as straw and button mushrooms.*

蟹肉扒蘭花

**292. Crab Meat over Broccoli:**
*A sauce made of crab meat is served over broccoli florets.*

清蒸蟹

**293. Steamed Crab:**
*A whole fresh crab is steamed, cut into pieces and served with a vinegar and shredded-ginger dip. Dismantle and eat the crab with fingers.*

豉椒蟹

**294. Crab with Black Beans:**
*Pieces of unshelled crab are fried, sautéed, then braised in a pungent black-bean sauce.*

薑葱蟹

**295. Crab with Ginger and Green Onions:**
Pieces of unshelled crab are fried, sautéed, then braised in a ginger and green-onion sauce.

奶油焗蟹

**296. Crab in White Sauce:**
Pieces of unshelled crab are fried, sautéed, then braised in a creamy coconut-flavored sauce.

椒鹽蟹

**297. Crab with Peppery Salt:**
Pieces of unshelled crab are fried, then tossed in a hot dry wok with salt, pepper and minced hot peppers.

釀蟹拑

**298. Stuffed Crab Claws:**
Crab claws are wrapped with a paste made of ground shrimp and pork, dipped in bread crumbs, then fried until golden brown.

酥炸蟹塔

**299. Stuffed Crab Shells:**
Crab meat, minced shrimp and pork are stuffed into small crab shells, which are steamed, then fried until golden brown.

網油蟹肉捲

**300. Crab Meat Rolls:**
A mixture of minced shrimp, pork and crab meat is rolled in a piece of caul, steamed, then fried until golden brown. The roll is sliced and served with a peppery salt dip and Worcestershire sauce on the side.

## 粵式炒鮮奶
**301. Sautéed Egg Whites and Crab Meat:**
*Crab meat is sautéed with beaten egg whites and milk until coagulated, then served over deep-fried crunchy rice vermicelli.*

## 金錢蟹盒
**302. Fried Crab Meat Toasts:**
*Crab meat and minced pork, mushrooms and ham are mixed into a paste, sandwiched between two small pieces of fatty pork or bread, then deep-fried until golden brown.*

## 生炒芙蓉蟹
**303. Crab with Egg Whites:**
*Pieces of unshelled crab are fried and sautéed with egg whites.*

## 蟹肉扒雙蔬
**304. Crab Meat and Two Kinds of Vegetables:**
*A white sauce made with crab meat is served over two types of sautéed vegetables.*

## 蟹肉扒荳苗
**305. Crab Meat and Snow-Pea Shoots:**
*The tender shoots of the snow pea are sautéed and topped with a white sauce made with crab meat.*

## 焗釀蟹蓋
**306. Baked Stuffed Crab Shells:**
*Crab meat, ham, black mushrooms and ground pork are stuffed into small crab shells, deep-fried and then baked.*

## 帶子鳳還巢
**307. Scallops in Bird's Nest:**
*Sautéed scallops and vegetables are served in a deep-fried shoestring potato or taro root basket. To eat, break up the nest with a spoon and take equal portions of filling and nest.*

## 油泡帶子
**308. Sautéed Scallops:**
*Marinated scallops are quick-fried and sautéed with minced garlic and ginger, sliced carrot and mushrooms.*

## 百花帶子
**309. Stuffed Scallops:**
*Scallops are wrapped with a seasoned ground-shrimp paste, then fried and braised in a transparent sauce with Chinese greens.*

## 崧子炒帶子
**310. Pine Nuts and Scallops:**
*Marinated scallops are sautéed with diced vegetables and fungi and served garnished with fragrant pine nuts.*

## 金錢帶子
**311. Layered Scallops:**
*Marinated scallops are layered with ham, black mushrooms, ground chicken and small pieces of bread, then fried until golden brown.*

## 雪豆帶子
**312. Scallops and Snow Pea Pods:**
*Marinated scallops are sautéed with crunchy sweet snow pea pods.*

## 油泡帶子
**313. Sautéed Scallops:**
*Marinated scallops are sautéed with minced garlic and ginger and with sliced carrots and mushrooms.*

## 生炸帶子
**314. Fried Scallops:**
*Marinated scallops are dipped in batter and deep-fried until golden brown.*

## 豉椒龍蝦
**315. Lobster with Black Beans:**
*Pieces of unshelled lobster are fried, then braised in a pungent and spicy black-bean sauce.*

## 白汁龍蝦
**316. Lobster in White Sauce:**
*Pieces of unshelled lobster are fried, then braised in a creamy coconut-flavored sauce.*

## 薑葱龍蝦
**317. Lobster with Ginger and Green Onions:**
*Pieces of unshelled lobster are fried, then braised in a ginger and green-onion sauce.*

## 上湯焗龍蝦
**318. Lobster Braised in Broth:**
*Pieces of unshelled lobster are fried, then braised in broth with minced garlic and ginger.*

## 雀 巢 海 鮮

**319. Seafood in a Bird's Nest:**
*Several types of seafood, such as shrimp and scallops, are sautéed with vegetables and served in a deep-fried shoestring potato or taro root basket. To eat, break up nest with a spoon and take equal portions of filling and nest.*

## 生 炒 蜆

**320. Sautéed Clams:**
*Fresh clams, still in the shell, are sautéed with garlic and ginger.*

## 豉 椒 炒 蜆

**321. Clams with Black Beans:**
*Fresh clams, still in the shell, are sautéed with black beans, garlic and ginger.*

## 白 灼 象 拔 蚌

**322. Poached Geoduck:**
*Geoduck, a giant west coast clam, is sliced paper-thin, poached and served with a black-bean dip.*

## 韭 菜 花 鮮 象 拔 蚌

**323. Geoduck and Chives:**
*Thin slices of geoduck are sautéed with pungent yellow or green chives.*

## 薑 葱 焗 生 蠔

**324. Oyster with Ginger and Green Onions:**
*Shelled oysters are sautéed with shredded ginger and green onions.*

酥 炸 生 蠔

325. Fried Oysters:
Shelled oysters are dipped in batter and deep-fried until golden brown.

蠔 豉 鬆

326. Dried Oyster Lettuce Wraps:
Dried oysters are minced and sautéed with a variety of minced vegetables and pork, and served over rice vermicelli with large lettuce leaves and hoi sin sauce on the side. To eat, smear the hollow of a leaf with hoi sin sauce, add a spoonful of filling, roll tightly and eat with fingers.

白 灼 響 螺 片

327. Poached Conch (or Whelk):
Thin conch slices are poached and served with a soy-based dip.

油 泡 響 螺 球

328. Sautéed Conch:
Conch slices are sautéed with minced garlic and ginger.

葡 汁 焗 響 螺

329. Baked Conch:
Cooked conch meat is minced, mixed with pork and seasonings, spooned into conch shells, covered with a curry-flavored sauce and baked.

紅 燜 海 螺

330. Red-Cooked Conch:
Shelled conch meat is slow-cooked with pork, wine and soy sauce, sliced thin and sautéed with bamboo shoots and black mushrooms.

## 蠔油響螺片
**331. Conch with Oyster Sauce:**
Sliced conch is poached in a seasoned liquid, sautéed with ginger, green onions and bamboo shoots and served over gai lan or choy sum.

## 咸酸菜吊片
**332. Squid and Pickled Mustard Greens:**
Squid slices are sautéed with shredded sour-tasting pickled mustard greens.

## 椒鹽吊片
**333. Squid with Peppery Salt:**
Fried squid pieces are tossed in a hot, dry wok with salt and pepper.

## 時菜吊片
**334. Squid with Seasonal Vegetables:**
Squid slices are sautéed with seasonal Chinese vegetables.

## 油泡鴛鴦魷
**335. Squid with Cuttlefish:**
Sliced squid and reconstituted dried cuttlefish are sautéed with minced garlic and ginger, and Chinese vegetables.

## 生炒魷魚
**336. Sautéed Cuttlefish:**
Dried cuttlefish is reconstituted, sliced and sautéed with garlic, ginger, bamboo shoots and Chinese greens.

鮑 魚 冬 菇
**337. Black Mushrooms and Abalone:**
*Sliced canned abalone is served with braised supple black mushrooms.*

蠔 油 鮑 片
**338. Abalone in Oyster Sauce:**
*Thinly sliced canned abalone is served over blanched lettuce with an oyster-based sauce.*

油 泡 鮮 鮑 片
**339. Sautéed Fresh Abalone:**
*Fresh abalone is sliced and sautéed with ginger and garlic. Chinese greens may be added to garnish the dish. Some restaurants use quick-frozen abalone.*

油 爆 墨 魚 花
**340. Sautéed Octopus:**
*Octopus slices are sautéed with ginger and garlic.*

清 蒸 豉 汁 墨 魚
**341. Steamed Octopus:**
*Octopus slices are steamed with a pungent black-bean sauce.*

海 棠 冬 菇 盒
**342. Stuffed Mushroom Caps:**
*Black mushroom caps are filled with minced pork, cuttlefish, dried shrimp and bamboo shoots, then steamed and served with their own juice. The hearts of mustard green or bok choy are sautéed and used as garnishes. Advance notice is required for this dish.*

## MAIN DISHES—VEGETABLES

### 清炒菜薳
**343. Sautéed Chinese Greens:**
Gai lan *or* choy sum *is sliced, blanched and sautéed.*

### 蠔油菜薳
**344. Chinese Vegetables with Oyster Sauce:**
*Blanched* choy sum *is served topped with oyster sauce. Toss before eating.*

### 蠔油芥蘭
**345. *Gai Lan* with Oyster Sauce:**
*Blanched* gai lan *is served with oyster sauce. Toss before eating.*

### 蠔油西生菜
**346. Lettuce with Oyster Sauce:**
*Blanched iceberg or romaine lettuce is served with oyster sauce. Toss before eating.*

### 素扒四寶
**347. Four Jewels:**
*Canned asparagus, blanched* choy sum, *sautéed black and straw mushrooms are served with a transparent sauce. (Some restaurants may use a different quartet of vegetables.)*

## 羅漢上素

**348. Buddha's Feast or *Lo Han* Combination:**
This dish consists of an assortment of vegetarian ingredients, such as bean-curd skin, gingko nuts, mushrooms, gluten, bamboo shoots, black moss and Chinese greens. They are sautéed in a flavorful sauce.

## 時菜扒北菇

**349. Black Mushrooms and Vegetables:**
Black mushrooms, braised in a brown sauce, are served over sautéed or blanched vegetables, such as bok choy or lettuce.

## 蠔油會三菇

**350. Three Kinds of Mushrooms with Oyster Sauce:**
Black, fresh and straw mushrooms are braised in a brown oyster sauce.

## 清炒豆苗

**351. Sautéed Snow-Pea Shoots:**
The tender shoots of the snow pea are sautéed in oil with salt and pepper. This dish is only available at certain times of the year.

## 紅燒北菇

**352. Braised Black Mushrooms:**
Black mushrooms are braised in a brown sauce until supple and tender.

## 素炒雙冬

**353. Sautéed Bamboo Shoots and Black Mushrooms:**
Sliced bamboo shoots and black mushrooms are sautéed together.

---

# SIDE DISHES

---

Dishes is this category are divided into six sub-sections: Congee, Fried Noodles, Lo Mein or Tossed Noodles, Noodles in Broth, Rice Dishes and Snacks or Miscellaneous Dishes. Most of these dishes can be found in fast-food won ton restaurants or in dim sum restaurants.

---

## CONGEE

---

*Congee* is a simple nourishing rice porridge, which can be eaten any time of the day. Fried Chinese Doughnuts (# 426 Canton Menu) are a frequent and filling accompaniment.

白粥

**354. Plain *Congee*:**
*Rice porridge is served steaming hot and slightly seasoned. Sprinkle with white-pepper powder.*

生滾牛肉粥

**355. Beef *Congee*:**
*Marinated beef slices are served in a bowl of hot* congee.

生滾碎牛肉粥

**356. Minced Beef *Congee*:**
*Marinated minced beef is served in a bowl of hot* congee.

滑鷄粥

357. Chicken *Congee*:
Chicken pieces, still on the bone, are served in a bowl of hot congee.

北菰鷄粥

358. Shredded Chicken and Black Mushroom *Congee*:
Shredded black mushroom and shredded marinated chicken meat are served in a bowl of hot congee.

鮑魚鷄粥

359. Abalone and Chicken *Congee*:
Shredded canned abalone and chicken meat are served in a bowl of hot congee.

生菜鯪魚球粥

360. Fish Ball *Congee*:
Shredded lettuce and fish balls are served in a bowl of hot congee.

魚生粥

361. Sliced Fish *Congee*:
Thin slices of raw marinated fish are scalded and served in a bowl of hot congee.

腰膶粥

362. Kidney and Liver *Congee*:
Sliced liver and kidney are served in a bowl of hot congee.

皮蛋瘦肉粥

363. Preserved Black Duck Egg and Pork *Congee*:
Chunks of preserved black duck eggs and salted pork are served in a bowl of hot congee.

## 艇仔粥

**364. Assorted Seafood or Sampan *Congee*:**
*Shredded pork, ham, cuttlefish, jellyfish, lettuce and fried peanuts are served in a bowl of hot congee.*

## 及第粥

**365. Assorted Meat *Congee*:**
*Liver, pork and kidney slices are served in a bowl of hot congee.*

---

# FRIED NOODLES

---

There are two main types of fried noodle dishes: *chow mein* are thin egg noodles, fried and served with a topping; *chow fun* are rice noodles, either flat or shaped like vermicelli, fried with meat and vegetables.

## 乾炒牛河

**366. Chow Fun or Fried Rice Noodles with Beef:**
*Slippery flat noodles are sautéed with sliced onions and beef.*

## 豉椒牛河

**367. Chow Fun or Fried Rice Noodles with Black Beans:**
*Flat rice noodles are sautéed and topped with sautéed sliced beef, green peppers and black beans.*

## 星州炒米

**368. Singapore Fried Rice Noodles or Vermicelli:**
*Vermicelli-like rice noodles are sautéed with shredded pork, onions and curry powder.*

# 廈門炒米

**369. Sweet-and-Sour Fried Rice Noodles or Vermicelli:**
*Vermicelli-like rice noodles are sautéed with shredded pork, vegetables, sweet pickles and sweet-and-sour flavorings. Some restaurants incorrectly add ketchup to these noodles.*

# 三絲炒麵

**370. Three Shredded Meats *Chow Mein*:**
*Shredded pork, chicken and black mushrooms are sautéed and served over crispy fried noodles.*

# 肉絲炒麵

**371. Shredded Pork *Chow Mein*:**
*Shredded, marinated pork is sautéed with vegetables, such as bean sprouts, and served over crispy fried noodles.*

# 招牌炒麵

**372. House Special *Chow Mein*:**
*Pork, vegetables, squid, pork rind and other ingredients are sautéed and served over crispy fried noodles.*

# 叉燒炒麵

**373. Barbecued Pork *Chow Mein*:**
*Barbecued pork slices are sautéed with vegetables and served over crispy fried noodles.*

# 菜心蝦球炒麵

**374. Prawns and Vegetables *Chow Mein*:**
*Shelled marinated prawns are sautéed with Chinese vegetables and served over crispy fried noodles.*

沙茶牛肉炒麵

375. Sar Char Beef Chow Mein:
Sliced marinated beef is sautéed in a spicy sar char sauce and served over crispy fried noodles.

菜蓮牛肉炒麵

376. Beef Chow Mein:
Sliced marinated beef is sautéed with Chinese vegetables and served over crispy fried noodles.

鷄絲炒麵

377. Shredded Chicken Chow Mein:
Shredded chicken is sautéed with bean sprouts and black mushrooms and served over crispy fried noodles.

豉椒鷄球炒麵

378. Chicken with Black Beans Chow Mein:
Marinated chicken pieces, still on the bone, are sautéed with black-bean sauce and served over crispy fried noodles.

## LO MEIN OR TOSSED NOODLES

*Lo mein* are thin won ton noodles that are boiled, drained and tossed. They are served on a plate with a variety of toppings. A bowl of broth is usually served on the side.

火鴨撈麵

**379. Barbecued Duck *Lo Mein*:**
*A plate of noodles is topped with a small portion of cut-up barbecued duck and blanched vegetables.*

叉燒撈麵

**380. Barbecued Pork *Lo Mein*:**
*A plate of noodles is topped with sliced barbecued pork and blanched vegetables.*

鷄鴨撈麵

**381. Chicken and Duck *Lo Mein*:**
*A plate of noodles is topped with small portions of poached chicken and barbecued duck. Both are still on the bone.*

薑葱撈麵

**382. Ginger and Green Onion *Lo Mein*:**
*A plate of noodles is topped with shredded ginger and green onions and drizzled with hot oil.*

蠔油撈麵

**383. Oyster Sauce *Lo Mein*:**
*A plate of noodles is topped with oyster sauce.*

牛腩撈麵

**384. Beef Brisket *Lo Mein*:**
*A plate of noodles is topped with stewed beef brisket.*

油鷄撈麵

**385. Chicken *Lo Mein*:**
*A plate of noodles is topped with poached white chicken or chicken cooked in soy sauce. The chicken is still on the bone.*

牛什撈麵

**386. Beef Organs *Lo Mein*:**
*A plate of noodles is topped with stewed beef, tripe and spleen.*

咖喱牛腩撈麵

**387. Curried Beef Brisket *Lo Mein*:**
*A plate of noodles is topped with curried beef-brisket stew.*

# NOODLES IN BROTH

These noodles are served in broth with a topping. There are two types of noodles to choose from: won ton noodles or *mein*, which are chewy and dark yellow in color, and rice noodles or *fun*, which are slippery and white. Won ton noodles can be ordered either thin or flat. Rice noodles come in three different shapes, thin, round and flat. When ordering, specify what type of noodles you want, then the topping.

燒鴨粉或麵
**388. Barbecued Duck over Noodles:**
*A small portion of barbecued duck is cut up and served over noodles in broth.*

叉燒粉或麵
**389. Barbecued Pork over Noodles:**
*A small portion of sliced barbecued pork is served over noodles in broth.*

燒鵝粉或麵
**390. Roasted Goose over Noodles:**
*A small portion of roasted goose, still on the bone, is cut up and served over noodles in broth.*

牛腩粉或麵
**391. Beef Brisket over Noodles:**
*Beef stew is served over noodles in broth.*

## 咖喱牛腩粉或麵
**392. Curry Beef Brisket over Noodles:**
*Curried beef stew is served over noodles in broth.*

## 雲吞粉或麵
**393. Won Tons over Noodles:**
*Pork- and shrimp-filled dumplings are served over noodles in broth.*

## 水餃粉或麵
**394. Shrimp Dumplings over Noodles:**
*Shredded pork, black fungi, bamboo shoots and shrimp are wrapped in dumplings and served over noodles in broth.*

## 魚蛋粉或麵
**395. Fish Balls over Noodles:**
*White fish balls are served over noodles in broth.*

## 牛肉粉
**396. Beef over Noodles:**
*Marinated beef slices are sautéed with vegetables and served over rice noodles in broth.*

## 牛丸粉或麵
**397. Beef Balls over Noodles:**
*Beef balls are served over noodles in broth.*

## 雙丸粉或麵
**398. Beef and Fish Balls over Noodles:**
*Beef balls and fish balls are served over noodles in broth.*

牛筋粉或麵
399. Beef Ligaments over Noodles:
*Stewed beef ligaments are served over noodles in broth.*

猪手粉或麵
400. Pig's Feet over Noodles:
*Stewed pig's feet are served over noodles in broth.*

---
RICE DISHES
---

Most of the dishes listed below are served on a dinner-sized plate; some come in a rice bowl.

楊州炒飯
401. Yangchow Fried Rice:
*Rice is sautéed with peas, eggs, ham, pork, shrimp and green onion.*

蝦仁炒飯
402. Shrimp Fried Rice:
*Rice is sautéed with shrimp, peas and eggs.*

蕃茄牛肉飯
403. Beef and Tomatoes over Rice:
*Marinated beef slices are sautéed with tomato slices and served over a plate of steamed rice.*

## 鴛鴦炒飯

**404. Two Types of Fried Rice:**
*One kind of fried rice is topped with a white chicken sauce, the other with a red sweet-and-sour shrimp sauce. This dish is considered quite special and is usually served at the end of a banquet.*

## 白切雞飯

**405. White Chicken over Rice:**
*A small portion of cut-up white chicken, still on the bone, is served over a plate or bowl of rice. A minced ginger and green-onion dip is served on the side.*

## 豉油雞飯

**406. Soy Sauce Chicken over Rice:**
*Chicken, still on the bone, is cooked in soy sauce. A small portion is served over a plate or bowl of rice.*

## 叉燒飯

**407. Barbecued Pork over Rice:**
*Slices of sweet barbecued pork are served over a plate or bowl of rice.*

## 燒味雙拼飯

**408. Combination Barbecued and Poached Meats over Rice:**
*The combinations may include White and Soy Sauce Chicken over Rice, Barbecued Pork and Duck over Rice, and White Chicken and Barbecued Duck over Rice. These dishes are usually ordered by the plate.*

時 菜 海 鮮 飯

**409. Seafood and Vegetables over Rice:**
*Marinated shrimp and scallops or squid are sautéed with Chinese vegetables and served over rice.*

時 菜 蝦 球 飯

**410. Prawns and Vegetables over Rice:**
*Large shelled, marinated shrimp are sautéed with Chinese vegetables and served over rice.*

咖 喱 蝦 球 飯

**411. Curried Prawns and Vegetables over Rice:**
*Marinated prawns, braised in a curried sauce, are served over rice.*

時 菜 班 球 飯

**412. Cod Fillets and Vegetables over Rice:**
*Boned, marinated cod pieces are fried and sautéed with Chinese vegetables and served over rice.*

北 菰 鷄 球 飯

**413. Chicken and Black Mushrooms over Rice:**
*Marinated chicken pieces, still on the bone, are sautéed with black mushrooms and served over rice.*

時 菜 牛 肉 飯

**414. Beef and Vegetables over Rice:**
*Marinated beef slices are sautéed with Chinese greens and served over rice.*

滑 蛋 碎 牛 飯

**415. Minced Beef and Egg over Rice:**
Minced beef is sautéed with beaten eggs and served over rice.

免 治 牛 肉 飯

**416. Minced Beef over Rice:**
Minced beef is sautéed with minced onion and green peas and served over rice. Some restaurants serve this dish with a fried egg on top.

咖 喱 牛 腩 飯

**417. Curried Beef Brisket over Rice:**
Curried beef brisket stew is served over rice.

柱 候 牛 腩 飯

**418. Beef Brisket over Rice:**
Beef brisket stew, made with *chi hau* sauce, is served over rice.

咖 喱 鷄 飯

**419. Curried Chicken over Rice:**
Chicken pieces, still on the bone, are cooked in a curried sauce and served over rice.

## SNACKS OR MISCELLANEOUS DISHES

淨雲吞

**420. Won Tons in Soup:**
*Dumplings stuffed with pork and shrimp are served in a seasoned broth.*

水餃

**421. Shrimp Dumplings in Soup:**
*Shrimp and shredded pork, bamboo shoots and black fungi are stuffed in large dumplings and served in a seasoned broth.*

猪腸粉

**422. Rice Noodles or** *Cheung Fun:*
*Long slippery rice noodles, speckled with dried shrimp and green onions, are served with soy sauce,* hoi sin *sauce and sesame seeds. The noodles are cut into small pieces just before serving.*

炸兩

**423. Stuffed Rice Noodles:**
*Long slippery rice noodles, stuffed with a savory fried Chinese doughnut, are served sliced. Dip in soy sauce before eating.*

鹹肉粽

**424. Salty Pork and Glutinous Rice Tamale or Sweet Rice Wrap with Pork:**
*Glutinous rice, stuffed with salted pork, is wrapped in bamboo*

leaves, boiled and served hot. To eat, unwrap the leaves, which are not edible, and sprinkle rice with soy sauce.

梘水粽

**425. Translucent Glutinous Rice Tamale or Sweet Rice Wrap:**
Glutinous rice, specially treated in a lye solution so that the rice becomes translucent, is wrapped in bamboo leaves, boiled and served hot. To eat, unwrap leaves, which are not edible, and sprinkle rice with white sugar.

炸油條

**426. Fried Chinese Doughnuts:**
A long savory doughnut is fried until golden brown. It is eaten as a bread for breakfast or for dunking in hot congee.

皮蛋

**427. Pei dan or Preserved Black Duck Egg:**
Erroneously called hundred-year-old egg, this is a duck egg that has been preserved in a brine for several weeks. The egg becomes black in color and has the pungency and texture of blue cheese. To eat, dip in soy sauce. In recent years, there has been controversy surrounding the chemical composition of the brine, which may not be safe for human consumption.

蘿白炆猪皮

**428. Stewed Pork Rind:**
Dried pork rinds are cooked until soft and spongy with soy sauce and pungent white Chinese radishes.

韭菜花猪紅

**429. Chives and Pig's Blood:**
Steamed, coagulated pig's blood is cut into cubes and served with poached chives and a soy-based sauce.

滑 鶏 球 窩 麵

**430. Chicken Wor Mein:**
Thin egg noodles are served in a large soup bowl with a sautéed chicken mixture and broth. This dish is enough for four to six people. You can also order Barbecued Meats Wor Mein or Won Ton Wor Mein.

乾 燒 伊 府 麵

**431. Braised E Mein:**
E mein is a beige-colored noodle prized for its lightness and crinkly texture. In this dish, E mein is braised in a little bit of liquid until soft, then served with black mushrooms and bean sprouts.

潮 州 乾 燒 伊 麵

**432. Chiu Chow E Mein:**
Usually, regular thin noodles are used for this dish. The noodles are pan-fried in one piece until crunchy. They are then cut into squares and served over a bed of Chinese chives. To eat, sprinkle with a pinch of sugar and a dash of vinegar. This dish is only available in Chiu Chow restaurants.

## DESSERTS

Advance notice may be required for some desserts.

生 果 盤

**433. Fruit Platter:**
This is a platter of peeled, sliced chilled fruits.

## 蜜瓜西米

**434. Honeydew and Tapioca:**
Cooked tapioca pearls, which have a soft and slippery texture, are served chilled with mashed honeydew melon.

## 椰汁西米露

**435. Coconut Milk and Tapioca:**
This is a hot dessert. Cooked tapioca is served in a sweet white soup laced with coconut flavor.

## 杏仁豆腐

**436. Almond Jelly:**
Almond-flavored white jelly cubes are served chilled with canned fruit cocktail or diced fresh fruits.

## 蓮子百合紅豆沙

**437. Sweet Red Mung Bean Soup:**
Red mung beans are cooked in sugar and water until they are almost completely dissolved. Lotus seeds and the petals of the lily bulb are added at the end.

## 杏仁露

**438. Almond Soup:**
This is a sweet, white, thick soup with an almond flavor. It is served hot.

## 蓮子湯

**439. Lotus Seed Soup:**
This is a sweet, white, thick soup studded with lotus seeds, and is served hot.

西米布丁

**440. Tapioca Pudding:**
This is a hot baked pudding of tapioca and eggs. Red mung bean or lotus-seed paste is sometimes used as stuffing.

鮮奶核桃露

**441. Walnut Soup:**
This is a sweet, beige soup made of milk and ground walnuts, and is served hot.

鮮奶花生露

**442. Peanut Soup:**
This hot, light-brown, thick soup is made of ground peanuts.

芝麻糊

**443. Black Sesame Seed Soup:**
This is a thick, black hot soup made of ground black sesame seeds. This soup is prized for its aroma and flavor.

# CHAPTER SIX

## A Peking Menu

Like the Tao symbol, Peking cuisine is a whole made up of two parts. One part is the decadent imperial cuisine, which uses exotic ingredients and elaborate methods. This style of cooking is appealing to many Chinese because of what it symbolizes: affluence and a state of well-being. The other more notable part is the common people's food. Robust, full-flavored and hearty, its ingredients are from the region and its recipes from the people.

The Peking culinary region, which includes the northern provinces of Shantung, Shansi, Honan, Hopei and Shensi, is a land of climatic extremes. The summers are oppressively hot and the winters cold, dry and frequented by dust storms. Northerners have limited access to fresh greens, so the primary vegetable used in most dishes is Chinese or Tientsin cabbage. The northern staple is wheat, not rice. Hence northerners eat a hefty diet of flour byproducts, such as steamed bread, noodles, flat bread, perogy-like dumplings and tortilla-like pancakes, which are used to wrap leeks, pork or duck. Especially popular in Peking cuisine is a dish called *lah mein*, or hand-pulled noodles. It is fascinating to watch these noodles being made by hand from a flour-and-water dough. The noodles are magically created from a slab of dough, which is kneaded, pulled and twirled by expert cooks into perfectly uniform strands in minutes. The noodles are boiled al dente, then either sautéed with shredded meat and cabbage or served in broth. Another special northern dish is dumplings or perogies. Pieces of soft, delicate dough are filled with minced beef, pork, lamb or shrimp, folded into crescents, then steamed or boiled. A tart vinegar-shredded ginger dip is served with the dumplings. Peking noodles and dumplings are so delicious it is hard to stop eating them. Northern Chinese men like to show off their machismo by boasting of the numbers of dumplings or bowls of noodles they can eat at a sitting.

Northerners use large quantities of garlic, leeks and onions for seasonings, which are believed to ward off infection and illness. Southerners often joke that this is why northerners are bigger and taller: they scare the germs away. Other favorite northern seasonings include *hoi sin* sauce, used in sautéed dishes or smeared on the pancakes that wrap Peking Duck; sugar, vinegar and soy sauce combined to create sweet and sour flavors; and wine residue juice, which is used to make aromatic sauces, such as the one used in Wine Residue Braised Fish.

Lamb and mutton figure prominently in Peking food. Many northerners were sheep farmers or nomadic shepherds and mutton was easy to get. The most famous lamb dish is Dipped Lamb. Paper-thin slices of lamb are dipped and cooked in a spectacular fondue called Mongolian Hot Pot, which was brought to China by the conquering Mongols in the thirteenth century. The hot pot is a charcoal-fueled brass fondue with a bubbling broth. Lamb and other ingredients, such as noodles, cabbage and bean curds, are scalded in the broth and eaten with a soy-garlic dip. The hot pot serves several purposes in a northern home: it cooks the food and warms the palate and stomach as well as the room. It is a welcome device in northern China, where often the only heat source is a brick sleeping platform under which coal or wood is burned.

Of the five northern provinces, Shantung is probably the

best known for its cooking. Shantung is on the coast, so it has a milder climate and access to seafood. Tsing Tao, on the Shantung Peninsula, is world-renowned for its large succulent prawns, sought after by gourmets everywhere, and its local beer, made in a brewery left behind by the Germans. Even today, Tsing Tao beer bears a remarkable resemblance to light German beers and is a refreshing accompaniment to the earthy cuisine of this region.

Imperial cuisine evolved in the royal courts of the north, which were the scene of many of China's past glories. Throughout history, China's rulers have usually been northerners, and all of its dynasties rose, prospered and crumbled in the north. China's first empire was created here. Its emperor, the ruthless Ch'in Chih Hwang Ti, unified the northern countries by brutal means. To protect his empire from the Mongols, he connected sections of the Great Wall, at considerable human cost. His regime (221 to 207 BC) was brief but powerful. Evidence of it can be seen today in Xian, his capital, where lavish symbols of might adorn his tomb. Archaeologists are still excavating the tomb, which he successfully kept hidden from grave robbers for twenty-two centuries. The intricate layout of the tomb and the sophisticated outfitting of the lifelike terracotta soldiers and war chariots suggest a rich culture that was technologically far ahead of its time.

Imperial cuisine is a reflection of the wealth and sophistication of ancient China. It relies heavily on rich seasonings such as wine and *kaoliang*, a grain alcohol, and extraordinary ingredients, such as shark's fins, fish lips, sea cucumbers, bird's nests, camel's hump and bear's paws. Even after elaborate preparation such as soaking, stewing and straining, most of these products are all texture and no taste. Other ingredients such as chicken, black mushrooms and Chinese ham are used to give them flavor.

While imperial cuisine has given Peking food style and diversity, the common people's food has given it character and substance. Few gastronomic experiences can be compared to that of eating a piping-hot bowl of *lah mein* in soup or a steaming plate of meat-stuffed dumplings with vinegar and shredded ginger. Our menu will introduce you to the many facets of Peking food.

# A PEKING MENU

## APPETIZERS

These appetizers can be ordered by themselves or in combinations of two, three or more depending on the number of diners.

羊糕

### 1. Lamb or Mutton Jelly:
*This is a lamb aspic usually served at the beginning of a northern meal. Mutton or lamb is slow-cooked until tender in a slightly sweet sauce with spices, such as cloves and cinnamon bark, and with Chinese radish and pork jelly. The mutton is then chilled into a jelly, cut into squares and served.*

燻鴿蛋

### 2. Smoked Pigeon Eggs:
*Soft-boiled pigeon eggs are shelled, marinated in a seasoned liquid and smoked. They are served at room temperature.*

## 糟 肉
**3. Pork with Wine Flavor:**
A piece of marbled pork is marinated in salt and wine, steamed with wine residue juice until tender, then thinly sliced.

## 五 香 醬 蹄
**4. Five Spices Pork Hock or Sliced Pig's Knuckle Peking Style:**
Pork hock is slow-cooked in soy sauce and five spices. It is then chilled and sliced paper-thin.

## 凍 鷄
**5. Chicken Jelly:**
Chicken meat is steamed with pork jelly, chilled and served cut in bite-sized pieces.

## 燻 鷄
**6. Smoked Chicken:**
Chicken is poached in a seasoned liquid, smoked—usually over wood chips—and served cut in bite-sized pieces.

## 拌 三 鮮
**7. Tossed Three Ingredients or Sliced Abalone, Prawns and Sea Cucumbers:**
Canned abalone, cooked prawns and sea cucumbers are tossed together in a salad, usually with a soy and sesame-oil dressing.

## 琥 皮 桃 仁
**8. Crunchy Walnuts:**
This dish is usually served on a combination plate with other appetizers. Skinned fried walnuts are cooked in a thick syrup with sesame oil, cooled, then served crunchy.

花 生 餞
### 9. Fried Peanuts:
*Shelled peanuts are fried, coated with a thick syrup, cooled and served. The syrup forms a crunchy crust.*

五 香 牛 肉
### 10. Five Spices Beef or Spiced Beef:
*Beef is cooked until tender in a seasoned liquid flavored with five-spices powder, cooled, then served sliced paper-thin.*

金 銀 鴨
### 11. Gold and Silver Duck:
*Shredded ham and duck meat are steamed with pork jelly, chilled in a mold and served cut in small pieces.*

水 晶 蝦 仁
### 12. Crystal Shrimp:
*This is a prawn aspic. Poached shrimp and shredded ham are chilled in a mold with melted pork jelly. It is served cut into small pieces.*

卷 尖
### 13. Smoked Omelet Rolls:
*Ground seasoned pork is stuffed in a thin omelet, rolled up, steamed and smoked over wood chips. It is brushed with sesame oil and served sliced.*

辣 黄 瓜 皮
### 14. Spicy Cucumbers:
*Cucumbers are cut into long thin slices, salted, and stuffed and rolled with a sautéed shredded mixture of green onions, ginger, hot peppers, bamboo shoots and black mushrooms. They are then marinated in a hot vinegary sauce.*

## 香椿拌豆腐
**15. Bean-Curd Salad:**
This is a cold bean-curd salad. Tender bean curds are mashed and mixed with sesame oil and minced heung chung, *salty preserved vegetables.*

## 鷄絲拌黃瓜
**16. Shredded Chicken and Cucumbers:**
*Shredded chicken meat is marinated, sautéed and served with shredded cucumbers and a soy and sesame-oil dressing.*

## 開洋熗芹菜
**17. Dried Shrimp and Celery Salad:**
*Shredded celery is parboiled, then tossed with minced dried shrimp and sesame-oil dressing.*

## 辣白菜
**18. Hot Chinese Cabbage:**
*Chinese cabbage is cut into long slivers, salted and pickled with a spicy marinade of hot red chilis, vinegar and Szechwan peppercorns.*

## 芥末鷄絲
**19. Shredded Chicken and Mustard Sauce:**
*Shredded chicken meat is marinated, sautéed and served with parboiled mung bean sprouts and a soy and yellow-mustard sauce.*

## 鷄絲拉皮
**20. Shredded Chicken and Tientsin Bean Sheet Salad or Shredded Chicken with Bean Vermicelli:**
*Shredded chicken is marinated, sautéed and tossed with*

shredded cucumbers and strips of Tientsin bean sheets and a soy and sesame-seed sauce. Yellow mustard is sometimes added to the sauce or served on the side. If you like pungent flavors, add a small dab of yellow mustard to your salad. A variety of ingredients is combined with Tientsin bean sheets to create other salad dishes; for example: Shredded Pork and Tientsin Bean Sheets and Shredded Poached Chicken and Omelet and Bean Sheets.

## 糖醋黃瓜
### 21. Sweet Vinegared Cucumbers:
*Small cucumbers are sliced open, seeded, salted and marinated in a sweet-and-sour sesame oil and Szechwan peppercorn sauce.*

## 鮮菱米熗對蝦仁
### 22. Poached Prawns and True Water Chestnuts:
*True water chestnuts are small, black-shelled nuts shaped with two horns. The meat is white and slightly sweet. Finely minced true water chestnuts and poached sliced prawns are tossed with a green-onion and Szechwan-peppercorn dressing.*

## 干貝豆苗松
### 23. Crispy Dried Scallops and Snow-Pea Shoots:
*Dried scallops are steamed, shredded and fried until crunchy. They are then tossed with the tender shoots of the snow pea, which have been deep-fried until crispy.*

## 鹽水胗
### 24. Salted Giblets:
*Chicken giblets are poached until tender in a savory liquid with ginger, green onions and Szechwan peppercorns. They are thinly sliced and served at room temperature.*

## 拌海蜇皮
### 25. Tossed Jellyfish (erroneously called Sea Blubber):
*Dried jellyfish is elaborately prepared—shredded, soaked, parboiled, then soaked again—and served with shredded cucumbers and a soy-based dressing with garlic and green onions. Jellyfish is prized for its crunchy texture.*

## 芥末腰花
### 26. Kidneys with Mustard Flavor:
*Pig's kidney slices are poached, arranged on a plate with sliced cucumber, then topped with a pungent and tangy yellow mustard dressing.*

## 熗腰花
### 27. Poached Kidneys:
*Slices of pig's kidney are cut in a crisscross pattern, poached and served with a shredded ginger and sesame-oil sauce.*

## 芝蔴鴨肝
### 28. Fried Duck's Livers:
*Duck's livers are sliced, marinated, dipped in an egg white batter, dredged in sesame seeds, then deep-fried.*

## 酒醉鴨肝
### 29. Drunken Duck Livers:
*Duck livers are poached in a seasoned liquid with ginger and green onions, then sprinkled with Mao Tai alcohol, sliced and served at room temperature.*

## 鴨掌拌西芹
### 30. Duck's Feet (erroneously called Webs) and Celery:
*Deboned poached duck's feet are tossed with parboiled sliced*

celery. Some restaurants serve this dish with a soy and sesame-oil sauce; others use a yellow-mustard dressing.

## 芥末鴨掌
### 31. Duck's Feet with Mustard Flavor:
*Poached duck's feet are boned and tossed in a salad with sliced cucumbers and a pungent yellow mustard sauce. Toss before eating.*

## 麻辣鴨膀
### 32. Mah Lah or Fragrant and Spicy Duck Wings:
*Duck wings are braised in sugar, wine, broth and sesame oil for fragrance and in Szechwan peppercorns for spiciness.*

## 醬肘花
### 33. Stuffed Pork Hock:
*A seasoned marbled pork dressing is stuffed into a deboned pork hock. The hock is then trussed, slow-cooked until tender, cooled and served thinly sliced.*

## 麻醬海螺
### 34. Sea Snails with Sesame-Seed Sauce:
*Sea snails are steamed, shelled, sliced paper-thin and arranged on a plate with cucumber slices. This dish is served with a dressing made with sesame-seed paste, vinegar, salt and sesame oil. Toss lightly before eating.*

## 醇香肚包
### 35. Stuffed Pig's Intestine:
*The pig's large intestine is stuffed with marinated pork and slow-cooked in a seasoned liquid. It is then removed from the liquid, flattened with weights, cooled and served thinly sliced.*

---

## SOUPS

---

## 清燉牛肉或甜牛肉

**36. Beef Consommé:**
A Peking special, this is a light and full-flavored broth with a few pieces of tender beef in it. This soup is usually served in deep individual bowls. It makes a wonderful starter to a Peking meal.

## 酸辣湯

**37. Hot and Sour Soup:**
This is a thick hot soup guaranteed to chase the winter chills away. An assortment of shredded ingredients—pork, carrots, bean curds, Szechwan kohlrabi, black fungi, bamboo shoots—is cooked in a tangy and spicy soup. Some traditional cooks also add shredded tripe and coagulated chicken-blood cubes. Chinese parsley, green onions and white-pepper powder are sprinkled over the soup.

## 醋椒魚湯

**38. Sour and Hot Fish Soup:**
A carp is pan-fried, cooked in a broth with ginger and green onions, and served in a soup bowl sprinkled with vinegar and white-pepper powder.

## 烤鴨骨熬白菜

**39. Duck Bones and Cabbage Soup:**
The leftover carcass of a Peking duck is cut up and slow-cooked in broth with Chinese cabbage, bean curds and slippery bean thread noodles. The duck bones are removed before the soup is served.

蛤蜊川蘿蔔絲桂魚湯

**40. Clams, Fish and Shredded Radish Soup:**
*A fish is cooked in a broth with ginger, green onions, shelled clams and shredded Chinese radish. The soup is milky white and pungent.*

川鷄片冬菇湯

**41. Chicken and Mushroom Soup:**
*Sliced marinated chicken meat and supple black mushrooms are served in a broth.*

川冬菇鴨掌湯

**42. Mushrooms and Duck's Feet (or Webs) Soup:**
*Duck's feet, cooked until tender, are served in a broth with black mushrooms.*

羊雜湯

**43. Sheep's Organs Soup:**
*Sheep stomach and intestines are sliced and slow-cooked until tender in a seasoned liquid.*

## MAIN DISHES—BEAN CURDS

鍋塌豆腐

**44. Pan-Fried Bean Curds:**
*Bean-curd slices are dipped in a batter, pan-fried, then braised in a brown sauce with ginger and green onions.*

蝦子豆腐

**45. Bean Curds with Shrimp Eggs:**
*Bean-curd pieces are marinated, dipped in scrambled eggs and deep-fried, then braised in a brown sauce with briny-tasting shrimp eggs.*

砂鍋凍豆腐

**46. Bean-Curd Casserole:**
*Bean curd is frozen so that it becomes spongy and chewy. It is then sliced and sautéed with bamboo shoots, black fungi and dried shrimp. This mélange is then poured into a Chinese casserole pot, topped with sautéed* tarp qwar choy, *a flat* bok choy, *and served bubbling.*

砂鍋腐竹

**47. Bamboo Skins Casserole:**
*Sticks of bamboo skins are softened, sautéed with ham, bamboo shoots and black fungi and served bubbling in a Chinese casserole topped with* tarp qwar choy, *a flat* bok choy.

## MAIN DISHES — BEEF

### 紅燒牛肉或小碗肉
**48. Red-Cooked Beef:**
A large chunk of beef is cooked until tender in soy sauce and spices, then sliced paper-thin. This beef is used to stuff Peking shaobing or Mandarin pancakes, or as a topping for noodles.

### 蝦子蹄筋
**49. Shrimp Eggs and Beef Ligaments:**
Beef ligaments are stewed until soft and gelatinous in a brown sauce with briny-tasting shrimp eggs, ginger and green onions.

### 五香扒牛肉
**50. Five Spices Braised Beef:**
Thick beef slices are cooked tender in a seasoned liquid of wine, broth and spices such as cloves and cinnamon bark. The beef is served in its own juice, which has been thickened.

### 生煎牛肉
**51. Pan-Fried Tender Beef:**
Medallion-sized pieces of sirloin or flank steak are marinated in a spicy sauce, dipped in scrambled eggs, then pan-fried. They are then braised in a sauce of minced garlic, sesame oil, soy sauce and red chilies.

### 紅煨牛筋
**52. Red Stewed Beef Ligaments:**
Beef ligaments are slow-cooked until almost melting with

*ginger, garlic, green onions, wine, cloves, cinnamon bark and soy sauce.*

## 鹽爆牛肚
**53. Sautéed Tripe or Sautéed Beef Tripe with Parsley and Garlic:**
*Beef tripe is cooked until tender, shredded, then sautéed with a lot of garlic and Chinese parsley.*

---

# MAIN DISHES — CHICKEN

---

## 北平燻雞或燒雞
**54. Smoked Chicken (Roasted Chicken):**
*A chicken is poached in a seasoned liquid, then smoked over tea leaves or wood chips. It is served cut in bite-sized pieces.*

## 童子雞
**55. Half-Grown Chicken:**
*A whole half-grown chicken, believed to be more tender than a full-grown chicken, is rubbed with salt and wine, stuffed with spices such as Szechwan peppercorns, tangerine peels and half a lotus leaf (for fragrance), steamed, cut up and served with its own juice. Some restaurants serve this chicken fried or roasted.*

## 醬爆核桃雞丁
**56. Chicken in Sauce with Walnuts or Diced Chicken and Walnuts in Bean Sauce:**
*Diced chicken meat is marinated, quick-fried, then sautéed in a sticky and sweet brown-bean sauce with fried walnuts.*

醬 爆 燻 雞 絲

**57. Smoked Chicken in Sauce or Fried Shredded Smoked Chicken:**
*The shredded meat of smoked chicken is marinated, fried until golden brown, then sautéed with shredded garlic, sesame oil and brown-bean sauce.*

燴 兩 雞 絲

**58. Braised Two Chicken Meats:**
*Chicken meat is shredded, marinated and sautéed with shredded smoked chicken and bamboo shoots.*

香 酥 雞 腿

**59. Crispy Chicken Legs:**
*Chicken legs are marinated in soy sauce and spices, steamed, then fried until golden brown. They are served with a peppery salt dip on the side. Sprinkle a little peppery salt over the chicken before eating.*

鍋 塌 雞 片

**60. Pan-Fried Chicken Slices:**
*Marinated chicken slices are dipped in flour and eggs, then pan-fried. Scrambled eggs are then added to make a large omelet. When the omelet is half-done, wine and seasoned broth are added, and the omelet is cooked covered. It is served cut in bite-sized pieces.*

芙 蓉 雞 片

**61. *Foo Yung* Chicken:**
*The term* foo yung *indicates that egg whites are used. Minced chicken meat is scrambled with egg whites, pan-fried to form a thin omelet, sliced, then braised in a light sauce*

with ham and green peas. *In some restaurants, egg whites are scrambled with minced chicken and sautéed like scrambled eggs. The cooked egg whites are topped with a sautéed mixture of chicken slices, ham and black mushrooms.*

## 山 東 燒 雞
### 62. Shantung Fried Chicken:
*Chicken is poached in a seasoned liquid, fried and served in bite-sized pieces. A spicy dip of hot peppers, Chinese parsley, shallots, soy sauce and sesame oil is served on the side. In some restaurants, a chicken is marinated, fried, stuffed with spices and steamed, then shredded and tossed with thin cucumber slices and a tart soy-based sauce.*

## 麻 辣 雞 翼
### 63. *Mah Lah* Chicken Wings:
*Chicken wings are sautéed in a spicy sauce of Szechwan peppercorns, dried chilies, wine and soy sauce.*

## 酒 蒸 肥 雞
### 64. Steamed Chicken:
*A chicken is steamed in a ceramic bowl with water, ginger, glutinous wine, fermented sweet wine and shaoshing wine. It is served whole with broth.*

## 砂 鍋 全 雞
### 65. Casserole Chicken:
*A whole chicken is slow-cooked in a Chinese casserole pot with black mushrooms, bamboo shoots, ham slices and* choy sum *(Chinese greens).*

## 鍋 燒 整 雞
### 66. Fried Whole Chicken:
*A chicken is deboned whole, poached in seasoned liquid,*

dipped in a batter and deep-fried. It is cut into bite-sized pieces, then served.

# 青椒鷄丁
## 67. Diced Chicken with Green Peppers:
Diced chicken meat is marinated, quick-fried, then sautéed with cubed green peppers and bamboo shoots.

# 乾爆鷄塊
## 68. Sautéed Chicken Pieces:
Chicken pieces are steamed with ginger, green onions and a slightly sweet wine sauce, then sautéed with green peas and diced ham, bamboo shoots and black mushrooms.

# 鷄裏爆
## 69. Sautéed Chicken and Pork Loin:
Slices of chicken and pork loin are dipped in batter, deep-fried and then sautéed with sesame oil and minced garlic, ginger and green onions.

# 茉莉鷄片
## 70. Jasmine and Chicken Meat:
Chicken meat is thinly sliced, marinated and sautéed with ginger, green onions and jasmine flower petals.

# 炒生鷄絲
## 71. Sautéed Shredded Chicken:
Shredded chicken meat is marinated and sautéed with julienned bamboo shoots.

# 扒三白
## 72. Braised Three Whites:
Slices of white chicken meat are marinated and sautéed in a

*transparent sauce with canned abalone slices and chunks of bamboo shoots.*

爆 全 丁

### 73. Sautéed Diced Combo:
*An assortment of diced ingredients — chicken meat and giblets, pig's stomach, pork, shrimp and bamboo shoots — is sautéed with a pungent sauce made with garlic, ginger and cheung qua (salty pickles).*

燴 全 丁

### 74. Braised Diced Combo:
*An assortment of diced ingredients — chicken, pig's stomach, pork, kidney, bamboo shoots, black mushrooms, ham, sea cucumbers and green soy beans — are sautéed and braised with wine, ginger, green onions and soy sauce.*

乾 炸 鷄 條

### 75. Fried Chicken Strips:
*Chicken meat is marinated, dipped in scrambled egg whites and cornstarch, deep fried until golden brown and served with peppery salt.*

鹽 爆 鷄 條

### 76. Salt-Sautéed Chicken Strips:
*Chicken strips are marinated in a batter, fried, then sautéed in a hot wok with salt and minced ginger, green onions and Chinese parsley.*

醬 爆 鷄 脯

### 77. Chicken Sautéed with Sauce:
*Diced chicken meat is marinated and quick-fried, then sautéed with a sticky sweet sauce of sugar and brown-bean sauce.*

爆 鷄 里 丁

**78. Sautéed Chicken and Pork Loin:**
Sliced chicken and pork loin are marinated, fried and sautéed with a yellow sauce made with cheung qua *(salty pickle) juice, green onions, garlic and broth.*

炒 子 鷄 丁

**79. Sautéed Chicken:**
Diced chicken is marinated and sautéed with diced black mushrooms and bamboo shoots.

鷄 油 三 白

**80. Three White Ingredients with Chicken Fat:**
Minced chicken is fried with scrambled egg whites to make an omelet. It is sliced, then braised in a transparent sauce with fresh mushrooms and bamboo shoots. The three ingredients are served side by side drizzled with rendered chicken fat.

鷄 油 四 寶

**81. Four Jewels with Chicken Fat:**
Minced chicken is fried with scrambled egg whites to form an omelet. It is sliced, then braised in a transparent sauce with sautéed choy sum (Chinese greens), sliced ham and bamboo shoots. These four ingredients are served side by side drizzled with chicken fat.

鷄 茸 豌 豆

**82. Minced Chicken with Peas:**
Minced chicken is marinated, mixed with broth and sautéed with green peas, then garnished with shredded ham.

## 雞 粥 豌 豆

**83. Mashed Chicken and Peas:**
*Mashed green peas and minced chicken are sautéed separately, then served side by side garnished with minced ham.*

## 香 菇 燜 雞 肫

**84. Black Mushrooms and Giblets:**
*Black mushrooms and chicken giblets are braised until tender in wine, sugar and soy sauce.*

## 鹽 爆 肫 花

**85. Sautéed Giblets:**
*Chicken giblets are halved, cut in a crisscross pattern, parboiled, then sautéed with wine and minced Chinese parsley, garlic, ginger and green onions.*

## 清 炸 肫 肝

**86. Fried Giblets:**
*Chicken giblets and livers are sliced, marinated, deep-fried until crunchy and served with peppery salt on the side.*

## 鹽 爆 雙 脆

**87. Sautéed Double Crunch:**
*Pig's stomach and chicken giblets are sliced and sautéed in a hot wok with a tangy sauce of minced garlic, ginger and green onions.*

## 糁

**88. Chicken and Rice Soup:**
*Chicken and crumbled rice are cooked in liquid. The chicken is removed and shredded. The rice soup is thickened,*

seasoned with a variety of ingredients — ginger, green onions, wine and five-spices powder — and served in small bowls with the shredded chicken. Season your rice soup with minced Chinese parsley and green onions, vinegar and sesame oil.

溜黃菜

**89. Scrambled Egg Yolks:**
Scrambled egg yolks are mixed with broth and sautéed, usually in pork fat, with minced water chestnuts and dried shrimp. Shredded ham is used as a garnish.

溜松花

**90. Fried Preserved Eggs:**
Pei dan, or preserved black duck eggs, are quartered, dredged in flour, deep-fried, then braised in a sweet-and-sour soy-based sauce.

燻鴿蛋

**91. Braised Pigeon Eggs:**
Hard-boiled pigeon eggs are deep-fried until golden brown, then braised with bamboo shoots and black mushrooms.

炸鴿子

**92. Fried Pigeon:**
Pigeon is marinated with soy sauce and spices, then deep-fried until golden brown. It is served cut in small pieces.

原鹵春鴿

**93. Poached Pigeon:**
Pigeon is fried until golden brown, then poached in a seasoned liquid of sesame oil, broth, ginger and green onions.

韭黄炒蛋

**94. Chives with Eggs:**
*Pungent one-inch sections of yellow chives are sautéed with scrambled eggs.*

---

## MAIN DISHES — DUCK

---

Duck has been eaten in northern China for millenia. It remains one of the most popular sources of protein for the northern Chinese. Earnest duck lovers, the northern Chinese have many novel ways of cooking duck.

北京烤鸭

**95. Peking Duck:**
*Traditionally, the duck used by the imperial cooks was force-fed. Nowadays, only in Peking are some ducks force-fed. After the duck's feathers have been removed and it has been cleaned, it is tied tightly at the neck. Air is pumped in from the tail end with bellows or a bicycle pump. The tail end is then sealed, so the duck is inflated with air. It is basted, hang-dried and roasted to a reddish brown. Most restaurants skip the air-pumping process. Only the skin, with a bit of meat attached, is served, with Mandarin pancakes, which are thin, like tortillas. To eat, smear one side of a pancake with hoi sin sauce, put on a large piece of duck skin and a piece of green onion. Roll the pancake tightly and eat with fingers. Peking Duck has a crispy skin, and the meat is full-flavored. You can order Peking Duck so that the whole duck is served. It is called Peking Duck Eaten Three Ways, and includes three separate dishes: the dish just described; Shredded Duck Sautéed with Bean Sprouts; and*

Duck and Cabbage Soup. Peking Duck, an elaborate dish, requires advance notice.

## 京葱燒鴨
**96. Braised Duck with Leeks (or Peking Onions):**
A duck is rubbed with soy sauce, fried, then slow-cooked in a slightly sweet pungent sauce of soy sauce, wine, cloves and leeks or green onions.

## 紅燒糯米鴨
**97. Red-Cooked Glutinous Rice Duck:**
A duck is rubbed with spices; stuffed with a mixture of giblets, vegetables and glutinous rice; sewn up; fried; then braised until tender with soy sauce. The waiter usually cuts the duck, which is served whole, at the table. Take equal portions of meat and stuffing.

## 黃燜鴨
**98. Yellow Stewed Duck:**
Unboned duck pieces are sautéed with ginger and green onions, then braised in wine, broth and soy sauce with black mushrooms and bamboo shoots.

## 燒鴨絲
**99. Fried Shredded Duck:**
Duck meat is coarsely shredded, marinated, dredged in flour and deep-fried. Strips of salty snow cabbage are also deep-fried until crunchy. The two ingredients are then tossed in a hot dry wok with sesame oil.

## 炒芽菜鴨絲
**100. Shredded Duck with Bean Sprouts:**
Cooked deboned duck meat is shredded and sautéed in a hot wok with crunchy mung-bean sprouts.

## 大葱扒鴨
**101. Duck Stewed with Leeks:**
*A whole duck is stewed tender in a brown sauce with julienned leeks.*

## 酒蒸鴨子
**102. Wine-Steamed Duck:**
*A duck is steamed in a large bowl with wine, broth, ginger and green onions.*

## 荷葉鴨子
**103. Duck in Lotus Leaves:**
*Duck is cut into bite-sized pieces, marinated in brown bean sauce and dredged in pulverized rice that has been roasted with spices such as cloves and cinnamon bark. The duck pieces are then wrapped in a large lotus leaf and steamed until tender. Before eating, unwrap the top part of the leaf, which is not edible.*

## 麻辣鴨
**104. *Mah Lah* Duck or Fragrant and Spicy Duck:**
*Pieces of unboned duck are braised in a mouth-tingling sauce of sesame oil, Szechwan peppercorns and dried red chilies. Traditionally, a wild duck was used for this dish, but restaurant cooks now use the domestic version.*

## 元寶鴨
**105. Duck with Eggs:**
*A duck is slit open along the backbone, rubbed with soy sauce and fried until golden brown. It is then slow-cooked in wine and broth and served with hard-boiled eggs that have been shelled and deep-fried.*

## 五香全鴨
**106. Five Spices or Spiced Stewed Duck:**
*A whole duck is slow-cooked in five spices and soy sauce.*

## 黃燜鴨肝
**107. Yellow Braised Duck Livers:**
*Duck livers are sautéed with choy sum (Chinese greens), bamboo shoots and fresh mushrooms.*

## 芝蔴鴨肝
**108. Fried Duck Livers:**
*Traditionally, the rich liver of the force-fed Peking duck was used for this dish; now ordinary duck livers are used. Duck livers are sliced, marinated, dipped in scrambled eggs and sesame seeds, then deep-fried until golden brown.*

## 糟溜鴨肝
**109. Wine Residue Braised Livers:**
*Slices of duck liver are parboiled, then sautéed in a fragrant transparent sauce of wine residue juice.*

## 糟蒸鴨肝
**110. Wine Residue Steamed Livers:**
*Duck livers are steamed with wine residue juice, ginger and green onions and served in their own juice.*

## 糟溜三白
**111. Wine Residue and Three White Ingredients:**
*The three white ingredients are poached duck livers, shelled hard-boiled pigeon eggs and bamboo shoots. They are braised in a fragrant transparent sauce of wine residue juice.*

紅燴鴨條

**112. Red-Braised Duck Strips:**
Cooked strips of duck meat are braised in a brown sauce made of sugar, soy sauce, green onions and white-pepper powder.

紅燒鴨翅

**113. Red-Cooked Duck Wings:**
Duck wings are fried, then slow-cooked in a syrupy sauce of sugar, wine, soy sauce and Szechwan peppercorns.

燴口蘑鴨掌

**114. Braised Duck Feet and Mushrooms:**
Deboned duck feet are cooked until tender, then sautéed in a hot wok with ginger, green onions and mushrooms.

燴鴨舌

**115. Braised Duck's Tongues:**
Duck's tongues are slow-cooked until tender and gelatinous, then braised with ginger and green onions.

油爆鴨舌

**116. Sautéed Duck's Tongues:**
Duck's tongues are slow-cooked until tender and gelatinous, then sautéed with garlic, green onions and a touch of vinegar.

炒鴨腸

**117. Sautéed Duck's Intestines:**
Duck's intestines, cut into sections, are fried, then sautéed with shredded ginger and leeks or green onions.

鴨 油 蒸 蛋

118. Duck Fat and Eggs:
*Scrambled eggs are mixed with broth and minced duck fat, then steamed to a soft custard and served piping hot. Serve with a spoon.*

燴 全 鴨

119. Braised Whole Duck:
*Duck meat, feet, testicles, giblets and tongue are braised with ham, mushrooms and choy sum.*

燴 鴨 腰

120. Braised Duck Testicles:
*Duck testicles are poached, then sautéed with bamboo shoots, mushrooms and small choy sum (Chinese greens).*

五 香 鴿 子

121. Five Spices Pigeon:
*Pigeon is poached in a seasoned liquid with spices such as Szechwan peppercorns, cloves, fennel and cinnamon bark. It is basted with honey and sesame oil and served in bite-sized pieces.*

琥 珀 鴿 蛋

122. Amber-Colored Pigeon Eggs:
*Hard-boiled pigeon eggs are shelled, fried to an amber color, then braised with mushrooms and bamboo shoots.*

# EXOTIC INGREDIENTS

These dishes reflect the influence of the imperial court on Peking food. The primary ingredients for most of these dishes are dehydrated. They are expensive and believed to have healing properties.

## 鷄汁排翅
**123. Chicken Juice and Shark's Fin:**
*A piece of shark's fin is steamed with chicken, pork, ham and broth. The meats are removed and the juice is strained and made into a sauce, which is served over the shark's fin.*

## 生鷄絲魚翅
**124. Shredded Chicken and Shark's Fin:**
*A shark's fin is braised until soft and gelatinous in a thick soup with shredded chicken.*

## 砂鍋鷄鮑翅
**125. Shark's Fin, Abalone and Chicken in a Casserole:**
*A piece of a shark's fin is cooked tender in broth, then served bubbling in a casserole with chicken and abalone.*

## 燴三鮮
**126. Braised Three Delicacies:**
*The three delicacies are chicken meat, sliced pork and sea cucumbers. They are braised in a brown soy-based sauce.*

紅燒海參

**127. Red-Cooked Sea Cucumbers (Beche-de-mer):**
Sea cucumbers are stewed until soft and spongy, then sautéed with green onions and soy sauce.

京蔥海參

**128. Sea Cucumbers and Leeks:**
Sea cucumbers are stewed until soft and spongy with leeks or green onions, sugar and soy sauce.

玉珠大烏

**129. Black Sea Cucumbers and Pigeon Eggs:**
Soft and spongy sea cucumbers are cooked in a brown sauce with hard-boiled pigeon eggs. The highlight of this dish is the contrast of colors. The sea cucumber is black and the eggs are white.

白汁大烏

**130. Black Sea Cucumbers in White Sauce:**
Black sea cucumbers are slow-cooked until soft and gelatinous, then braised in a white sauce with sliced ham and choy sum.

蔥扒大烏

**131. Green Onions and Sea Cucumbers:**
Sea cucumbers are slow-cooked until soft and gelatinous with chicken, pork, ginger and green onions. The sea cucumbers are drained, then braised in their own juice with leeks and deep-fried green onions.

山東海參

132. Shantung Sea Cucumbers:
Sea cucumbers are braised in a brown sauce and served with thin slices of omelet and pork.

蝴蝶海參

133. Butterfly Sea Cucumbers:
A large whole sea cucumber is made to resemble a butterfly. The wings are made of ham, black mushrooms and bamboo shoots; the eyes are green peas. Stuffed with minced chicken and shrimp, the sea cucumber is then steamed and served with a transparent sauce. This is an elaborate dish, which requires a skilled chef and advance notice.

紅燒干貝

134. Red-Cooked Dried Scallops:
Dried scallops are steamed, shredded and sautéed with minced ginger and green onions, wine and soy sauce.

奶湯干貝蘿蔔球

135. Scallops and Chinese Radish:
Dried scallops are steamed and cooked in a milky-white soup with Chinese radish balls.

鷄茸干貝

136. Minced Chicken and Dried Scallops:
Dried scallops, chicken and ham are shredded and arranged into a bird's-nest shape with snow-pea shoots. This arrangement is gently poached in broth, drained, then served with its own juice.

芙蓉干貝

**137. *Foo Yung* Dried Scallops:**
*Egg whites are sautéed with shredded dried scallops and garnished with shredded ham and green peas.*

干貝四絲

**138. Dried Scallops and Four Shredded Ingredients:**
*The four ingredients are pork, chicken, ham and bamboo shoots. They are sautéed and topped with shredded dried scallops and a transparent sauce.*

紅燒魚唇

**139. Red-Cooked Fish Lips:**
*Dehydrated fish lips are slow-cooked until soft and gelatinous, then braised in a brown sauce with* choy sum, *black mushrooms and bamboo shoots.*

酸辣魚唇

**140. Hot and Sour Fish Lips:**
*Slivers of fish lips are soaked, boiled, washed, then slow-cooked until soft and gelatinous in a thickened broth and served with vinegar, white pepper, green onions and Chinese parsley.*

奶汁魚唇

**141. Fish Lips in White Sauce:**
*Dehydrated fish lips are slow-cooked until soft and gelatinous, then braised in a white sauce with shredded ham and* choy sum.

## 鶏汁魚肚

**142. Fish Bladder (or Maw) with Chicken Juice:**
*Sliced dehydrated fish bladder is braised in a thickened sauce with shredded black mushrooms, ham,* choy sum *and minced chicken.*

## 鶏茸魚肚

**143. Fish Bladder (or Maw) and Minced Chicken:**
*Dehydrated fish bladder is sliced, slow-cooked until soft and spongy, then braised in a white sauce with minced chicken, black mushrooms, bamboo shoots and* choy sum.

## 紅燒魚肚

**144. Red-Cooked Fish Bladder (or Maw):**
*Dehydrated fish bladder is sliced, slow-cooked until soft and spongy, then braised with black mushrooms,* choy sum *and ham.*

## 高湯燕菜

**145. Fine Broth with Bird's Nest:**
*The bird's nest is actually hardened bird saliva picked from nests. Believed to have health-giving qualities, it goes through elaborate processing before it reaches the kitchen, where it is slow-cooked until soft and noodle-like, drained, topped with minced ham and parboiled snow-pea shoots, then served with a bowl of broth on the side. When you are ready to eat, the bird's nest is poured into the hot broth. Chinese parsley sprigs are served on the side. If you like pungent flavors, add a sprig to your bowl of broth.*

芙 蓉 官 燕

**146. *Foo Yung* Bird's Nest Soup:**
Dehydrated bird's saliva is cooked until soft and noodle-like, then served in a thickened soup with scrambled egg whites.

鍋 塌 鮑 魚 盒

**147. Pan-Fried Abalone Slices:**
Canned abalone slices are sandwiched with a stuffing of ground shrimp and pork, pan-fried, then braised in a clear sauce.

燴 鮑 魚 片

**148. Braised Abalone:**
Canned abalone slices are sautéed with Chinese greens, ham and mushrooms.

芙 蓉 鮑 魚 片

**149. *Foo Yung* Abalone Slices:**
Scrambled egg whites are sautéed with minced chicken and abalone slices.

蔴 醬 鮑 魚

**150. Abalone with Sesame-Seed Sauce:**
Canned abalone is thinly sliced and served drizzled with a nutty sesame-seed dressing.

奶 油 鮑 魚

**151. Abalone with White Sauce:**
Canned abalone slices are braised in a white sauce.

## 清湯銀耳
**152. Silver Ears in Broth:**
*Silver ears or white fungi, a type of mushroom, are cooked in broth until soft but chewy.*

## 葱爆兔肉
**153. Rabbit with Green Onions:**
*Rabbit meat is fried and then slow-cooked with ginger, wine, tangerine peels, leeks or green onions and soy sauce.*

## 汽鍋元甲
**154. Turtle in Yunnan Casserole:**
*Turtle meat is put into a Yunnan steam pot with ham, bamboo shoots and broth, then steamed until the meat is tender.*

## 奶湯蛤仕蟆
**155. Frog Fat in White Sauce:**
*Lentil-sized kernels of fat, allegedly extracted from hibernating frogs, are cooked in a cream soup with sliced ham, black mushroom, bamboo shoots and* choy sum. *Frog fat is believed to have rejuvenating qualities.*

## MAIN DISHES — FISH

In general, most Chinese fish dishes are served whole or unboned. Tell your waiter if you want the fish boned.

Most of these fish dishes are available in Chinese restaurants all over the world. The Chinese characters in some of the dishes listed specify Asian fish which may not be available. When ordering, you can ask your waiter to substitute fresh indigenous fish.

糟 溜 魚 片

**156. Wine Residue Braised Fish or Sliced Yellow Croaker in Rice Wine Sauce:**
*Slices of boned fish (yellow croaker, cod or snapper) are marinated, quick-fried, then braised with black fungi in a fragrant sauce made with wine residue juice and sweet glutinous rice wine.*

醬 汁 鰤 魚

**157. Brown Sauce Braised Fish:**
*A whole fish is fried until golden brown, then braised in a sauce of brown beans, sugar and broth.*

網 油 板 魚

**158. Caul Fried Fish or Fried Fish with Net Lard:**
*Boned fish slices are marinated, wrapped in small pieces of caul, dipped in a batter and deep-fried until golden brown. They are served sliced with peppery salt on the side.*

## 乾爆桂魚

**159. Braised Fish or Mandarin Fish:**
*A whole fish is fried until golden brown, then braised in a sauce with peas and sliced ham, bamboo shoots and black mushrooms.*

## 煎蒸黃魚

**160. Pan-Fried Steamed Fish or Yellow Croaker:**
*A whole fish is salted, dipped in scrambled eggs and fried. It is then placed on a plate, garnished with shredded ginger and green onions and steamed.*

## 乾煎黃魚

**161. Pan-Fried Fish or Yellow Croaker:**
*A whole fish is salted, dipped in scrambled eggs, fried and served covered with a garlicky brown sauce.*

## 白汁桂魚

**162. Fish in White Sauce:**
*A whole Mandarin fish is braised in a milky-white sauce with sliced ham, bamboo shoots and* choy sum. *Sometimes rendered chicken fat is drizzled over for additional flavor.*

## 五柳魚

**163. Sweet-and-Sour Carp with Five Shredded Ingredients:**
*A whole grass carp, or unboned carp pieces, is poached in a broth with ginger and green onions, then topped with a sweet-and-sour sauce made with shredded ham, ginger, green onions, black mushrooms and bamboo shoots. Sometimes shredded pickled vegetables are also added.*

酸 辣 燉 魚 塊

**164. Hot-and-Sour Braised Fish Pieces:**
*Pieces of unboned yellow croaker are dipped in a batter, deep-fried, then cooked in a broth with sliced pork, bamboo shoots and black fungi. The finished dish is served in a soup bowl and sprinkled with white-pepper powder, vinegar and Chinese parsley.*

菊 花 桂 魚

**165. Chrysanthemum Fish Slices:**
*Mandarin fish slices are marinated, dredged in cornstarch, fried until golden brown and served with a sweet-and-sour sauce. An omelet is shredded and arranged to resemble a chrysanthemum, for garnish.* Choi sum *is served around the fish.*

蒸 原 汁 桂 魚

**166. Steamed Mandarin Fish:**
*A Mandarin fish is placed in a deep bowl and topped with dried shrimp, shredded fatty pork and black mushrooms. The bowl is then filled with seasoned broth, sealed with paper and steamed. The fish is served directly in the bowl.*

乾 燒 黃 魚

**167. Pan-Fried Yellow Croaker:**
*A yellow croaker is fried until golden brown, then braised in a wok with ginger, green onions, snow cabbage, diced bamboo shoots, soy sauce and broth.*

醬 汁 瓦 塊 魚

**168. Fish in Brown-Bean Sauce:**
*A whole fish is fried until golden brown then braised in a sauce of brown beans, wine, green onions, sugar, vinegar and broth.*

## 醋溜瓦塊魚
**169. Sweet-and-Sour Fish Slices:**
Large fish slices are dipped in a batter, fried and served with a sweet-and-sour sauce.

## 芝蔴桂魚
**170. Sesame Seed Fish:**
Boned Mandarin fish slices are marinated, dipped in eggs and sesame seeds, then deep-fried until golden brown.

## 鍋塌銀魚
**171. Pan-Fried White Bait:**
Little white bait, smaller than anchovies, are dipped in a batter, pan-fried into a thick squarish pancake, then braised in a bit of broth with ginger and green onions.

## 紅燒鯉魚
**172. Red-Cooked Carp:**
A carp is pan-fried until golden brown, then braised in broth with ginger, green onions, sugar and soy sauce.

## 糟溜魚卷
**173. Wine Residue Fish Roll:**
Slices of boned fish with the skin still attached are stuffed with minced pork and shrimp, rolled, dipped in an egg-white batter and deep-fried. These rolls are then braised with black fungi in a fragrant sauce of wine residue juice, broth, salt and sugar. Advance notice is required for this dish.

## 清蒸鰣魚
**174. Steamed Fish:**
A fish is steamed with shredded ham, ginger, marbled pork, black mushrooms, bamboo shoots and green onions. The fish

juice is strained, cooked with broth and sprinkled over the fish together with green peas. Sometimes a piece of caul is used to wrap the fish and its garnishes before it is steamed.

## 炸 板 魚
### 175. Deep-Fried Fish Slices:
Bite-sized pieces of fish are marinated, dipped in eggs and bread crumbs, deep-fried until golden brown and served with two dips: a peppery salt dip, and soy sauce laced with red chilies.

## 雙 味 桂 魚
### 176. Sweet-and-Sour Whole Fish or Mandarin Fish:
A fish is boned whole. It is marinated, dredged in cornstarch, deep-fried until golden brown, then served with a red sweet-and-sour sauce studded with pine nuts, peas, diced ham and bamboo shoots.

## 抓 炒 魚 片
### 177. Sautéed Fish Slices:
Fish slices are marinated, quick-fried, then sautéed in a tangy ginger and green-onion sauce.

## 鍋 塌 魚
### 178. Pan-Fried Fish Slices:
Large fish slices are marinated, dipped in beaten eggs, pan-fried until golden brown, then braised in broth and soy sauce.

## 糖 醋 鯉 魚
### 179. Sweet-and-Sour Carp:
A whole carp is deep-fried, then served with a garlicky sweet-and-sour sauce with shredded red peppers and black mushrooms.

## 滑炒魚片
**180. Tender Sautéed Fish Slices:**
*Fish slices are marinated, fried briefly, then sautéed with* choy sum *and crunchy black fungi.*

## 松鼠黃魚
**181. Squirrel Fish or Deep-Fried Yellow Croaker á la Squirrel:**
*A yellow croaker is boned whole, marinated, dusted with cornstarch and deep-fried. It is served covered with a sweet-and-sour sauce with diced ham, peas, black mushrooms and bamboo shoots. This dish serves at least four people.*

## 葱烤鯽魚
**182. Leeks with Fish or Braised Golden Carp with Onions:**
*Two small golden carp—about three-quarters of a pound each—are pan-fried. They are then braised in broth with soy sauce, garlic, julienned leeks or green onions, and ginger.*

## 茄汁魚片
**183. Fish Slices in Tomato Sauce:**
*Fish slices are marinated, fried and served with a sweet-and-sour tomato sauce.*

## 松子魚條
**184. Fish with Pine Nuts:**
*Marinated carp slices are fried, then braised in a slightly sweet sauce with pine nuts.*

## 椒麻魚條
**185. Peppery Fragrant Fish:**
*Marinated carp slices are fried, then braised in a sauce of sesame oil, Szechwan peppercorns, ginger and green onions.*

酥 魚

**186. Tender Fish:**
Three or four small fish are layered in a casserole with sliced garlic, ginger and leeks and spices such as cloves and cinnamon bark, and slow-cooked in broth and soy sauce until even the bones are soft.

珊 瑚 魚 條

**187. Coral Fish:**
Sliced carp or a similar fish is marinated, fried and braised in a sauce with shredded hot peppers, bamboo shoots, ginger, green onions and black mushrooms.

高 麗 魚 條

**188. Fried Fish Strips:**
Fish meat is cut into strips, marinated, dipped in batter, deep-fried and served with two dips, a peppery salt dip and a spicy soy dip.

賽 螃 蟹

**189. Imitation Crab Meat:**
This dish is created to resemble crab meat. Boned fish meat is diced, marinated, fried, shredded, then sautéed with a bit of broth and scrambled eggs.

糟 溜 魚 肝 丁

**190. Wine Residue Fish and Livers:**
Diced fish meat is marinated, fried, then sautéed with poached duck liver and a fragrant wine residue sauce.

爆炒鱔片

**191. Sautéed Eel:**
*Slices of boned eel are fried, then sautéed with garlic, ginger, wine and soy sauce.*

---

## MAIN DISHES — LAMB

---

Originally sheep farmers, the northern Chinese have had lamb and mutton in their diet for a long time. In fact, lamb is more popular than pork or beef in northern China.

葱爆羊肉

**192. Leeks and Lamb:**
*This is a pungent dish of thinly sliced lamb sautéed with lots of garlic and shredded leeks or green onions.*

烤羊肉

**193. Barbecued or Pan-Fried Lamb:**
*Though called barbecued, this dish is actually pan-fried on a grill. Thin slices of lamb are marinated in green onions, Chinese parsley, vinegar, sugar and soy sauce, then pan-fried on a grill. The pan-frying is usually done either on a large grill by a cook or at the table by the patron. Side dishes such as shredded Chinese cabbage and chives are served with the lamb.*

涮羊肉

**194. Dipped Lamb or Peking Mongolian Hot Pot:**
*This is one of the most spectacular northern dishes, which*

the ancient Chinese learned from their Mongol conquerors. Raw lamb and other ingredients — bean thread noodles, bean curds, Chinese cabbage, spinach — are served on small plates around a Mongolian hot pot, which is a charcoal-fueled fondue. The fondue pot is filled with broth, which is brought to a rolling boil. Dip or drop each ingredient gently in the boiling broth until done. Remove and dip it in a sauce, which is either provided by the restaurant or mixed by you at a sauce table. At the sauce table, a dozen or so seasonings are available for you to choose from: soy sauce, wine, hot chili oil, vinegar, sesame oil, shrimp oil, sesame-seed paste and minced garlic, green onions and Chinese parsley. Mix your own sauce in a bowl and bring it back to your table. At a Mongolian hot pot meal, it is customary to cook and eat small portions of food a bit at a time. After the meal, drink the broth. It is delicious after all the cooking. Other dishes, such as fish or pork balls and sliced meat or shellfish, can also be ordered with the hot pot.

## 它似蜜
### 195. It's Like Honey or Sweet Sautéed Lamb:
This is a sweet-tasting dish. Thin slices of lamb are marinated in sweet bean sauce, fried in sesame oil, then sautéed in a syrupy sauce of sugar, vinegar and soy sauce.

## 煨汆羊肉片黄瓜
### 196. Braised Lamb with Cucumbers:
Thin slices of lamb are marinated in a soy-based sauce laced with ginger and Chinese parsley. The lamb is then braised in broth with a touch of vinegar and sesame oil, drained and tossed with thin cucumber slices.

## 羊肉糊
### 197. Braised Lamb Slices:
Thin slices of lamb are sautéed in hot oil with garlic, then

braised in a thickened sauce and served sprinkled with vinegar, white-pepper powder and Chinese parsley.

## 清燉羊肉
### 198. Slow-Cooked Lamb:
*A large piece of lamb is slow-cooked with ginger, green onions, cloves and pungent Chinese radish; the lamb is cut into small pieces, then braised in a wok with broth, garlic and ginger.*

## 粉蒸羊肉
### 199. Rice Powder Steamed Lamb:
*Marbled lamb slices are marinated in soy and sweet bean sauces, dredged in rice that has been roasted and pulverized with Szechwan peppercorns and cloves, then steamed until tender.*

## 紅燒羊肉
### 200. Red-Cooked Lamb:
*Lamb meat is cubed, marinated, sautéed with ginger and green onions and slow-cooked with spices, soy sauce and sugar. It is served garnished with chopped green onions. This lamb makes a good topping for either rice or noodles.*

## 砂鍋羊肉
### 201. Lamb in a Casserole:
*A lamb stew, cooked in a brown-bean sauce, is served bubbling in a Chinese casserole pot.*

## 醬爆羊肉
### 202. Lamb Sautéed with Sauce:
*Thin slices of lamb are marinated, then sautéed with minced garlic and sweet-bean (or hoi sin) sauce.*

宫保羊肉

**203. Kung Pao Lamb:**
This is a spicy dish. Lamb is cubed, marinated, quick-fried and sautéed in a hot and pungent sauce with dried chilies, garlic, wine, soy sauce, sugar and vinegar.

炒羊肉絲

**204. Sautéed Shredded Lamb:**
Shredded lamb is marinated, quick-fried and sautéed with shredded carrot, bamboo shoots, spinach and crinkly bean thread noodles, which have been deep-fried.

醋溜羊肉片

**205. Vinegar-Braised Lamb:**
Thin slices of lamb are marinated and sautéed in a sweet-and-sour sauce of ginger and green onions.

芙蓉羊肉片

**206. *Foo Yung* Lamb Slices:**
Foo Yung *indicates that egg whites are used in a dish.* Minced lamb is mixed and sautéed with scrambled egg whites, then served with sautéed lamb slices.

乾炸羊里脊

**207. Fried Lamb Tenderloin:**
Lamb tenderloin is sliced, marinated in a batter, fried until golden brown and served with a peppery salt dip on the side.

滑溜羊里脊

**208. Sautéed Lamb Tenderloin:**
Lamb tenderloin is sliced, marinated, quick-fried, then sautéed in a transparent sauce with garlic and ginger.

## 醬爆羊肉丁
**209. Diced Lamb with a Brown Sauce:**
*Lamb tenderloin is diced, marinated, quick-fried, then sautéed with minced garlic and a sweet sticky sauce.*

## 鐵板羊肉
**210. Teppan Lamb:**
*A teppan is a cast-iron dish used by Japanese cooks. Here, lamb slices are marinated, sautéed and served sizzling on a heated teppan dish with sliced green onions and a pungent sauce.*

## 鍋燒羊肉
**211. Fried Lamb:**
*Cooked strips of lamb are dipped in batter, pan-fried into a pancake, cut into bite-sized pieces and served with peppery salt on the side.*

## 炸羊肉捲
**212. Fried Lamb Rolls:**
*Slices of lamb tenderloin are stuffed with sautéed shredded chicken, bamboo shoots and black mushrooms, dipped in batter, deep-fried, then braised in a brown soy-based sauce.*

## 水爆羊肚或肚仁
**213. Parboiled Tripe:**
*Lamb tripe is cut into thin strips, parboiled, then served with a dip of soy sauce, sesame-seed paste, Chinese parsley and green onions.*

## 油爆羊肚
**214. Sautéed Tripe:**
Strips of lamb tripe are sautéed in sesame oil and a tart garlic sauce.

## 鹽爆羊肚
**215. Sautéed Lamb's Stomach:**
Lamb's stomach is shredded and sautéed with ginger, garlic, green onions, sesame oil, vinegar and wine.

## 燴蒜泥羊肚
**216. Garlic and Lamb's Stomach:**
Lamb's stomach is slow-cooked until tender, shredded and sautéed with minced garlic and a transparent sauce.

## 爆三樣
**217. Sautéed Three Kinds:**
Lamb's liver, kidney and meat are sliced and sautéed with choy sum, black fungi and bamboo shoots and a tangy garlicky sauce.

## 燴銀絲爛蒜
**218. Braised Silver Threads and Garlic:**
The section connecting the stomach and small intestine is used. It is stewed until tender, cut into thin strips and sautéed with a lot of mashed garlic and a sesame-oil-flavored sauce.

## 羊雜碎
**219. Assorted Lamb:**
Lamb heart, lung, spleen, stomach, intestine and carcass, cut into small pieces, are cooked until tender in a seasoned liquid.

全羊席

**220. A Lamb Banquet:**
This is a rare banquet only available in specialty restaurants with plenty of advance notice. An entire lamb is eaten in a series of banquet courses. Almost every part of the lamb is used, including the brain, the tail, the organs and ligaments. A number of cooking methods are used to create a variety of tastes.

## MAIN DISHES — PORK

京醬肉絲

**221. Shredded Pork with Sweet Peking Sauce:**
Shredded pork is marinated, quick-fried, then sautéed in a sweet sticky sauce with shredded green onions.

醬爆白肉絲

**222. Shredded Pork with Brown-Bean Sauce:**
Strips of cooked pork are marinated in brown-bean sauce, dredged in flour, fried, then sautéed with soy sauce, sugar and hot green peppers.

木樨肉

**223. *Mooshu Roo*, or Shredded Pork with Eggs, or Quick Fried Shredded Pork with Egg:**
Shredded pork, bamboo shoots, black fungi and an omelet are sautéed together with golden needles. This dish is usually served with Mandarin pancakes and hoi sin *sauce*. To eat, spread out a pancake, smear one side with hoi sin *sauce*, fill with the sautéed mixture, roll up and eat with fingers.

和 菜 戴 帽

**224. Shredded Pork and Assortment Topped with an Omelet, or Peking Chop Suey with Egg:**
*This dish is used as stuffing for Mandarin pancakes. Shredded pork is sautéed with softened bean-thread noodles and shredded black mushrooms, golden needles and cabbage. The sautéed mélange is topped with a large omelet. Break up omelet and follow the previous instructions to eat this dish.*

榨 菜 炒 肉 末

**225. Minced Pork with Preserved Kohlrabi (or Chinese Pickles):**
*Ground pork is marinated and sautéed with minced spicy preserved kohlrabi. This dish can be eaten by itself or used as stuffing for Peking Shaobing (#333 A Peking Menu), a rectangular-shaped hollow bread with sesame seeds.*

軟 炸 里 脊

**226. Fried Tenderloin, or Soft Fried Fillet of Pork:**
*Pork tenderloin is sliced, marinated in an egg-white batter, deep-fried to a golden brown and served with a peppery salt dip on the side.*

過 油 肉

**227. Pork Sautéed with an Assortment:**
*Thin pork slices are marinated, then sautéed with bamboo shoots, black fungi, green soy beans and pungent seasonings: ginger, garlic, green onions, wine, vinegar and Szechwan peppercorns.*

炸 溜 里 脊

**228. Fried Tenderloin:**
*Pork loin is thinly sliced, marinated, sautéed with sliced*

bamboo shoots and mushrooms and seasoned with wine and soy sauce.

## 椒 鹽 里 脊
**229. Tenderloin with Peppery (or Spiced) Salt:**
*Pieces of pork loin are marinated and deep-fried until golden brown. They are then tossed in a hot wok with salt and pepper.*

## 椒 鹽 排 骨
**230. Spareribs with Peppery (or Spiced) Salt:**
*This is similar to the tenderloin above, except unboned strips of pork rib are used.*

## 炸 醬 肉 丁
**231. Diced Pork with Sweet Peking Sauce:**
*Diced pork is quick-fried, then sautéed with soy and sweet bean sauces until sweet and sticky. This dish makes a tasty topping for noodles.*

## 酥 炸 肉 丸
**232. Fried Meatballs:**
*Ground marbled pork is seasoned, shaped into meatballs, deep-fried and served with a peppery salt dip on the side.*

## 醋 溜 丸 子
**233. Vinegar-Braised Meatballs:**
*Ground marbled pork is seasoned, shaped into meatballs, fried, then braised in a brown sweet-and-sour sauce.*

## 捲 尖
**234. Smoked Omelet Rolls:**
*Seasoned minced pork is wrapped in a thin omelet, steamed,*

炸溜肉丸

**235. Braised Meatballs:**
Marbled pork is minced, shaped into meatballs and fried. The meatballs are then braised with bamboo-shoot slices, black fungi, garlic and a soy-based sauce.

酥丸子

**236. Tender Meatballs:**
Ground pork balls are fried, then braised in a sauce made of broth, vinegar, Chinese parsley and sesame oil.

里脊絲粉皮

**237. Pork and Tientsin Bean Sheets:**
Shredded pork is marinated, then sautéed with shredded green onions and served over slippery Tientsin bean sheets with a vinegar-sesame oil dressing.

醬爆里脊丁或絲

**238. Diced or Shredded Pork in a Sweet Sauce, or Shredded Pork with Bean Sauce:**
Diced or shredded pork is marinated in a batter, fried and sautéed in a sticky, syrupy brown-bean sauce.

青椒里脊片

**239. Sliced Pork Loin and Green Peppers:**
Thinly sliced pork loin is marinated and sautéed with ginger, green onions and green peppers.

荷葉粉蒸肉

**240. Pork Steamed in Lotus Leaves:**
Marbled pork chunks are marinated in wine, soy and

brown-bean sauces, dredged in rice that has been roasted and pulverized with cloves and star anise, wrapped in a lotus leaf for fragrance, then steamed until tender. Unwrap the leaf, which is not edible, before eating.

## 罈子肉
**241. Pork in a Container:**
A piece of marbled pork belly is barbecued over a flame until brown and crinkly, dipped in water, and trimmed. It is then sliced and put into a ceramic container with ginger, green onions, wine and broth, sealed with paper and steamed. The ceramic container is served directly at the table.

## 糖醋里脊
**242. Sweet-and-Sour Pork Loin, or Sweet-Sour Fillet of Pork:**
Pieces of pork loin are marinated in a batter, fried, and served with a sweet-and-sour sauce.

## 乾爆肉條
**243. Sautéed Pork Strips:**
Marbled pork strips are steamed with a sweet wine sauce, then drained and sautéed with bamboo shoots, black mushrooms, ham and peas.

## 油爆里脊丁
**244. Sautéed Diced Pork Loin:**
Diced pork loin is marinated, then sautéed with wine and minced garlic and ginger.

## 滑溜里脊片
**245. Sautéed Pork-Loin Slices:**
Sliced pork loin is marinated, quick-fried, then sautéed with bamboo shoots and fresh sliced mushrooms.

清炸里脊

**246. Fried Pork Loin:**
*Pieces of pork loin are marinated in wine, fried until golden brown and served with a peppery salt dip on the side.*

鍋塌里脊

**247. Pan-Fried Pork Loin:**
*Pork-loin slices are marinated, dredged in flour, dipped in scrambled eggs, arranged in a pan and pan-fried. Broth, wine, minced ginger and green onions are then added, and the pork is braised briefly.*

紅燒肘子

**248. Red-Cooked Pork Hock:**
*A whole pork hock is rubbed with soy sauce, fried until golden brown, then slow-cooked until tender in a liquid with rock sugar, soy sauce and cloves.*

鍋燒肘子

**249. Fried Pork Hock:**
*A pork hock is poached in a seasoned liquid until tender, deboned, smeared with a batter and deep-fried until golden brown. It is served cut into bite-sized pieces with a peppery salt dip on the side.*

水晶肘子

**250. Crystal Pork Hock:**
*A pork hock is deboned, sliced, cooked until tender with Szechwan peppercorns, ginger, green onions and pork jelly. It is then chilled in a mold and served cut into bite-sized pieces. Some restaurants serve this dish with a spicy soy-garlic dip.*

## 全 爆
### 251. Sautéed Combo:
Shelled shrimp, diced chicken and pork are marinated, quick-fried and sautéed in a thick garlicky soy-based sauce with a diced assortment of giblets, pig's stomach, kidney and bamboo shoots.

## 蜜 汁 火 方
### 252. Honeyed Ham:
Sliced ham is steamed with rock sugar and Chinese wine. The juice is strained, thickened and served over the ham.

## 葱 爆 三 樣
### 253. Sautéed Three Types, or Sautéed Pork, Liver and Kidney with Green Onions:
Sliced pork, liver and kidney are sautéed with garlic and green onions.

## 爆 炒 腰 花
### 254. Sautéed Pig's Kidneys:
Kidney slices are sautéed with an assortment of bamboo shoots, choy sum, black fungi, garlic and ginger.

## 醋 溜 腰 花
### 255. Vinegar-Braised Kidneys:
Sliced pig's kidneys are sautéed in sesame oil with bamboo shoots, black fungi and a garlicky vinegar sauce.

## 炸 腰 花
### 256. Fried Kidneys:
Kidney slices are marinated, then deep-fried until crunchy. A peppery salt dip is served on the side.

## 清燴蹄筋
**257. Stewed Pig's Ligaments:**
Dehydrated pig's ligaments are slow-cooked until soft and gelatinous, then braised in a thickened sauce with mushrooms and ham slices.

## 肥腸扒白菜
**258. Intestine and Cabbage:**
Pig's large intestine is slow-cooked in a seasoned liquid, cut into small pieces, braised with shredded Chinese cabbage and served with its own thickened sauce.

## 醬肚
**259. Pig's Stomach with Sauce:**
Pig's stomach is slow-cooked in soy sauce and spices, such as cloves and cinnamon bark, until tender. It is served thinly sliced at room temperature.

## 湯爆肚片
**260. Poached Pig's Stomach:**
Pig's stomach is thinly sliced, poached in boiling water, drained and served piping hot in a seasoned broth with hot green peppers.

## 九轉肥腸
**261. Stuffed Pig's Intestine:**
A long piece of pig's large intestine is cut into sections. The sections are stuffed one inside the other until there are five layers, which are slow-cooked in a seasoned liquid, sliced, then braised in a sweet-and-sour sauce.

焦 溜 大 腸

**262. Sautéed Intestine:**
Pig's large intestine is cooked until tender, cut into small pieces, dipped in batter, fried, then sautéed with bamboo shoots, black fungi, garlic and green onions.

脆 皮 大 腸

**263. Crispy Intestine:**
Pig's intestine is cooked until tender in a seasoned liquid, drained, deep-fried until golden brown and served sliced.

## MAIN DISHES — SHELLFISH

Each year, the northern Shantung peninsula harvests enormous amounts of shrimp and prawns, which are exported to other provinces and countries. Since other parts of northern China do not have access to seafood, most of these dishes are of Shantung origin.

乾 爆 大 蝦

**264. Sautéed Prawns:**
Large unshelled prawns are cut into sections and sautéed until bright red with garlic, ginger, wine and soy sauce.

溜 大 蝦 片

**265. Braised Prawns:**
Prawn slices are marinated, coated with egg and cornstarch, deep-fried, then braised in a sauce with ginger, green onions, wine and broth.

燻 大 蝦

266. Spicy Prawns:
*Prawns are braised in a sauce spiced by Szechwan peppercorns, ginger and green onions, drained, then smoked over wood chips and served thinly sliced.*

熗 大 蝦

267. Parboiled Prawns:
*Prawn slices are parboiled and served with shredded ginger and a soy-based sauce.*

木 樨 蝦 仁

268. Mooshu Shrimp:
*Shelled shrimp are sautéed with green onions and a shredded omelet.*

水 晶 大 蝦

269. Crystal Prawns:
*Poached prawn slices are arranged decoratively in a bowl, steamed with pork jelly and chilled. The dish may be served in a mold or cut into small pieces.*

胡 辣 明 蝦

270. Peppery Prawns:
*Prawn slices are sautéed in wine and broth with green onions, prawn roe and white-pepper powder.*

茄 汁 蝦 仁

271. Shrimp in Tomato Sauce:
*Shelled shrimp are marinated, quick-fried, then sautéed in a sweet-and-sour red sauce.*

## 軟炸蝦仁
**272. Fried Shrimp or Soft Fried Prawns:**
Shelled medium shrimp are dipped in batter, then deep-fried until golden brown.

## 清炒蝦仁
**273. Sautéed Shrimp or Fried Fresh Shrimp:**
This dish is of Shanghai origin. Shelled shrimp are marinated, quick-fried, then sautéed with ginger, garlic and a touch of wine.

## 芙蓉蝦仁
**274. Shrimp *Foo Yung* or Scrambled Egg Whites with Shrimp:**
Shelled shrimp are marinated and sautéed with scrambled egg whites.

## 炒蝦仁鮮蘑
**275. Sautéed Shrimp and Mushrooms:**
Shelled prawns are sliced, fried, then sautéed with minced garlic, ginger and fresh mushroom slices.

## 炸蝦球
**276. Fried Shrimp Balls:**
Shrimp and fat pork are minced, seasoned and mixed thoroughly. The paste is shaped into small balls, dredged in bread crumbs, then deep-fried until golden brown.

## 生燜明蝦
**277. Braised Prawns:**
Prawns, with the shells still attached, are sautéed with minced ginger, green onions and broth until bright red in color and piping hot.

## 煎 蝦 餅
**278. Shrimp Cakes:**
Minced shrimp, marbled pork and water chestnuts are mixed thoroughly, formed into patties, fried until golden brown, then sautéed with sliced black mushrooms, bamboo shoots and choy sum.

## 鍋 塌 明 蝦
**279. Pan-Fried Prawns:**
Shelled shrimp are marinated, dipped in flour and eggs, pan-fried, then braised in broth and wine with green onions.

## 炸 鳳 尾 蝦
**280. Fried Phoenix-Tailed Prawns:**
Large prawns are shelled except for the tails, marinated, dipped in a batter (or in eggs and bread crumbs), deep-fried and served with a spicy soy dip and a peppery salt dip.

## 炒 蟹 黃 蝦 仁
**281. Crab Meat and Shrimp:**
Shelled shrimp are marinated, quick-fried, then sautéed with crab meat and crab roe.

## 抓 炒 蝦 仁
**282. Sautéed Shrimp:**
Shelled shrimp are marinated, fried, then sautéed in a transparent sweet-and-sour sauce.

## 綢 油 明 蝦
**283. Prawns in Caul:**
Prawns are shelled except for the tails, stuffed with minced pork and shrimp, wrapped with small pieces of caul, dipped in a batter and deep-fried.

## 鍋貼蝦仁
**284. Fried Shrimp Toasts:**
*Minced shrimp is marinated, smeared onto pieces of bread, garnished with minced ham and Chinese parsley and deep-fried until golden brown.*

## 油爆鷄蝦球
**285. Shrimp and Chicken Balls:**
*Minced shrimp, fat pork and chicken are combined, formed into balls, fried, then sautéed with minced garlic and Szechwan peppercorns.*

## 三鮮鍋巴
**286. Three Ingredients over Sizzling (or Crispy) Rice:**
*This is actually two dishes in one. One consists of shrimp, pork, sea cucumbers, peas and mushrooms sautéed in a transparent sauce. The other is pieces of rice crust that have been deep-fried. At the table, the waiter pours the assortment over the piping-hot rice crusts to produce a sizzling sound. Rice crusts that don't sizzle have not been fried at the right temperature. This dish should be eaten immediately or the rice crusts will become soggy.*

## 醬爆蟹
**287. Crab Braised in a Brown Sauce:**
*Unshelled crab pieces are dipped in flour, fried, then braised in sweet-bean sauce, ginger and green onions.*

## 炒全蟹
**288. Sautéed Crab:**
*Crab meat and crab roe are sautéed with marbled minced pork, ginger and green onions and garnished with crispy fried green onions.*

炸 板 全 蟹

**289. Crab Meat Patties:**
*Crab meat, fat pork, ginger and green onions are mixed together, formed into patties, wrapped in caul, dipped in a batter and deep-fried until golden brown. They are then served cut into small pieces.*

芙 蓉 蟹 黃

**290. Foo Yung Crab Meat:**
*Crab meat and crab roe are sautéed with wine, broth and scrambled egg whites.*

蟹 黃 扒 白 菜

**291. Crab Meat over Cabbage:**
*Chinese cabbage is sautéed until soft, then served with a thickened sauce of crab meat and crab roe.*

水 炒 蠣 黃

**292. Sautéed Oysters:**
*Small shucked oysters are mixed with scrambled eggs and short strands of chives, then sautéed with oil and a bit of broth.*

油 爆 魷 魚 卷

**293. Sautéed Cuttlefish:**
*Reconstituted dried cuttlefish is sliced, then sautéed with minced garlic and green onions, salty pickles and a tangy sauce.*

鍋 塌 蟶 子

**294. Fried Clams:**
*Shelled clams are marinated, dipped in flour and eggs, then*

deep-fried. They are then braised in a bit of broth with ginger and green onions.

蒸芙蓉蛤仁
### 295. Foo Yung Steamed Clams:
Scrambled egg whites are steamed until coagulated and topped with sautéed clam meat, ham, bamboo shoots, black mushrooms and peas.

蟹裏藏珠
### 296. Crab with Jewels:
This is an elaborate dish that requires advance notice. Crab meat is sautéed in a thickened sauce with hard-boiled pigeon eggs, and served garnished with the crab shell. Vegetables and fried shoestring potatoes are placed around the crab shell to simulate sea grass.

## MAIN DISHES—VEGETABLES

The northern Chinese live in a temperate climate, and do not have much access to fresh greens. Chinese or Tientsin cabbage figures prominently in most Peking menus.

北菇扒津菜
### 297. Braised Black Mushrooms and Chinese (or Tientsin) Cabbage:
Chinese cabbage is cooked until soft and wilted, then topped with supple-textured black mushrooms and a brown sauce.

## 金 腿 扒 津 菜

**298. Chinese Ham and Chinese Cabbage, or Yunnan Ham and Tientsin Cabbage:**
*Chinese cabbage is cooked until soft and wilted and topped with shredded Chinese ham and a transparent sauce.*

## 奶 油 津 白

**299. Braised Chinese Cabbage with White Sauce:**
*Chinese cabbage is cooked until wilted and served with a thickened white sauce.*

## 鷄 油 津 白

**300. Braised Chinese Cabbage with Chicken Fat:**
*Chinese cabbage is cooked until wilted and served drizzled with rendered chicken fat.*

## 二 鬆 筍 桃 仁

**301. Two Crisps with Walnuts, or Crispy Fried Shredded Dried Scallops, Walnuts, Bamboo Shoots and Salted Cabbage:**
*Dried scallops are steamed, shredded and deep-fried with snow cabbage until both ingredients are crunchy. They are served with fried walnuts and shredded bamboo shoots.*

## 鷄 油 絲 瓜

**302. Squash with Chicken Fat:**
*Angled or ridged squash is peeled, cut into chunks and braised until tender with ginger and green onions in a seasoned broth. Rendered chicken fat is drizzled over before serving. Angled squash has a taste and texture similar to zucchini.*

白汁菜心

**303. Chinese Vegetables with White Sauce:**
A Chinese vegetable such as Chinese cabbage is braised until tender in a milky-white sauce.

素燒茄子

**304. Sautéed Eggplants:**
Chunks of Oriental or Western eggplants are deep-fried, then sautéed in a brown sauce with green soybeans, sliced mushrooms and bamboo shoots.

糟燴鮮蘑豆腐

**305. Mushrooms and Bean Curds:**
Bean-curd and mushroom slices are braised in a sauce of seasoned broth and wine residue juice.

乾燒冬筍

**306. Sautéed Bamboo Shoots:**
Chunks of bamboo shoots are sautéed with snow cabbage and soy sauce.

口蘑鍋巴

**307. Mushrooms over Sizzling Rice:**
This is two dishes in one. In one, sliced mushrooms, bamboo shoots and choy sum are sautéed together in a transparent sauce. The other is pieces of rice crusts that have been deep-fried. At the table, the waiter pours the sautéed mushrooms over the hot rice crusts to produce a sizzling sound. Rice crusts that don't sizzle have not been fried at the right temperature. This dish should be eaten immediately or the rice crusts will become soggy.

醋溜白菜

308. Vinegar-Braised Cabbage:
*Chinese cabbage is sliced and sautéed until wilted with dried shrimp, shredded hot peppers and a sweet vinegar sauce.*

蝦子春笋

309. Bamboo Shoots with Shrimp Eggs:
*Chunks of bamboo shoots are sautéed in a brown sauce with tiny briny-tasting shrimp eggs.*

辣冬筍

310. Hot Bamboo Shoots:
*Shredded bamboo shoots are sautéed in a spicy sauce of red chili oil, shredded red peppers, ginger and green onions.*

燒二冬

311. Sautéed Two Vegetables, or Braised Bamboo Shoots and Black Mushrooms:
*Black mushrooms and bamboo shoots are sautéed in soy sauce and a bit of broth.*

乾煸筍塊

312. Sautéed Bamboo Shoots:
*Chunks of bamboo shoots are sautéed with snow cabbage in a seasoned broth. Both ingredients are then deep-fried until the shoots are golden brown and the snow cabbage is crunchy. They are served tossed together.*

糟煨冬筍

313. Bamboo Shoots in Wine Residue:
*Chunks of bamboo shoots are sautéed in oil, then braised in broth and wine residue juice.*

鷄 油 菜 心

**314. Chinese Vegetables with Chicken Fat:**
A Chinese vegetable is sautéed in rendered chicken fat with straw mushrooms.

素 十 香 菜

**315. Vegetarian Ten Ingredients:**
Shredded carrots, Chinese radish, celery, bamboo shoots, black mushrooms, fried bean curd, gluten and green peppers are sautéed with soybean sprouts and golden needles. This dish can be used as a vegetarian stuffing for Mandarin pancakes. To eat, smear one side of a pancake with hoi sin sauce, add a piece of green onion and a spoonful of stuffing, roll tightly and eat with fingers.

鷄 油 四 寶

**316. Four Jewels with Chicken Fat:**
Fresh mushrooms, bamboo shoots, canned abalone and small bok choy are poached, arranged side by side decoratively on a plate and served with a transparent sauce.

椒 油 茄 子

**317. Eggplants and Spicy Oil:**
Whole Oriental eggplants are steamed, drained, deep-fried and served with a soy and Szechwan-peppercorn dressing.

奶 油 小 白 菜

**318. Braised Bok Choy with White Sauce:**
Bok choy is sautéed and served with a creamy white sauce. Sometimes shredded ham is sprinkled over the dish.

扒四蔬

**319. Braised Four Vegetables, or Sautéed Vegetables Four Treasures:**
The four "treasures" are any four of the following vegetables: black mushrooms, straw mushrooms, Chinese cabbage, bamboo shoots, canned asparagus and choy sum. They are braised or sautéed, then served with a transparent sauce.

## SNACKS OR SIDE DISHES

水餃

**320. Boiled Dumplings:**
These perogy-like dumplings are a northern Chinese mainstay. They are usually stuffed with ground pork, Chinese cabbage and green onion. They are then boiled, drained and served with a vinegar and shredded-ginger dip. You can add soy sauce and hot chili sauce to the dip for extra zest. These crescent-shaped dumplings may also be stuffed with lamb, beef or minced pressed bean curds, eggs and chives.

蒸餃

**321. Steamed Dumplings:**
These dumplings are similar to the boiled dumplings above except that the skin is made differently and the dumplings are steamed. Some steamed dumplings are wrapped into squares or rectangles. The most common stuffing is of ground pork and Chinese cabbage. You can also order these dumplings with a vegetarian stuffing.

鍋貼

**322. Fried Dumplings:**
These dumplings are pan-fried. They are crunchy at the bottom and soft and pliable on top. They are usually stuffed with pork and cabbage. Eat with a soy-vinegar dip.

炸春段

**323. Fried Omelet or Fried Egg Rolls:**
A thin omelet is stuffed with sautéed chicken, bamboo shoots and spinach, dredged in flour, then deep-fried. It is served cut into small slices.

拉麵

**324. Lah Mein, or Hand-Pulled Noodles:**
A northern specialty, these noodles are handmade from a flour-and-water dough. The cook kneads and pulls the dough until it turns into thin spaghetti-like strands. The noodles are then boiled, drained and sautéed or served in soup. Lah mein *may be served with shredded pork; shredded three ingredients (chicken, pork and ham); or with meat, seafood and vegetables.*

大滷麵

**325. Noodles in Soup with an Assorted Topping:**
A satisfying one-dish meal, these noodles are served in a small soup bowl with broth and sautéed pork slices, black fungi, black mushrooms and scrambled eggs. Eat with hot chili sauce. Sometimes other ingredients are added, such as shrimp, sea cucumbers and bamboo shoots.

川滷麵

**326. Noodles with a Szechwan Assortment:**
Diced pork is sautéed with diced black mushrooms, bamboo

shoots, sea cucumbers, shrimp, scrambled eggs and spicy seasonings and served as topping over a small bowl of noodles in broth.

炸 醬 麵

327. Pork with Sauce over Noodles, or Noodles with Szechwan Sauce:
*Drained thin noodles are served with a savory topping of minced pork sautéed with green onions and brown-bean and* hoi-sin *sauces.*

熱 湯 麵

328. Hot Broth Noodles:
*Minced dried shrimp, green onions and* choy sum *are sautéed together, then braised with fat noodles in soy sauce and broth.*

韭 菜 盒 子

329. Chive Pies:
*A flour-and-water dough is rolled out thin, cut into small rounds, stuffed with a savory mixture of pork, shrimp and chives, then pan-fried until golden brown.*

撈 餅

330. Pork Pies:
*These are like chives pies, except a mixture of seasoned minced pork and vegetables is used as stuffing.*

葱 油 餅

331. Green Onion Cake:
*A flour-and-water dough is stuffed and rolled with shortening and green onions. It is cut, flattened into pancake shape, then pan-fried until golden brown and cut into pizza-like wedges.*

## 蘿蔔絲餅
**332. Chinese Radish Cakes:**
*These are small flat pies about two inches in diameter. They are made with a flaky pastry and filled with shredded Chinese radish, dried shrimp, ham and pork fat. Chinese radish cakes are pan-fried and served warm or at room temperature.*

## 京式燒餅
**333. Peking *Shaobing*:**
*This is a rectangular pocket of bread topped with sesame seeds. It is usually stuffed with cold sliced beef and pickled cabbage, or with sautéed minced beef and preserved kohlrabi.*

## 銀絲捲
**334. Silver Thread Bread or Steamed Plain Roll:**
*A northern staple, this yeasted bread is served steamed or deep-fried. This bread is made in an unusual way: the raised bread dough is wrapped and steamed in a thin sheet of dough. The roll is served sliced in small pieces. Remove paper on the bottom of the bread before eating.*

## 花捲
**335. Flower Bread:**
*This yeasted bun is rolled into a pinwheel and cut ornately to resemble a flower. Usually two to an order, steamed flower bread has a slightly sweet taste.*

## 饅頭
**336. Mantou or Plain Buns:**
*These round yeasted buns are steamed. Usually two to an order, they are slightly sweeter than Western bread.*

羊 肉 包 子

**337. Lamb Bun:**
A white yeasted bun is stuffed with minced lamb and cabbage, then steamed.

油 條

**338. Fried Doughnuts:**
These are eaten throughout China. Strips of yeasted dough are deep-fried into long doughnuts. They are crunchy, savory and delicious by themselves or dunked in rice porridge or hot soybean milk.

大 餅

**339. Pan-Fried Pancakes:**
This is a huge pizza-like flat bread with no topping. Green onions and shortening are used as filling. The pancake is pan-fried and sold in large triangular wedges.

牛 肉 包 子

**340. Beef Bun:**
Seasoned ground beef is stuffed in a yeasted bun. It is steamed or pan-fried until golden brown at the top and bottom.

苟 不 理

**341. Pork Bun:**
Minced pork and bok choy are stuffed and steamed in a small yeasted bun.

天 津 包

**342. Tientsin Buns:**
These are small buns made with a flour-and-water dough and stuffed with a savory filling of minced pork. They are served steamed.

# DESSERTS

Although the Chinese are not known for their desserts, northern desserts tend to be a little more interesting than desserts from other regions.

## 拔絲蘋果，香蕉或山藥
**343. Apple, Banana or Yam Fritters or Fried Apple, Bananas or Yams with Honey:**
Sliced apple, banana or yam is dipped in batter, deep-fried and dunked in syrup. This dish is served with a bowl of cold water on the side. Dip a piece of fritter in the cold water for two or three seconds until the syrup hardens and becomes crusty.

## 拔絲脂油芝蔴
**344. Pork Fat Fritters:**
Pieces of pork fat are dipped in batter, deep-fried, dunked in syrup and sprinkled with sesame seeds. They are served as above with a bowl of cold water on the side.

## 杏仁豆腐
**345. Almond Jelly:**
This is an almond-flavored jelly cut into cubes and served with canned fruit cocktail.

## 豆沙鍋餅
**346. Red-Bean Fried Crêpe or Crispy Red-Bean Pancake:**
A crêpe is stuffed with sweet red-bean filling, wrapped and then fried until crispy. It is served sliced.

## 棗泥鍋餅

**347. Dates Fried Crêpe or Crispy Date Pancake:**
This dish is similar to the one previous except that mashed dates are used as a filling.

## 荷花酥

**348. Lotus-Shaped Flaky Pastry:**
Small flaky pies are stuffed with red-bean paste, clipped at the top to resemble a budding lotus flower and deep-fried until golden brown.

## 涼糕

**349. Glutinous Rice Cakes:**
Steamed glutinous rice is flattened and layered with red-bean paste and sesame seeds mixed with sugar and cranberry-flavored pudding. The rice is shaped into squares, then cut into small pieces and dusted with sugar.

## 愛窩窩

**350. Glutinous Rice and Yellow-Bean Powder:**
Steamed glutinous rice is mashed, then used as a dumpling skin for sweet red-bean paste. The dumplings are shaped into small round patties and dredged in yellow-bean powder.

## 炒三泥

**351. Sautéed Three Mashed Ingredients:**
Lotus seeds, red beans and peas are cooked separately with sugar and shortening, then served side by side glazed with syrup.

## 三不粘

**352. Sautéed Egg Yolks or Not Sticky to Three Things:**
When well made, this dessert does not stick to the spoon, bowl or teeth. Egg yolks are mixed with sugar, water and cornstarch, then sautéed in shortening or chicken fat over very low heat until a glutinous consistency is achieved.

## 酥盒子

**353. Flaky Pies:**
Flaky pastry is stuffed with sweet red-bean paste, shaped into small patties and deep-fried.

## 高力豆沙

**354. Fried Red-Bean Paste:**
Sweet red-bean paste is shaped into small balls, dipped in an egg-white batter and deep-fried. They are served sprinkled with white sugar.

## 高力豆沙香蕉

**355. Banana Fritters or Soufflé Balls with Mashed Red Bean and Banana:**
Banana chunks, stuffed with sweet red-bean paste, are dipped in an egg-white batter and deep-fried. They are served sprinkled with white sugar.

## 猪油水晶包

**356. Transparent Buns:**
These buns have a thin transluscent skin. A thin dough is used to make the small buns, which are filled with a sweet stuffing of minced melon seeds and sugar, then steamed.

蓮 子 糕

357. Lotus Seed Cake:
*Lotus seeds are cooked, mashed, then mixed with sugar and gelatin and chilled to form a jelly. It is served cut in small pieces.*

核 桃 酪 圓 子

358. Walnut Soup and Dumplings:
*Glutinous rice flour is used to make dollar-sized dumplings, which are filled with minced sweetened gingko nuts or red-bean paste. The dumplings are boiled, drained and served with a sweet milky soup made with ground walnuts.*

核 桃 酪

359. Walnut Soup or Sweetened Mashed Walnut Cream:
*This is a sweet milky-white soup made with ground walnuts.*

琥 珀 蓮 子

360. Amber-Colored Lotus Seeds:
*Lotus seeds are cooked in syrup until golden brown, layered with glutinous rice and red-bean paste, then steamed. This dish is served in a dome shape, then topped with a syrup.*

# CHAPTER SEVEN

# A Shanghai Menu

The Shanghai culinary region, which includes the provinces of Chekiang, Kiangsu, Kiangsi and Anhwei, is an agricultural land of plenty. It has a mild climate, fertile soil and lots of water, and is one of China's largest rice- and vegetable-producing areas. It is close to the sea and has many fresh-water lakes, so fish is a frequent addition to the diet. The Shanghainese also have access to the best tea: Dragon Well (*Lung Jang*) tea, which grows lush in the hills of Hangchow. The Yangtze River, with its many canals and tributaries, is the driving force in the region. For centuries it has provided the water needed to grow food, and has transported people and goods. Shanghai, which is on the Yangtze delta, is the largest city and trading center in China and the cooking capital of the region. Shanghainese cooks have created recipes with ingredients brought in from the outside as well as those produced in their own rich environment.

The region also excels in food-products manufacturing. In the city of Jinjiang, in Kiangsu province, specialists with ancient skills make Jinjiang vinegar, a dark rice-wine vinegar prized for its mellow flavor. The rice wines in the region are arguably the best in China. The city of Shaoshing is known for its aromatic glutinous rice wine, used throughout the country. Soochow, a neighboring city, not to be outdone, claims to make an even better rice wine called *far dew*.

These products figure prominently in many Shanghai dishes. The Shanghainese sauté Dragon Well tea in a sizzling-hot wok with shelled fresh shrimp, producing a delicate, fragrant dish called Shrimp with Dragon Well Tea. With so much excellent wine in the region, it is not surprising that the people use it liberally in their cooking. They marinate raw shellfish in wine and coarse salt and call it "Drunken Shellfish." Poached chicken is marinated in wine and broth and called "Drunken Chicken." These dishes are served chilled as appetizers. The Shanghainese also cook with the residue left from making glutinous rice wine. Wine residue (called *joh*) is actually fermented glutinous rice still in the husk. Wrapped tightly in muslin, it is added to simmering poaching liquids for a rich, perfumy and distinctly Shanghai flavor. Another wine by-product often used by the Shanghainese is the wine vinegar of Jinjiang. It is used in well-known dishes, such as Vinegar-Braised Fish, to produce a tangy, mouth-watering sauce.

Shanghai is a seaport and a major railway junction between northern and southern China and is connected to the vast interior by the great Yangtze. Its people boast that "all things come to Shanghai." Preserved kohlrabi, a crunchy spicy pickled vegetable, is from Szechwan; yet the Shanghainese use it so often many of them think it is a local product. Curry Chicken is originally Indian; the people of Shanghai acquired the taste from British-Indian soldiers who were stationed there. From the northern Chinese, whose staple is wheat, not rice, the Shanghainese learned to enjoy meat-filled dumplings and hefty noodles dishes.

More hearty than delicate, Shanghai food is rich and robust. It sometimes resembles certain European dishes, which may be why some Westerners prefer it to the other regional cuisines. More red meat is featured on the menu, and the Shanghainese will frequently serve whole fowl and roasts rather than bite-sized pieces. The saying about getting hungry right after you eat Chinese food is nowhere less true than in authentic Shanghainese restaurants. Lion's Head, which resembles cabbage rolls, is meatballs wrapped and simmered in Chinese cabbage, but the meatballs are the size of baseballs. Steamer Dumplings are perogy-like dumplings stuffed and steamed with juicy ground pork; they are intended to be eaten in large quantities. Red-Cooked Pork Hock looks like and has the substance of a pot roast, though it is not roasted, but stewed until tender in soy sauce and rock sugar.

Like the Cantonese, the Shanghainese also stir-fry and steam dishes, but their favorite cooking method is red-cooking—a unique way of simmering meat in soy sauce and sugar. Meat or fish done this way tends to be brown in color, full-flavored, and slightly sweet in taste. To many diners, red-cooked fish is a stimulating alternative to Cantonese steamed fish. It is first pan-fried until crunchy, then braised in a garlicky sauce of broth, sugar and soy sauce.

The Shanghainese consider themselves to be extremely fortunate; they believe their cuisine reflects the best of all China. Thankfully, you don't have to go all the way to Shanghai to sample the food. Good Shanghai restaurants exist in many cities of the world. This menu will help you order some truly authentic Shanghai dishes.

# A SHANGHAI MENU

## APPETIZERS

Shanghai appetizers are usually served at room temperature. The Shanghainese like to enjoy them with beer, Scotch or brandy; a sweet aperitif such as sherry is also compatible with these appetizers.

油 炸 花 生

### 1. Fried Peanuts:
Shelled peanuts, sometimes with the membrane still attached, are fried and salted. This dish is commonly eaten at breakfast with congee (rice porridge). Considered a humble man's appetizer, it is usually available in small diners.

鹹 烤 花 生

### 2. Salted Peanuts:
Peanuts are cooked in the shell in salty water until soft. Before eating, remove shells with fingers.

茶 葉 蛋

### 3. Tea Eggs:
Hard-boiled eggs with cracked shells are poached with soy sauce, star anise and tea leaves. These eggs, usually served whole, have interesting coffee-colored marbled patterns and a tasty anise flavor. Before eating, remove shells and cut into quarters.

燻 蛋

4. Smoked Eggs:
Soft-boiled eggs are shelled and smoked until light brown. The smoky-flavored egg white and the runny yolk make these eggs a very special treat. Season with salt before eating.

醉 鷄

5. Drunken Chicken:
A poached chicken is marinated in broth and wine. (Discriminating cooks use only Shaoshing wine for drunken dishes.) Drunken chicken is served chilled, in small pieces with bone and skin still attached.

凍 鷄

6. Chilled Chicken or Chicken Jelly:
Chicken is cooked until tender with pork jelly and spices such as cloves and Szechwan peppercorns. It is then deboned, chilled until it forms a gelatin and served thinly sliced.

大 轉 彎

7. Soy Chicken Wings:
Chicken wings are poached in wine and soy sauce and served at room temperature.

滷 胗

8. Poached Giblets:
Chicken giblets are poached in soy sauce and star anise.

鹽 水 鴨

9. Salty Water Duck or Salted Duck:
The commonest method of preparing this duck is to marinate it with salt and spices, such as star anise and Szechwan

*peppercorns, and then steam it. Salty Water Duck is served at room temperature, in bite-sized pieces and on the bone. Order a whole, a half or a quarter of a duck.*

## 醬鴨

**10. Saucy Duck or *Soochow*-Style Duck:**
*Duck is poached in red-colored rice (used for coloring) and spices, such as ginger and cassia bark. This rosy-colored duck is slightly sweet in taste and served in bite-sized pieces and on the bone. Order a whole, a half or a quarter of a duck.*

## 鹵鴨舌或脚

**11. Poached Duck's Tongues or Feet:**
*Tiny duck's tongues or feet are poached until soft and gelatinous in soy sauce and spices. They are served unboned and at room temperature.*

## 紅燒鴨脚

**12. Red-Cooked Duck's Feet:**
*Duck's feet, with the claws removed, are poached until tender in spices and soy sauce. The texture of the meat is fatty and gelatinous.*

## 醬肉

**13. Sauced Pork:**
*Marbled pork is marinated in sweet bean sauce, then poached until tender in spices and soy sauce. This meat is then chilled into a jelly and served sliced or julienned.*

## 鯌肉

**14. Preserved Pork:**
*A pork hock is deboned, rubbed with salt and saltpeter, then*

poached. It is chilled to a jelly and served in small pink rectangular pieces.

## 白切猪肚
### 15. Poached Pig's Stomach:
Pig's stomach is poached until white and tender, sliced and served with a soy and Chinese-parsley dip. Pig's stomach has a chewy texture and a gamy flavor.

## 燻猪腦
### 16. Smoked Brain:
Pig's brain is poached, smoked to a light brown and served cold and sprinkled with salt. This dish has a smoky but otherwise bland flavor and a soft crumbly texture.

## 燻魚
### 17. Smoked Fish:
The fish is not really smoked, but is prepared so that it has a slight smoky taste. Fish steaks (usually cod) are fried until crunchy, then braised in a syrup of sugar, soy sauce and five spices. Smoked fish has a sweet anise flavor and is delicious as a cold appetizer or as a topping on noodles.

## 油爆蝦
### 18. Sautéed Shrimp:
Medium shrimp are sautéed in oil with sugar and soy sauce, then served at room temperature.

## 脆鱔
### 19. Crunchy Eel:
The slender, snake-like yellow eel is a favorite of the Shanghainese because of its supple, tasty meat. Boned shredded eel is fried until crunchy, then braised in a sweet syrup of sugar and soy sauce.

醉 蟹

## 20. Drunken Crab:
The Shanghainese are fond of preparing seafood by pickling with salt. The crab is cleaned, cut and marinated in wine and coarse salt for several days. It is then served chilled and raw. The meat of the crab is jelly-like and very salty. Eat with fingers. (It is risky to eat raw shellfish in countries where the water may be badly polluted.)

醉 蚬 或 螺

## 21. Drunken Shellfish:
A variety of shellfish such as cockles, clams and tiny sea snails are pickled raw, in coarse salt and wine, and served chilled. The meat of the shellfish is tender, juicy and salty. (It is risky to eat raw shellfish in countries where the waters may be badly polluted.)

油 爆 蛤 蜊

## 22. Sautéed Clams:
Shelled large clams are sautéed with minced garlic and ginger.

灼 蛏 子

## 23. Poached Clams:
Clams are poached, removed from the shells and served with a garlic-ginger dip.

拌 蛏 肉

## 24. Clams Cold Plate:
An assortment of poached clam meat, black mushrooms, ham, peas and mung-bean sprouts is arranged on a plate and served at room temperature. A soy-ginger sauce is drizzled over the ingredients before serving. Toss well before eating.

## 糟田螺

**25. Snails in Wine Residue:**
*Escargot are shelled and braised in wine residue and spices and served at room temperature.*

## 拌海蜇皮

**26. Jellyfish Salad:**
*This is a cold crunchy salad of jellyfish, shredded green onions and Chinese white radish. Oil, salt and pepper are used in the dressing. Sometimes shredded Chinese ham is also included.*

## 素鴨

**27. Vegetarian Duck:**
*Bean-curd sheets are folded into a roll, steamed and sometimes pan-fried. They are served cut in small pieces, sometimes with a sauce of soy and sesame oil.*

## 素鷄

**28. Vegetarian Chicken:**
*Tender Shanghai bean-curd skins are used for this dish. The skins are folded into a rectangular roll, trussed and steamed. It is served sliced, sometimes with a mixture of soy sauce and sesame oil. This dish is also called Vegetarian Ham.*

## 拌黃瓜

**29. Cucumber Salad:**
*Peeled cucumbers are seeded, sliced and pickled in salt, sugar and vinegar.*

拌雙筍

**30. Tossed Shoots:**
Young bamboo shoots are cut into chunks, parboiled and tossed with a soy and green-onion dressing with pieces of salted stem lettuce.

---
## SOUPS
---

As a matter of tradition, the Shanghainese prefer to have soup at the end of a meal, to clean the palate. For this reason, most of their soups tend to be lighter than those of other regional cuisines.

油豆腐絲粉湯

**31. Fried Bean-Curd and Bean-Thread Noodle Soup:**
This soup is often eaten as a noodle dish at lunchtime. A clear broth is served with pieces of fried bean curd, slippery bean thread noodles and dried shrimp.

榨菜肉絲湯

**32. Shredded Pork and Preserved Kohlrabi Soup, or Szechwan Pickles and Pork Soup:**
Shredded pork, dried shrimp and crunchy, spicy preserved kohlrabi are cooked in a clear broth. Sometimes transparent bean thread noodles are also added. This is a spicy and pungent soup.

## 雪菜肉絲湯

**33. Shredded-Pork and Snow-Cabbage Soup, or Salt Vegetables and Pork Soup:**
Salty preserved cabbage, called snow cabbage, is cooked in a clear broth with shredded pork and bamboo shoots.

## 三絲湯

**34. Three Kinds of Shredded-Meat Soup:**
Shredded pork, ham, chicken, bamboo shoots and black mushrooms are cooked in clear broth.

## 咖喱牛肉湯

**35. Curry Beef Soup:**
The Shanghainese learned to like Indian flavors from British-Indian soldiers stationed in Shanghai. Beef chunks are cooked until tender and served in a curry-flavored broth with bean-thread noodles.

## 紫菜蝦米湯

**36. Seaweed and Dried-Shrimp Soup:**
Seaweed or nori, used by the Japanese to wrap sushi, is cooked in clear broth with briny dried shrimp. Other ingredients, such as shredded pork or scrambled eggs, may also be added. Because this dish is usually home-cooked, it is not always available in restaurants.

## 蛋捲粉絲湯

**37. Stuffed Omelet Soup:**
Seasoned ground pork is rolled in an omelet and steamed. The omelet is sliced and served in broth with slippery bean-thread noodles, dried shrimp and greens.

# 醃篤鮮
**38. Ham and Pork Combo:**
*A whole ham, a pork hock, bamboo-shoot slices and pork-stuffed Shanghai bean-curd skins are cooked in a delicious broth. A meal in itself, this hefty soup is usually served in the winter, around Chinese New Year. Advance notice may be required for this dish.*

# 雪菜冬筍湯
**39. Snow-Cabbage and Bamboo-Shoots Soup:**
*Shredded bamboo shoots and minced salty snow cabbage are cooked in clear broth.*

# 薺菜豆腐羹
**40. Shepherd's Purse and Bean-Curd Thick Soup:**
*Shepherd's purse, a vegetable like watercress, is served in a thickened soup with shrimp and bean-curd cubes. This dish is sometimes unavailable because shepherd's purse is seasonal.*

# 蛤蜊燉蛋
**41. Egg-Custard Soup with Clams:**
*Eggs, scrambled with broth or water, are steamed to a soft custard then topped with clams. This delicate soup also makes a wholesome main dish.*

# 川鯽魚湯
**42. Fried and Boiled Fish Soup:**
*A fish, for example bream, is fried, then cooked in broth with shredded Chinese white radish. Shredded ham is sometimes added. After prolonged cooking, the soup turns white. A vinegar and shredded ginger sauce is served on the side. Sprinkle a teaspoon of the sauce over the soup before eating.*

## 杭州清湯魚圓
**43. Hangchow Fish-Ball Soup:**
*Small, finely textured fish balls are cooked in broth with sliced ham and black mushrooms.*

## 大湯黃魚或黃魚雪菜湯
**44. Fish and Snow-Cabbage Soup:**
*A yellow croaker is cut up, fried and cooked in broth with bamboo shoots and snow cabbage. After prolonged cooking, the broth turns white.*

## 特別黃魚羹
**45. Special Yellow Croaker Thick Soup:**
*This is an elaborate thick soup containing diced fish, chicken, bamboo shoots, ham, peas and clams.*

## 莧菜黃魚羹
**46. Yellow Croaker and *Heen Choy* Thick Soup:**
*This soup, thickened with cornstarch, is served with sliced fish, bamboo shoots and* heen choy *(water spinach).*

## 扣三絲
**47. Arranged Three Shredded Meats Soup:**
*Thinly shredded pork, ham, omelet, chicken and black mushrooms are arranged attractively in a bowl and steamed. The bowl is then turned upside down into a deep plate and the ingredients are topped with a clear chicken broth. This is an elaborate dish that requires advance notice.*

## 鷄鴨血湯
**48. Coagulated-Chicken-and-Duck-Blood Soup:**
*Chicken and duck blood are coagulated, steamed, cut into*

cubes, then cooked in broth with giblets, fried bean curds, soybean sprouts and salted bamboo-shoot tips.

大血湯

49. Blood Soup:
*Chicken or pig blood is coagulated, steamed, cut into cubes, then cooked in broth with shredded pork and shrimp.*

## MAIN DISHES—BEAN CURD

Bean curd is a favorite among the Chinese because of its delicate texture and protein and calcium content. Because bean curd by itself tastes bland, Shanghai cooks like to prepare it with full-flavored sauces.

什錦豆腐

50. Bean Curd with an Assortment, or Braised Deluxe Bean Curd:
*Bean-curd cubes, ham, mushrooms, bamboo shoots and sea cucumbers are braised with Chinese greens.*

蝦子豆腐

51. Bean Curd with Shrimp Eggs:
*This is a briny dish of soft bean-curd cubes braised in a brown sauce with tiny, salty shrimp eggs. In a variation, the bean curd is sliced, pan-fried, then braised with shrimp eggs, bamboo shoots and black mushrooms.*

雪菜豆腐

52. Snow Cabbage and Bean Curd:
*Soft bean-curd cubes are braised with shredded pork and salty, crunchy snow cabbage.*

## 紅燒豆腐

**53. Red-Cooked Bean Curd or Braised Bean Curd:**
*Bean-curd cubes are braised in a brown sauce with chopped or sliced pork, bamboo shoots and black fungi. This dish is good with steamed rice.*

## 三蝦豆腐

**54. Bean Curd with Three Types of Shrimp:**
*Shelled shrimp, shrimp roe and shrimp eggs are braised in a brown sauce with bean-curd cubes.*

## 蟹粉豆腐

**55. Bean Curd with Crab Meat:**
*Bean-curd cubes are braised in a thickened sauce laced with crab meat. Green peas and sliced mushrooms are often added to garnish the dish.*

## 清湯珍珠豆腐

**56. Thick Soup with Bean Curds:**
*Bean-curd cubes and ground chicken are cooked in a thickened broth. Because of its thick consistency, this dish is mostly eaten as a main dish and not as a soup.*

## 四喜豆腐

**57. Four Happiness Bean Curd:**
*Bean curd is mashed with egg whites and broth, then sautéed with an assortment of chopped chicken, ham, black mushrooms and walnuts. Because of the time-consuming cooking methods, this dish is rarely available in restaurants.*

芙蓉豆腐

**58. Bean Curd *Foo Yung*:**
*The term* foo yung *denotes the use of egg whites in the dish. Bean curd is mashed with milk and egg whites, steamed, sliced, then served at room temperature with ham, peas and black mushrooms. This dish is seldom available in restaurants.*

蒸臭豆腐

**59. Stinky Bean Curd:**
*A Shanghai favorite, this bean curd has been fermented in snow-cabbage juice until very pungent, then steamed with chopped snow cabbage and green soybeans. This bean curd has a taste that resembles blue cheese and is only available in Asia.*

## MAIN DISHES — BEEF

Few beef dishes exist in Chinese cuisine. But there is a simple way of getting beef in your Chinese food: ask your waiter to substitute beef in any of the pork dishes.

紅燒牛肉

**60. Red-Cooked Beef:**
*Stewing beef or beef shanks are stewed in a slightly sweet soy-based sauce. As with any good beef stew, this is a hearty, filling dish appreciated most in cold weather. The beef should be tender and full-flavored. It makes a tasty topping over noodles or rice.*

## 紅燒牛筋
**61. Red-Cooked Beef Ligaments:**
Gelatinous ligaments are stewed until tender in soy sauce. Sometimes star anise and dried red chilies are added.

## 洋蔥牛肉絲
**62. Shredded Beef and Onions:**
This dish, from Yangchow, consists of marinated beef strips sautéed with sweet shredded onions.

## 咖喱牛肉
**63. Curry Beef:**
Beef chunks are cooked until tender in a curry-flavored sauce with onions and potatoes.

# MAIN DISHES—CASSEROLES

Especially warming in wintry weather, Chinese casseroles are served at the table in a covered pot. The waiter removes the lid at the table; the casserole should be bubbling hot.

## 砂鍋魚頭
**64. Fish-Head Casserole:**
The head section of a large fish is cut up, fried, then braised in a casserole with ginger, bamboo shoots, broth, black mushrooms, fried bean curds and transparent Tientsin bean sheets.

# 全家福

**65. Family Hot Pot:**
This is a casserole with a bit of everything from the kitchen: chicken, ham, pig's stomach, meatballs, bamboo shoots, giblets, black mushrooms, sea cucumbers, shrimp, Chinese cabbage and pork-stuffed omelet rolls. A mixture of soy sauce and hot chili sauce is customarily used as a dip.

# 砂鍋油豆腐鷄

**66. Chicken and Fried Bean-Curd Casserole:**
Chicken pieces are braised in a casserole with fried bean curds and chives.

# 砂鍋全魚

**67. Fish Casserole:**
A Shanghai classic, this dish is satisfying and full-flavored. A whole unboned fish, such as rock cod or snapper, is cut up, fried and cooked in a garlicky brown sauce with slippery Tientsin bean sheets and bamboo shoots.

# 獅子頭

**68. Lion's Head:**
Baseball-sized meatballs are braised in a casserole with Chinese cabbage or large bok-choy leaves. In fancy Shanghai restaurants, the meatballs are wrapped in the leaves of the bok choy, or Chinese cabbage.

# 什錦鍋

**69. Casserole with Assorted Meats:**
Some restaurant cooks do not differentiate between this casserole and the Family Hot Pot. This dish is made with meatballs, sea cucumbers, chicken, ham, fried pork rinds and vegetables, served in a broth.

## 一品鍋
**70. First-Rate Casserole:**
*Pork hock, chicken and ham are cooked in a broth.*

## 粉皮魚頭
**71. Bean Thread Sheets and Fish Head:**
*A large meaty fish head is cut up and cooked in a Chinese casserole with broth, soy sauce and slippery Tientsin bean sheets.*

## 什錦暖鍋
**72. Shanghai Mongolian Hot Pot:**
*Traditionally, a brass coal-burning Mongolian hot pot is used for this dish, although some restaurants may use electric hot pots or Western-style fondues. This dish, ideal for winter, contains small meatballs, fish balls, bean thread noodles, Chinese cabbage, pork-stuffed omelet rolls, ham and shrimp, all cooked in a bubbling broth. May require advance notice.*

---

# MAIN DISHES — CHICKEN AND EGGS

---

## 紙包雞
**73. Paper-Wrapped Chicken:**
*Deboned sliced chicken is marinated, layered with ham and black mushrooms, wrapped in parchment paper and deep-fried. To eat, unwrap the paper. Sometimes edible wafers are used to wrap the chicken. When fried, these wafers turn white and crispy and contrast nicely with the tender meat inside.*

叫化鷄

## 74. Beggar's Chicken:
*Allegedly a hobo's invention, this is a stuffed chicken baked in clay. A whole chicken is partially deboned, rubbed with spices and stuffed with pork, onions and preserved vegetables. It is then wrapped with caul, lotus leaves and wet clay and baked in hot coals or an oven. Beggar's Chicken is served with ceremony. It is brought to the table still wrapped in clay. The waiter breaks open the clay with a small hammer, transfers the chicken to a plate, opens the lotus leaves and cuts the chicken into small pieces. Beggar's Chicken is difficult to prepare: if the heat is too high, the meat is overdone and becomes dry and chewy. This is an elaborate dish and requires advance notice.*

紙封鷄

## 75. Paper-Sealed Chicken:
*Chicken meat is placed in a Chinese ceramic container with salted giblets, black mushrooms, ham and broth, sealed and steamed.*

卷筒鷄

## 76. Tube-Shaped Chicken:
*Diced chicken and black mushrooms are rolled into small tubes with caul, dipped in batter and deep-fried. A spicy, soy-based sauce is served as a dip. Because of the elaborate cooking methods, this dish is not always available in restaurants.*

銀芽炒鷄絲

## 77. Shredded Chicken with Silver Sprouts:
*Silver sprouts are mung-bean sprouts with the roots and heads removed. Shredded chicken is sautéed with julienned ham, hot peppers and silver sprouts.*

## 栗子鷄

**78. Chestnut Chicken:**
Marinated chicken pieces are stewed with soy sauce, green onions and shelled chestnuts. The chestnuts make this dish rich and slightly sweet.

## 炸八塊

**79. Fried Eight Pieces:**
A chicken is cut into eight pieces, marinated in batter and deep-fried. The chicken pieces are then sautéed with salt, pepper, chopped green onions and sesame oil.

## 炒鷄片或丁

**80. Sautéed Chicken Slices or Cubes:**
Chicken meat is marinated and sautéed with bamboo shoots.

## 芋艿鷄骨醬

**81. Taro Root Chicken:**
Chicken pieces are braised with chunks of taro root, ginger, green onions and soy sauce. Because of the taro root, this dish is slightly sweet and greyish in color. Taro root is seasonal.

## 八寶鷄

**82. Eight Precious Chicken:**
The chicken is partially deboned; stuffed with chopped black mushrooms, ham, lotus seeds, chestnuts, bamboo shoots and glutinous rice; and then steamed and topped with a brown sauce. Some restaurants fry the chicken after the steaming to give it a crispier skin. Advance notice is required for this dish.

# 桃 仁 鷄 片

**83. Walnut Chicken Slices:**
*Marinated chicken meat is dredged in crushed walnuts and deep-fried. A salt-and-pepper dip is served on the side.*

# 鷄 火 白 菜

**84. Chicken Sautéed with Cabbage:**
*Marinated chicken meat is sautéed with ham and Chinese cabbage.*

# 芝 蔴 鷄 排

**85. Sesame Chicken Toast:**
*Ground chicken is smeared on toast, topped with sesame seeds and fried. A salt-and-pepper dip is served on the side.*

# 紅 燴 鷄 排

**86. Red-Braised Chicken:**
*Marinated chicken pieces are fried and braised with onions, wine and ketchup.*

# 紅 燜 鷄 塊

**87. Red-Stewed Chicken Pieces:**
*Marinated chicken pieces are fried, then braised with black mushrooms, bamboo shoots and soy sauce.*

# 紅 燒 全 鷄

**88. Red-Cooked Whole Chicken:**
*A chicken is stewed in sugar and soy sauce.*

## 貴妃鷄

**89. Empress Chicken:**
*Named after the decadent empress Yang Kwei-Fei, this dish consists of pieces of chicken (most restaurants use wings) that are braised with black mushrooms, bamboo shoots and a slightly sweet wine sauce.*

## 咖喱鷄

**90. Curry Chicken:**
*The Shanghainese have been eating curry dishes for decades. In this dish, chicken pieces are braised with curry powder, onions and potatoes.*

## 翡翠鷄片

**91. Jade Chicken Slices:**
*Ground chicken is seasoned, tinted green with spinach leaves, steamed, sliced and braised with black mushrooms, bamboo shoots and ham. This dish is seldom available because of the elaborate preparation required.*

## 炒鷄腰

**92. Sautéed Chicken Testicles:**
*A rare specialty served in few restaurants, chicken testicles are sautéed with black mushrooms, bamboo shoots and Chinese greens. Advance notice is required. (Duck testicles are cooked in a similar way.)*

## 韭黃炒蛋

**93. Chives and Eggs:**
*Scrambled eggs are sautéed with pungent yellow chives.*

# A SHANGHAI MENU

蝦仁炒蛋

**94. Shrimp and Eggs:**
*Scrambled eggs are sautéed with small shrimp.*

蟶肉炒蛋

**95. Clams and Eggs:**
*This is a thick omelet made of scrambled eggs and clam meat. Sometimes minced pork is also included.*

木須銀魚

**96. Eggs with Small Fish:**
*Scrambled eggs are sautéed with tiny white bait.*

## MAIN DISHES—DUCK AND QUAIL

京冬鴨

**97. Peking Winter Vegetables with Duck:**
*A duck is browned, then braised in soy sauce and broth. A pungent sauce made of shredded pork and* gain don choy *(Peking preserved vegetables) is served over the duck.*

紅燒鴨

**98. Red-Cooked Duck:**
*A whole duck is stewed until tender in sugar and soy sauce. Sometimes onions are added for more sweetness.*

## 芋芳鴨塊
**99. Duck with Taro Root:**
*Duck pieces are poached, then sautéed with soy sauce, rock sugar and taro root.*

## 糟鴨
**100. Red-Braised Deboned Duck:**
*A duck, cut open along the backbone, is fried, then braised in soy sauce and spices. It is served deboned, in small pieces and with a brown sauce. Advance notice is required for this dish.*

## 八寶脆皮鴨
**101. Eight Precious Crispy Skin Duck:**
*A deboned duck is stuffed with a variety of delicacies, such as ham, black mushrooms and glutinous rice. The duck is steamed, then fried until crispy. It is served whole in a salt-and-pepper dip on the side. To eat, cut duck open along the breast, and serve meat with equal amounts of stuffing. Advance notice is required for this dish.*

## 清炖八寶鴨
**102. Steamed Eight Precious Duck:**
*A whole duck is deboned and stuffed with glutinous rice and other delicacies, such as lotus seeds and ham. It is then steamed and topped with its own sauce. To eat, cut duck open along the breast, and serve meat with equal amounts of stuffing. Advance notice is required for this dish.*

## 葫蘆八寶鴨
**103. Gourd-Shaped Eight Precious Duck:**
*A duck is deboned, stuffed with a savory glutinous rice filling, tied with a string in the midsection to resemble a*

gourd, then fried and steamed. It is served whole. To eat, cut open the duck along the breast, and take equal amounts of duck and stuffing. Advance notice is required for this dish.

油燜鵪鶉

**104. Braised Quail:**
Pieces of quail are fried, then braised with bamboo shoots, green onions and soy sauce. The dish is served with sautéed tender shoots of snow peas.

---

## MAIN DISHES—EXOTIC INGREDIENTS

---

These dishes are exotic delicacies to the Chinese. Many of the primary ingredients, such as shark's fin and fish bladder, are dehydrated, and require elaborate preparation. Many Chinese believe these ingredients have medicinal value and are good for general health and well-being; they can be expensive.

蝦子海參

**105. Sea Cucumbers with Shrimp Eggs:**
Reconstituted dried sea cucumbers, spongy and gelatinous, are braised until soft with briny-tasting minute shrimp eggs.

雞茸魚翅

**106. Shredded Chicken with Shark's Fin:**
Shark's fin is cooked in chicken broth until soft and noodle-like, then thickened and served with minced chicken meat.

蟹 粉 魚 翅

**107. Crab-Meat and Shark's Fin:**
*Shark's fin is cooked in chicken broth until soft and noodle-like, then served with crab meat and crab roe.*

紅 燒 魚 肚

**108. Red-Cooked Fish Bladder:**
*Reconstituted dried fish bladder, spongy and gelatinous, is shredded and braised in a thick soup with shredded pork, ham, black mushroms and bamboo shoots.*

紅 燒 海 參

**109. Red-Cooked Sea Cucumbers or Braised Sea Cucumbers with Brown Sauce:**
*Dried sea cucumbers are reconstituted, then stewed until soft and gelatinous in soy sauce and sugar.*

炒 櫻 桃

**110. Sautéed Frog Legs:**
*Frog legs are sautéed with ginger, onions and five-spices powder.*

醬 爆 田 鷄

**111. Frog Legs Sautéed with Sauce:**
*Marinated frog legs are coated in flour, then fried and sautéed with garlic and sweet bean sauce.*

紅 燒 圓 菜

**112. Red-Cooked Turtle:**
*Turtle meat is steamed until tender, then braised with bamboo shoots and black mushrooms in rock sugar and soy sauce. This dish is rare because few cooks know how to prepare turtles. Advance notice is required for this dish.*

炒 裙 邊

**113. Sautéed Turtle Meat:**
*Only the side meat of the turtle, considered to be superior, is used for this dish. The meat is poached until tender, then sautéed with garlic, bamboo shoots, black mushrooms and red-cooked pork chunks. Advance notice is required for this dish.*

海 參 燴 蹄 筋

**114. Sea Cucumbers and Pig's Ligaments:**
*The ligaments of the pig are stewed until tender with sea cucumbers in soy sauce. After prolonged cooking, both ingredients turn crunchy. Advance notice is sometimes required for this dish.*

---

# MAIN DISHES — FISH

---

The Shanghainese prefer strong flavors with their seafood. Many Shanghai seafood dishes are braised in brown sauces made up of sugar and dark soy sauce with preserved vegetables, or in wine residue. Shanghainese restaurants sometimes serve frozen fish, so if you want fresh fish be sure to ask for it. Unless otherwise specified, most fish is served whole.

紅 燒 划 水

**115. Red-Cooked Fish Tail Section:**
*The tail section of the fish, considered a delicacy by the Shanghainese because of its firm meat, is fried, then braised in a pungent sauce of green onions, soy sauce, sugar and broth.*

## 糖醋黃魚

**116. Vinegar-Sweet Fish or Sweet-and-Sour Fish:**
*A yellow croaker, usually frozen, is most often used for this recipe. The whole fish is fried and topped with a garlicky sweet-and-sour sauce. Some restaurants fry the fish in batter, which makes it crunchy but somewhat heavy.*

## 雪菜黃魚

**117. Fish with Snow Cabbage:**
*A yellow croaker is pan-fried, then braised in a broth with salty snow cabbage and bamboo shoots.*

## 蒜子紅燒黃魚

**118. Red-Cooked Garlic Fish:**
*A yellow croaker is pan-fried, then braised with soy sauce, garlic, sugar and broth. Fish such as snapper or rock cod can also be used in this dish.*

## 紅燒魚塊

**119. Red-Cooked Fish Slices:**
*Unboned fish slices are fried and braised in soy sauce, sugar and broth.*

## 炒魚片

**120. Sautéed Fish Slices:**
*Deboned fish slices are quick-fried, then sautéed with black mushrooms, bamboo shoots and the tender shoots of snow peas. Often frozen peas or snow pea pods are used as a substitute.*

## 芝蔴魚排
**121. Sesame Fish:**
Deboned fish slices are marinated, dredged in sesame seeds and deep-fried.

## 松鼠黃魚
**122. Squirrel Fish:**
A whole fish is deboned, deep-fried in batter, and served with a sweet-and-sour tomato-based sauce garnished with peas, shrimp and pine nuts. The dish is usually made with yellow croaker.

## 西湖醋魚
**123. West Lake Vinegar Fish:**
Named after Hangchow's West Lake, where carp is still abundant, this fish is steamed or poached, and served with a sauce of sugar, vinegar and soy.

## 下巴划水
**124. Chin and Tail Sections:**
The cheek, chin and tail sections of a large fish are fried, then braised in sugar and soy sauce.

## 紅燒頭尾
**125. Red-Cooked Head and Tail:**
Only the head and tail sections of a fish are used. The fish pieces are marinated, fried and braised in a garlicky, soy-based sauce with black fungi and bamboo shoots.

## 苔條拖黃魚
**126. Fish Fritters:**
Boned fish slices are dipped in batter flavored with toi tew (dried seaweed flakes), and deep-fried. A salt-and-pepper dip

is served on the side. *Toi tew* has a rich seafood flavor and is delicious when fried.

## 雪菜蒸黃魚
**127. Snow Cabbage Steamed Fish:**
A whole fish is steamed and served with a brown sauce and salty snow cabbage. Most restaurants use yellow croaker for this dish.

## 醋溜魚
**128. Vinegar Fish:**
A whole fish is fried, then braised in a sweet-and-sour brown sauce.

## 醋溜魚片
**129. Vinegar Fish Slices:**
Boned fish slices are fried and braised in a sweet-and-sour brown sauce.

## 紅燒肚當
**130. Red-Cooked Fish Belly:**
The belly section of a carp is braised in sugar broth, and soy sauce.

## 苔條乾煎黃魚
**131. Seaweed and Yellow Fish:**
A yellow croaker is salted and pan-fried with *toi tew* (dried seaweed flakes).

## 川糟青魚
**132. Wine-Residue-Flavored Fish:**
Fish slices are marinated in ambrosial wine residue, then braised with soy sauce and bamboo shoots. Carp or buffalo fish may be used.

糟 鹵 划 水

**133. Wine-Residue-Flavored Fish Tail Section:**
*Believed to be firmer than the rest of the fish, the fish tail is much prized by the Shanghainese. The tail section of a fish, such as carp, is marinated in ambrosial wine residue, then steamed with ham and bamboo shoots.*

八 寶 桂 魚

**134. Eight Precious Fish:**
*The backbone of a fish is removed. The fish is stuffed with chopped ham, giblets, shrimp and dried scallops, breaded and then fried. This dish is seldom available because of its elaborate preparation, but a good restaurant should be able to prepare this dish with advance notice.*

炒 鱔 糊

**135. Sautéed Chinese Eel:**
*A real Shanghai specialty, this is a pungent dish of delicious shredded yellow eel, which has a supple texture. Boned shredded eel is sautéed in hot oil with lots of garlic and silver sprouts (mung-bean sprouts with heads and roots removed). It is customary to sprinkle white-pepper powder over the eel right before eating. Plain noodles in broth are the best accompaniment for this dish.*

蒜 子 油 泡 大 鱔

**136. Eel in Garlic Sauce:**
*Sliced white eel is fried, then sautéed with garlic, bamboo shoots and carrot slices.*

韭 黃 炒 鱔 絲

**137. Yellow Chives with Shredded Eel:**
*Boned shredded yellow eel is sautéed with garlicky flat yellow chives.*

糖醋鱔絲

138. Vinegar-Braised Shredded Eel:
*Boned shredded yellow eel is marinated, quick-fried and sautéed in a garlicky sweet vinegared sauce.*

---

MAIN DISHES — PORK

---

糖醋排骨

139. Sweet Vinegar Spareribs:
*Spareribs are sliced, fried and then braised in a sweet and tangy sauce. Sometimes ketchup is added to the sauce.*

百葉炒肉絲

140. Shredded Pork with Shanghai Bean-Curd Skin:
*Shredded pork is sautéed with soft, beige-colored shredded Shanghai bean-curd skin.*

青椒邊尖炒肉絲

141. Salted Bamboo Shoots with Shredded Pork:
*Salted bamboo-shoot tips are shredded and sautéed with hot green peppers and shredded pork. This dish is pungent, salty and spicy.*

雪菜炒肉絲

142. Snow Cabbage with Shredded Pork:
*Minced salty snow cabbage is sautéed with shredded pork and bamboo shoots. It is delicious over plain noodles in broth.*

榨菜炒肉絲

143. Preserved Kohlrabi with Shredded Pork:
*Pork, preserved kohlrabi and bamboo shoots are shredded and sautéed together. This is a pungent, spicy dish that goes well with noodles.*

冬筍肉絲

144. Shredded Pork and Bamboo Shoots:
*Marinated pork shreds are sautéed with strips of bamboo shoots.*

冰糖元蹄

145. Rock Sugar with Pork Hock:
*A whole pork hock is stewed until tender with plenty of rock sugar and soy sauce.*

紅燒元蹄

146. Red-Cooked Pork Hock:
*A whole pork hock is stewed with soy sauce and sugar until the meat is almost falling off the bone.*

醬豬肉

147. Red Arranged Pork:
*Pork belly is poached, arranged neatly on a plate and steamed with sugar, spices and red preserved bean curds.*

醬排骨

148. Red Spareribs:
*Pork ribs are braised until tender in sugar, spices and red preserved bean curds.*

## 香糟扣肉

**149. Wine Residue Arranged Pork:**
*Pork belly is poached, arranged neatly on a plate and steamed with spices and wine residue.*

## 梅菜扣肉

**150. Preserved Vegetables and Arranged Pork, or Sliced Pork with Preserved Vegetables:**
*Pork belly is poached, arranged on a plate and steamed with mui choy, a brown salted preserved vegetable.*

## 椒鹽排骨

**151. Spicy Spareribs:**
*Small pieces of marinated pork chop are fried until crunchy, then tossed in a hot dry wok with salt and pepper.*

## 肉片菜心

**152. Pork Slices and Vegetables:**
*Marinated pork slices are sautéed with* choy sum, *a Chinese vegetable like spinach.*

## 五香排骨

**153. Five Spices Spareribs:**
*Fried spareribs are braised in a sauce of soy and five spices. In another version of this dish, spareribs are marinated in five spices, eggs and cornstarch, then fried until crunchy.*

## 芋艿肉骨醬

**154. Ribs with Taro Root:**
*In this recipe from Ningpo, spareribs are cooked until tender with soy sauce, sugar and chunks of gray taro root.*

## 八寶辣醬
**155. Eight Precious Hot Saucy Pork:**
Diced pressed bean curds, bamboo shoots, black mushrooms, dried shrimp, chicken, ham, pork and giblets are diced and sautéed in a thick, salty and spicy sauce. This dish is particularly good with plain noodles in broth.

## 獅子頭
**156. Lion's Head:**
Baseball-size meatballs are wrapped in Chinese cabbage or bok choy leaves and simmered in a Chinese casserole. This dish is sometimes served on a plate and not in a casserole.

## 蜜汁火腿
**157. Honey-Sauce Ham:**
Chinese ham is sliced, arranged on a plate and steamed with rock sugar. The sauce is then thickened and served over the ham. In most restaurants, canned salty Yunnan ham is used for this dish.

## 走油元蹄
**158. Fried Pork Hock:**
Pork hock is poached, fried, immersed in water so that the skin wrinkles, then stewed with sugar and soy sauce.

## 雪菜肉絲百葉
**159. Snow Cabbage, Pork and Shanghai Bean-Curd Skins, or Shredded Pork with Salted Vegetables and Dry Bean Curd:**
Chopped snow cabbage, shredded pork and soft beige-colored bean-curd skins are sautéed together.

## 麵筋百葉

**160. Gluten and Shanghai Bean-Curd Skins:**
*Fried gluten balls and Shanghai bean-curd skins are stuffed with seasoned ground pork and simmered in broth. Bamboo shoots and black mushrooms are added as garnishes.*

## 炒乾絲

**161. Sautéed Shredded Pork and Pressed Bean Curd, or Shredded Bean Cake with Pork:**
*Chewy pressed bean curd, bamboo shoots and pork are shredded, then sautéed together.*

## 韭菜炒乾絲

**162. Yellow Chives with Pressed Bean Curd:**
*Chewy pressed bean curds are shredded and sautéed with strips of pork and pungent yellow chives.*

## 油麵筋塞肉

**163. Red-Cooked Stuffed Gluten:**
*Fried gluten balls are stuffed with seasoned ground pork, then braised in soy sauce and sugar.*

## 洋葱排骨

**164. Pork Chops with Onions:**
*Sliced onions are braised until soft with pork chops and soy sauce.*

## 紅燒肉煮蛋

**165. Red-Cooked Pork and Eggs:**
*Chunks of pork are cooked until tender in sugar and soy sauce. At the end, hard-boiled eggs are added and cooked until they turn brown.*

無錫肉骨頭

**166. Wuxi Spareribs:**
*Originating in Wuxi, this is a dish of long pork ribs marinated in sugar, soy sauce and spices such as cloves and star anise. The ribs are slow-cooked until tender.*

乾切鹹肉

**167. Sliced Dry Salty Pork:**
*Pork is pickled in salt, Szechwan peppercorns and other preservatives, steamed and served thinly sliced at room temperature.*

枸杞肉絲

**168. Shredded Pork with Chinese Box Thorn:**
*Shredded pork is sautéed with julienned bamboo shoots and the tender leaves of Chinese box thorn. This dish is seldom available because of the difficulty of getting box thorn, which tastes like watercress.*

黃雀塞肉

**169. Yellow Birds:**
*These are bean-curd rolls stuffed with shredded pork, pressed bean curds and chives. They are pan-fried and served with a sauce.*

豆苗圈子

**170. Sautéed Circles:**
*The large intestine of the pig is cut up into little rings, cooked until tender, then sautéed. The rings are served with sautéed tender shoots of snow peas. If shoots are not available, spinach is used.*

## 脆皮圈子

**171. Crispy Circles:**
*Pig's intestine is poached and fried until crispy, then served with fried toi tew (dried, flaked seaweed). A vinegar dip and a salt-and-pepper dip are served on the side.*

## 鷄燒圈子

**172. Chicken with Circles:**
*Pig's intestine is poached, sliced and braised with chicken pieces.*

---

### MAIN DISHES — SHELLFISH

---

## 龍井蝦仁

**173. Shrimp with Dragon Well Tea:**
*Created in Hangchow, where Dragon Well tea farms proliferate, this dish consists of small shelled shrimp sautéed with fragrant and clean-tasting Dragon Well tea. The tea leaves are not edible.*

## 椒鹽蝦仁

**174. Spicy Fried Prawns:**
*Medium or large shrimp are dredged in flour, fried and tossed in a hot dry wok with salt and pepper.*

## 醋溜蝦仁

**175. Vinegar Shrimp:**
*Marinated shelled shrimp are sautéed with ginger and onions and served in a sweet tangy soy-based sauce.*

## 蝦仁雙腰
**176. Shrimp, Kidney and Cashews:**
Shelled marinated shrimp are sautéed with kidney slices and crunchy fried cashews.

## 蝦爆鱔片
**177. Shrimp and Eel:**
Shelled marinated shrimp are sautéed with supple-textured sliced eel.

## 酥炸蝦餅
**178. Shrimp and Pork Cakes:**
Shrimp and ground pork are formed into small cakes and fried. A salt-and-pepper dip is served on the side.

## 紅燒明蝦
**179. Red-Cooked Prawns:**
Prawns are sautéed in the shell with garlic and onions, then braised in a slightly sweet-and-sour sauce of sugar, vinegar and soy sauce. Some restaurants serve pricy but delicious Tsing Tao prawns in this dish.

## 苔條拖蝦仁
**180. Seaweed and Shrimp Fritters:**
Marinated large shrimp are dredged in a batter laced with dried seaweed flakes (toi tew), then deep-fried to a golden brown. Dried seaweed, which has a pungent herbal taste, is prized by the Shanghainese. Sautéed Chinese greens are sometimes used as garnishes.

## 清炒蝦仁
**181. Sautéed Shrimp:**
This dish is a Shanghai specialty. Small shelled shrimp are

marinated then sautéed in a transparent sauce flavored with sesame oil and Shaoshing wine.

## 炒 蝦 蟹
**182. Sautéed Shrimp and Crab Meat:**
*Small shrimp and crab meat are sautéed together.*

## 清 炒 龍 蝦 片
**183. Sautéed Lobster:**
*Sliced lobster meat is marinated and sautéed.*

## 大 閘 蟹
**184. Shanghai Big Lake or Hairy Crab:**
*These are small crab from the Shanghai region, which are only available in the autumn. Prized for their rich yellow-colored roe, these crab are served steamed with a shredded-ginger-and-vinegar dip. To eat, pull the shell away from the body, remove and discard the gills, and eat the roe and meat. It is acceptable to eat crab with fingers.*

## 炒 蟹 粉
**185. Sautéed Crab Meat:**
*Cooked crab meat is sautéed with ground pork. Broth and then cornstarch are added to create a thick sauce. A vinegar-and-shredded-ginger sauce is served on the side. Drizzle a teaspoon of vinegar sauce onto the crab meat before eating.*

## 芙 蓉 青 蟹
**186. Crab *Foo Yung*:**
*Foo Yung means a dish has egg whites in it. Pieces of unshelled crab are fried, then sautéed with ginger, onions and beaten egg whites.*

## 醬燒青蟹
**187. Crab with Sauce:**
*Floured crab pieces are fried and sautéed with sweet bean sauce and soy sauce. This dish is crunchy and slightly sweet.*

## 溜黃青蟹
**188. Yellow Crab:**
*Crab pieces in the shell are fried, then sautéed with scrambled eggs.*

## 蟹粉菜心
**189. Crab Meat and Greens:**
*Sautéed Chinese greens, such as bok choy or choy sum, are topped with a white sauce with crab meat in it.*

## 麵拖蟹
**190. Floured Crab:**
*Crab pieces are dredged in batter, fried, then braised in broth.*

## 酥炸蟹黃
**191. Crunchy Crab:**
*Crab pieces in the shell are dredged in an egg-white batter and deep-fried. A vinegar or salt-and-pepper dip is served on the side. This dish is seldom available in restaurants because of its elaborate preparation.*

## 炒蟹黃
**192. Sautéed Crab Roe:**
*Yellow crab roe is sautéed in oil with ginger and green onions to a thick, rich sauce. This dish is seldom available outside Asia because it is difficult to get fresh crab roe.*

蟹 粉 菜 心

**193. Crab Roe and Greens:**
*Sautéed Chinese greens, such as* bok choy *or* choy sum, *are topped with a sauce of white crab meat and yellow crab roe. This dish is seldom available outside Asia because it is difficult to get fresh crab roe.*

炸 蝦 包 子

**194. Fried Shrimp Rolls:**
*Chopped shrimp, pork, preserved kohlrabi and water chestnuts are wrapped in small pouches made of caul and deep-fried. This dish is seldom available in restaurants because of its elaborate preparation.*

炒 蝦 腰

**195. Sautéed Shrimp and Kidney:**
*Small shelled shrimp and kidney slices are sautéed with shredded ginger and green onions.*

田 螺 塞 肉

**196. Stuffed Snails:**
*Small snail shells are stuffed with minced pork and snail meat. They are then sautéed and braised with garlic, soy sauce and star anise.*

# MAIN DISHES—VEGETABLES

## 毛豆子炒雪菜

**197. Snow Cabbage and Green Soybeans:**
*Chewy green soybeans are shelled and sautéed with salty snow cabbage, a Shanghai favorite. This is usually eaten as a side dish.*

## 拌乾絲

**198. Tossed Pressed Bean Curd:**
*Shredded pressed bean curd, which has a chewy meaty texture, is tossed with a dressing and an assortment of shredded ham and omelet. The textural contrast of the different ingredients is the highlight of this dish. It is served at room temperature.*

## 炒二冬

**199. Sautéed Two Vegetables:**
*Black mushrooms and bamboo shoots are sautéed with soy sauce and broth. This dish is delicious when made with fresh bamboo shoots, which have a refreshing milky flavor.*

## 炒三冬

**200. Sautéed Three Vegetables:**
*Bamboo shoots, black mushrooms and salty Peking winter vegetables are sautéed together.*

## 炒白菜

**201. Sautéed *Bok Choy*:**
*Bok choy is cut into bite-sized pieces and sautéed in oil with salt and garlic.*

## 炒上海白菜
**202. Sautéed Shanghai *Bok Choy*:**
*Shanghai* bok choy, *which has a green rather than a white stem, tastes like a cross between spinach and* bok choy. *When fresh and properly prepared, it is sweet and delicious. Here it is sautéed in oil with salt and pepper.*

## 糟黃豆芽
**203. Wine Residue with Soybean Sprouts:**
*Chewy soybean sprouts are braised until tender with fried bean curds, black fungi and wine residue. The dish is served at room temperature.*

## 蝦子冬筍
**204. Bamboo Shoots with Shrimp Eggs:**
*Chunks of bamboo shoots are braised with briny shrimp eggs. When made with fresh bamboo shoots, this dish is very tasty.*

## 雪菜冬筍絲
**205. Shredded Bamboo Shoots with Snow Cabbage:**
*Shredded bamboo shoots are sautéed with finely chopped salty snow cabbage.*

## 素什錦
**206. Vegetarian Ten Mix:**
*An assortment of mushrooms, bamboo shoots, black moss, gingko nuts, fried bean-curd, gluten and bean-curd shoots are sautéed and braised with hearts of* bok choy *or* choy sum.

乾燒茄子

207. Fried Eggplant:
Chunks of eggplant are sautéed in a pungent sauce of garlic, ginger and soy sauce. This dish is especially good when made with long, sweet Oriental eggplant.

冬筍青菜心

208. Bamboo Shoots with Chinese Greens:
Sliced bamboo shoots are sautéed with the hearts of bok choy or choy sum.

百葉炒雪菜

209. Shanghai Bean-Curd Skins and Snow Cabbage:
Soft Shanghai bean-curd skins are shredded and sautéed with salty snow cabbage.

冬筍炒豆苗

210. Sautéed Tender Shoots:
The sweet tender shoots of snow peas are sautéed with bamboo shoots and black mushrooms. Snow-pea shoots are not widely available.

生煸枸杞

211. Sautéed Chinese Box Thorn:
The small leaves of the box thorn, which are slightly bitter, are sautéed in oil with garlic, salt and pepper.

生煸莧菜

212. Sautéed *Heen Choy*:
Heen choy *(Chinese spinach)* has purple or green leaves. Here it is sautéed with garlic, salt and pepper.

## 素黃雀
**213. Vegetarian Yellow Birds:**
Pieces of bean-curd sheets are stuffed and wrapped with an assortment of sautéed ingredients such as pressed bean curd, spinach, preserved kohlrabi, bamboo shoots and black mushrooms. These rectangular rolls are then pan-fried. Some restaurants serve these rolls with a sauce.

## 紅燒烤麩
**214. Red-Cooked *Korfu*:**
Korfu is coarse-grained gluten. In this dish, chunks of korfu are braised with black fungi, bamboo shoots and soy sauce. This is a satisfying dish with lots of substance.

## 素紅燒獅子頭
**215. Vegetarian Red-Cooked Lion's Head:**
Lion's Head usually means a dish of large meatballs wrapped in vegetables. In this dish, mashed bean curds are mixed with minced gluten and vegetarian chicken, formed into balls, fried, wrapped in cabbage leaves and served bubbling in a casserole pot. Black mushrooms, bamboo shoots, golden needles, black fungi and soy sauce accompany the vegetarian meatballs.

## 薺菜冬筍
**216. Shepherd's Purse and Bamboo Shoots:**
Shepherd's purse, a vegetable like watercress, is sautéed with bamboo shoots.

## 油燜筍
**217. Braised Bamboo Shoots:**
Bamboo shoots are braised in sugar and soy sauce. This dish is served at room temperature.

發芽豆

218. Braised Broad Beans:
*Dried broad beans are stewed until soft and crumbly with snow cabbage. This dish is served at room temperature.*

炒蠶豆

219. Sautéed Green Broad or Fava Beans:
*Green fava beens are sautéed with green onions and the tips of bamboo shoots.*

炒塌棵菜

220. Sautéed *Tarp Qwar Choy:*
*A Shanghai specialty, these small flat vegetables, which are like* bok choy, *are sweet and juicy when sautéed by themselves or with bamboo shoots.*

冬筍塌菜

221. Bamboo Shoots and *Tarp Qwar Choy:*
*Juicy* tarp qwar choy, *a Shanghai vegetable similar to baby* bok choy, *is sautéed in oil with slices of bamboo shoots.*

乾煸草頭

222. Fried Chinese Clover:
*Tiny tender shoots of Chinese clover, a plant indigenous to Shanghai, are sautéed in oil. They are accompanied by a sweet soy dip.*

---

## SNACKS OR SIDE DISHES

---

These are savory dishes, ideal as one-dish meals or luncheon dishes. They can also be ordered as side dishes for dinners.

### 蘇州湯飽
### 223. *Soochow* Soup Dumplings, or Steamed Buns with Soup:
*Served in large bamboo steamers, these dumplings, called* tong bow, *are usually served ten to an order. They are dainty round dumplings stuffed with seasoned ground pork, then steamed. Some restaurants also add crab roe to the pork filling. A small bowl of clear broth is served on the side. Dip dumpling in broth before eating.*

### 小籠飽
### 224. Steamer Dumplings:
*These dumplings are a little larger than the soup dumplings above, and are wrapped differently. They are round and stuffed with ground pork. A vinegar and shredded-ginger dip is served on the side. To eat, put a dumpling on a spoon, bite a hole in the skin, drain the broth from the dumpling onto the spoon, dip the dumpling in the ginger sauce, eat the dumpling and drink the broth.*

### 南翔饅頭
### 225. Southern Steamed Dumplings:
*These steamer dumplings originated from an area in the Shanghai region known for its delicate dumplings. They are stuffed and steamed with juicy ground pork. Leftover*

Southern Steamed Dumplings are fried and served in the afternoon at some Shanghai restaurants, and are called Fried Southern Dumplings.

生 煎 飽

226. San Jeen Bow, or Pan-Fried Round Dumplings:
Small yeast dumplings are stuffed with ground pork, topped with sesame seeds or green onions, then pan-fried. These dumplings have a crunchy bottom, soft skin and juicy filling.

菜 肉 雲 吞

227. Shanghai Won Tons:
A seasoned filling of minced pork and bok choy is wrapped in ravioli-like pouches, boiled and served in clear broth.

蝦 或 鷄 肉 蒸 雲 吞

228. Steamed Won Tons:
Shanghainese are also fond of steaming instead of boiling won tons. Shrimp and chicken meat are used as fillings. Dip won tons in soy sauce and hot chili sauce before eating.

湯 年 糕

229. Glutinous Rice Noodles in Soup, or Pork with Rice-Cake Soup:
Neen go, Shanghai glutinous rice noodles, are small flat noodles that tend to stick to the teeth. In this dish, they are cooked in broth with shredded pork and Chinese vegetables.

炒 年 糕

230. Sautéed Glutinous Rice Noodles, or Pork Fried with Rice Cake:
Neen go, flat, sticky Shanghai glutinous rice noodles, are sautéed with shredded pork, Chinese cabbage and soy sauce. Eat with hot chili sauce.

## 二面黃

**231. Two-Side Yellow, or Crunchy *Chow Mein*:**
*"Two-side yellow" means thin egg noodles that have been pan-fried until both sides are light brown and crunchy. These noodles are served topped with sautéed shredded pork, black mushrooms and Chinese cabbage.*

## 肉絲炒麵

**232. Shredded Pork *Chow Mein*:**
*Soft noodles, like spaghetti, are sautéed with shredded pork and vegetables. Eat with hot chili sauce.*

## 三鮮炒麵

**233. Three Sorts of Meat with Noodles:**
*Soft noodles, like spaghetti, are sautéed with shredded pork, chicken and ham. Sometimes vegetables such as black mushrooms and bean sprouts are added.*

## 上海粗炒麵

**234. Shanghai *Chow Mein*:**
*A robust dish that is typically Shanghai, this* chow mein *is a must. Thick noodles are sautéed with shredded pork, Chinese cabbage and spinach and served piping hot.*

## 上海湯麵

**235. Shanghai Noodles in Soup:**
*Thick noodles are served in broth with a topping of sautéed pork, Chinese cabbage and spinach.*

## 榨菜肉絲湯麵

**236. Preserved Kohlrabi with Pork over Noodles, or Pork with Chinese Pickles Noodle Soup:**
*Sautéed shredded pork and spicy preserved kohlrabi are served over thin noodles in broth.*

雪菜肉絲湯麵

237. Pork with Snow Cabbage and Noodles in Soup:
*Sautéed shredded pork, bamboo shoots and salty snow cabbage are served over thin noodles in broth.*

嫩鷄煨麵

238. Chicken with Noodles in Soup, or Chicken with Braised Noodle Soup:
*Soft, vermicelli-like noodles are served in a creamy soup with shredded chicken meat and* bok choy.

陽春麵

239. Plain Noodles in Soup:
*Thin, plain noodles are served in broth. This dish can be ordered in place of rice.*

過橋麵

240. Side Dish Noodles:
*A bowl of thin plain noodles is served with a side dish, such as shredded pork with snow cabbage or sautéed eel. Specify the side dish you want.*

大肉麵

241. Big Pieces of Pork Noodles:
*Thin noodles are served in a bowl of broth with big slices of red-cooked pork.*

小肉麵

242. Small Pieces of Pork Noodles:
*A bowl of thin noodles is served in broth with sautéed diced pork, bamboo shoots and pressed bean curd.*

## 素什錦麵

**243. Vegetarian's Delight Noodles:**
*Thin noodles are served in a bowl of broth and topped with sautéed gluten, bamboo shoots, black mushrooms and greens.*

## 小澆麵

**244. Vegetarian Noodles with Fried Bean Curds:**
*Thin noodles are served in a bowl of seasoned broth topped with sautéed bean curds and black mushrooms.*

## 排骨湯麵

**245. Noodles in Soup with Pork Chop, or Pork Chop Noodle Soup:**
*Thin noodles are served in a bowl of seasoned broth topped with a piece of fried pork chop.*

## 燻魚湯麵

**246. Noodles in Soup with Smoked Fish:**
*Thin noodles are served in a bowl of seasoned broth topped with crunchy fish steaks that have been braised in soy sauce and five-spices powder.*

## 鱔湖麵

**247. Sautéed Eel over Noodles in Soup:**
*Thin noodles are served in a bowl of broth and topped with sautéed Chinese yellow eel and silver sprouts. Sometimes the topping is served on a separate dish.*

## 冷麵

**248. Cold Noodles:**
*Eaten by the Shangainese in the summer, this is a cold pasta dish. Boiled noodles are served cold with parboiled bean*

sprouts and a peanut butter sauce on the side. Sautéed shredded pork is often used as part of the topping. To eat, transfer a portion of the noodles to your plate or bowl, top with bean sprouts, shredded pork and peanut sauce. Mix well before eating.

## 肉絲湯麵

**249. Shredded Pork with Noodles in Soup:**
*Thin noodles are served in a bowl of broth topped with sautéed shredded pork.*

## 滷鴨麵

**250. Poached Duck with Noodles:**
*Thin noodles are served in a bowl of broth with pieces of seasoned poached duck still on the bone.*

## 脆鱔麵

**251. Crispy Eel with Noodles:**
*Thin noodles are served in a bowl of broth topped with crunchy fried yellow eel.*

## 青菜煨麵

**252. Vegetable with Noodles in Soup, or Vegetable with Braised Noodles Soup:**
*Soft, vermicelli-like noodles are served in soup topped with shredded bok choy. Sometimes shredded pork is also added.*

## 肉絲煨麵

**253. Shredded Pork with Soft Noodles in Soup, or Pork with Braised Noodles Soup:**
*Soft, vermicelli-like noodles are served in a creamy soup with sautéed shredded pork.*

## 楊州炒飯

**254. Yang Chow Deluxe Fried Rice:**
Cooked long-grain rice is sautéed with diced pork, shrimp, peas and scrambled eggs.

## 上海月餅

**255. Shanghai Moon Cakes:**
Shanghai moon cakes are small and patty-shaped, and are covered in a beige-colored flaky pastry. They have a savory filling of pork and sometimes shrimp.

## 菜肉飽

**256. Steamed Bun with Pork and Vegetables:**
A white bun made with yeast and flour is filled with chopped pork and bok choy, then steamed. The Chinese equivalent of the hot dog, this is eaten as a quick snack.

## 素菜飽

**257. Vegetarian Steamed Bun:**
A white bun made with yeast and flour is stuffed with minced bok choy, pressed bean curds, black mushrooms and bamboo shoots, then steamed.

## 粢飯

**258. Glutinous Rice Bundles:**
Cooked glutinous rice is shaped into a long pouch and stuffed with Chinese fried doughnuts. To eat, unwrap the pouch and sprinkle with white sugar. Rewrap the rice tightly around the doughnut and eat with fingers.

## 蟹殼黃

**259. Baked Flaky Pastry, or Baked Sesame-Seed Bun:**
This is a sesame-seed-topped flaky pastry that may be ordered

either sweet or savory. The sweet ones are filled with white sugar and the savory with green onions and shortening. The pastry is very light and the savory stuffing pungent; the cakes come two to an order.

## 蘿蔔絲餅

**260. Turnip Flaky Pastry:**
Shredded Chinese white radish, savory and pungent, is stuffed in flaky pastry and baked to a golden brown.

## 春卷

**261. Spring Rolls:**
These crispy paper-thin rolls are stuffed with shredded pork and Chinese cabbage, then fried. The rolls make a tasty appetizer for any meal. Dip in vinegar and soy sauce before eating.

## 鮮肉粽

**262. Chinese Tamale with Pork, or Sweet Rice with Pork:**
Glutinous rice is stuffed with soy-flavored chunks of pork, wrapped in bamboo leaves and boiled. To eat, unwrap the leaves and eat the rice and pork with hot chili sauce.

## 豆沙粽

**263. Chinese Tamale with Sweet Bean Paste, or Sweet Rice with Sweet Bean:**
Glutinous rice is stuffed with sweet and rich red-bean paste, wrapped in bamboo leaves and boiled. Unwrap the leaves before eating.

## 梘水粽

**264. Chinese Tamale with Transluscent Rice:**
Glutinous rice, made translucent by soaking in a solution, is wrapped in bamboo leaves and boiled. Unwrap the leaves and sprinkle the rice with white sugar before eating.

## 猪 肉 湯 糰

**265. Tong Yuen, or Glutinous Rice Dumplings with Pork, or Boiled Rice-Powder Bun with Pork:**
Tong Yuen *are dumplings the size of a dollar made with a glutinous rice-flour dough. They are stuffed with seasoned ground pork, boiled and served in hot broth.*

## 粢 飯 糕

**266. Fried Glutinous Cake:**
*Steamed glutinous rice, garnished with dried shrimp, is pressed into a mold, sliced and deep-fried until golden brown. These cakes are often sold by street vendors.*

## 咸 豆 漿

**267. Savory Soybean Milk:**
*Milk extracted from soybeans is served steaming hot with chopped peanuts, dried shrimp and preserved kohlrabi. This is a popular breakfast soup. Add vinegar and soy sauce and mix well before eating.*

## 甜 豆 漿

**268. Sweet Soybean Milk:**
*Soybean milk is sweetened with sugar and served steaming hot. This is a popular breakfast drink.*

## 炸 臭 豆 腐

**269. Fried Stinky Bean Curds:**
*Bean curds are fermented until pungent in snow-cabbage juice, then deep-fried and served with* hoi sin *and hot chili sauces. These bean curds are usually sold by street vendors.*

## DESSERTS

Like most Chinese desserts, Shanghai desserts tend to be sweet and bland.

## 猪 油 年 糕
### 270. Lard Pudding:
*Glutinous rice flour is mixed into a dough, steamed, sliced, dipped in egg and fried. This pudding has a crispy skin and sticks to the teeth.*

## 綠 豆 糕
### 271. Green-Bean Pudding:
*Green-bean flour is mixed into a dough, molded into small cakes and steamed. Red-bean paste is sometimes used as filling.*

## 雪 花 銀 耳
### 272. Sweet Snow Fungi:
*White fungi, a dehydrated mushroom, are believed to possess medicinal properties. The fungi are cooked into a sweet, thick but bland soup with rock sugar.*

## 酒 釀 圓 子
### 273. Glutinous Rice Wine (Sweet) with Dumplings, or Boiled Rice Powder with Wine Rice:
*Sticky tiny glutinous rice dumplings are served in a sweet syrup laced with glutinous rice wine. A scrambled egg and dried* gwai far *blossoms are sometimes added to the syrup.*

## 熱 酒 釀

**274. Hot Glutinous Rice Wine (Sweet) or Hot Wine Rice:**
*Sweet glutinous rice wine, made from soured glutinous rice, is served hot as a dessert soup.*

## 凍 酒 釀

**275. Cold Glutinous Rice Wine or Cold Wine Rice:**
*This is the same as the dish above except it is served chilled as an after-dinner aperitif.*

## 豆 沙 湯 糰

**276. Glutinous Rice Dumplings with Red-Bean Paste Filling, or Boiled Rice-Powder Bun with Red Bean:**
*Dollar-sized glutinous rice dumplings, stuffed with sweet red-bean paste, are boiled and served in clear hot water. The dough sticks to the teeth, and the filling is extremely sweet. After eating the dumplings, drink the water to clean your palate.*

## 芝 蔴 湯 糰

**277. Glutinous Rice Dumplings with Black Sesame-Seed Filling, or Boiled Rice-Powder Bun with Black Sesame Seeds:**
*Dollar-sized glutinous rice dumplings, stuffed with aromatic black sesame-seed paste, are served in clear hot water. The dough sticks to the teeth, and the filling is sweet and fragrant. Drink the water after eating the dumplings to clean your palate.*

## 擂 沙 圓

**278. Dipped Glutinous Rice Dumplings:**
*Red-bean paste or black sesame-seed-filled glutinous rice dumplings are boiled, then dredged in sweet red-bean powder. These dumplings are eaten warm.*

鬆 糕

**279. Fluffy Pudding:**
*Glutinous rice flour dough is mixed with red dates and walnuts, stuffed with red-bean paste, poured into molds, then steamed.*

綠 豆 湯

**280. Green Mung-Bean Soup:**
*Green mung beans are cooked in water with sugar until the beans have almost completely dissolved. Served either hot or chilled, this drink makes a sweet but refreshing summer beverage.*

紅 豆 湯

**281. Red Mung-Bean Soup:**
*Red mung beans are cooked in water with sugar until the beans have almost completely dissolved. This drink, served either hot or chilled, makes a sweet but refreshing summer beverage.*

八 寶 飯

**282. Eight Precious Rice:**
*Cooked glutinous rice is pressed into a mold with an assortment of dried fruits such as dates and lotus seeds, steamed, then served piping hot. To eat, take a small bowlful. Advance notice is required for this dish.*

定 勝 糕

**283. Steamed Pudding:**
*Glutinous rice and rice flour dough are tinted pink, mixed with walnuts and dates, poured into small molds and steamed. These puddings are for celebrations such as birthdays.*

# CHAPTER EIGHT

# A Szechwan Menu

Tucked away in a corner and cut off from the rest of China by mountain ranges, Szechwan is a land of mystery even to many Chinese. Until the twentieth century, the only way to get in and out of Szechwan was over the mountain ranges and through turbulent gorges of the Yangtze. The Szechwanese became a self-sufficient and fiercely independent people, with their own ways of doing things, and with a cuisine unlike any other in China.

The character of the Szechwanese is best revealed in the way they have overcome their environment. Though Szechwan has some of the richest soil in China and its climate is wet and mild, only five percent of its land is flat and arable. The rest is all steep hills. Undaunted, the tough-minded Szechwanese learned to farm the hills by terracing them. They became proficient at terraced farming, and are major producers of rice, sugar, citrus fruits, mushrooms and spices, such as Szechwan peppercorns, star anise and hot peppers. Hot peppers play an important role in Szechwan cuisine. It is believed that they were brought to Szechwan in the first century by Indian monks who came to spread Buddhism. Many people believe that the monks also taught the early Szechwanese the art of blending spices, a culinary practice unknown in other parts of China. The Szechwanese added their own spices and developed an aromatic but distinctly Chinese cuisine.

# A SZECHWAN MENU

Szechwan food has several intriguing flavors not found in other Chinese cuisines, the best-known of which is *lah* or "spicy-hotness." *Lah* is created by using a variety of spices, such as fresh and dried hot peppers, chili sauces and red chili oil. These hot spices are believed to facilitate perspiration in a hot, humid climate and to sensitize the palate to flavors that emerge after the initial fire dies down. Peppering Chicken, for example, is spicy at first; then other taste sensations — the crunchiness and sweetness of the water chestnuts and the savoriness of the chicken meat — come through, their flavors intensified by the spicy hotness.

Another uniquely Szechwan flavor is produced by a remarkable little peppercorn called *fagara*, or Szechwan red peppercorn. Indigenous to Szechwan, it gives off a strange mix of sensations, a flowery aroma and a tingling in the mouth called *mah*. Szechwan cooks roast and crush these peppercorns and sprinkle them liberally on food. A recently invented dish, Chungking Beef, is tender beef slices sautéed with dried chilies and crushed Szechwan peppercorns. Another dish flavored with peppercorns is Szechwan Peppercorn Chicken: chicken cubes are marinated in powdered Szechwan peppercorns, sautéed with more peppercorns and served with deep-fried spinach leaves.

Another mouth-watering Szechwan flavor is found in a sauce with the somewhat misleading name of "fish-fragrant." This sauce, a hot and tangy combination of vinegar, soy and chili sauces, contains no fish at all. Nor does it taste like fish. But to the landlocked Szechwanese, who rarely have access to seafood, the term "fish-fragrant" reflects their craving for seafood and their love of this spicy, tangy sauce. A dish that goes well with either rice or noodles, Fish-Fragrant Pork is finely shredded pork sautéed in a pungent sauce of garlic, ginger, vinegar and hot chilies. Also cooked in a fish-fragrant sauce is Fish-Fragrant Eggplant. Chunks of peeled eggplant are sautéed with minced pork and a sauce that is thick, spicy and vinegary.

Proud of the spicy flavors of their cuisine, the Szechwanese love to watch outsiders try their food for the first time. They even have a private joke about picking out tourists in restaurants. Before a meal begins, most restaurants in Szechwan provide a glass of water and a wet towel. The water is to rinse the burning palate, the towel to mop a progressively sweaty brow. Tourists unfamiliar with the spiciness of Szechwan cuisine are easily spotted. Before the meal arrives, they have consumed all their water and have used the towel to wipe their hands.

Szechwan food is often spicy, but spiciness is not its only feature. Many restaurant cooks, untrained in Szechwan cooking, misunderstand the principles, and overload dishes with chilies. But Szechwan food is not just hot Chinese food; it is also pungent, aromatic and texturally interesting. One bite of an authentic Szechwan specialty is not simply a taste; it is an eruption of tastes, aromas and textures that at first seems overwhelming, but then is immensely satisfying.

Szechwan cuisine is not as diverse as the cuisines of Canton or Shanghai, but its tastes and textures are original. Many people believe that once you have been introduced to Szechwan food, you will become a Szechwan food lover for life, and will find other Chinese food bland and uninteresting. This menu includes some of Szechwan's best dishes. If you're lucky enough to find a restaurant where they are well prepared, you're bound to get hooked on the flavors of this high-spirited cuisine.

# A SZECHWAN MENU

## APPETIZERS

Szechwan appetizers are usually served cold or at room temperature, and are intended to whet the appetite. These items can be ordered by themselves or in combinations of two, three or four.

棒 棒 鶏

**1. Bong Bong Chicken or Baun Baun Chicken:**
*"Bong Bong" means pieces cut like matchsticks. Poached chicken meat is shredded into strips, then served with sliced cucumbers or with Tientsin mung-bean sheets, which have a slippery texture. A spicy sauce made of soy sauce, chili sauce and sesame-seed paste or peanut butter is drizzled over the chicken.*

怪 味 鶏

**2. Strange Taste Chicken, or Spiced Chicken:**
*In most restaurants, Strange Taste Chicken is made the same way as Bong Bong Chicken, except that crushed peanuts are added. But authentic Strange Taste Chicken consists of diced poached chicken meat served with fried crunchy peanuts, green onion chunks and a spicy soy-based sauce.*

椒 麻 鶏

**3. Peppercorn Aromatic Chicken:**
*Poached shredded chicken meat is served with slippery bean*

thread noodles and topped with a vinegar and Szechwan peppercorn sauce. Szechwan peppercorns are aromatic and create a tingling sensation in the mouth.

蒜泥白肉

**4. Garlic Pulp White Pork, or Sliced Pork with Garlic Sauce:**
Marbled pork is poached, sliced paper-thin and served with a soy-garlic dip.

芝麻醬拌腰片

**5. Sliced Kidney with Sesame-Seed Sauce:**
Poached crunchy pig's kidney slices and Tientsin bean sheets are topped with a fragrant sauce of sesame paste, vinegar and soy sauce. Toss lightly before eating.

泡菜

**6. Szechwan Pickled Vegetables:**
Real Szechwan pickled vegetables are tart and spicy. A variety of vegetables, such as carrots, cucumbers, Western cabbage, Chinese white radishes and hot peppers, are pickled in a salty brine and served chilled. Szechwan pickles have to be made on the premises, so many restaurants do not serve them.

辣白菜

**7. Pickled White Cabbage:**
Slivers of Chinese white cabbage, siu choy, are marinated until wilted in salt, garlic, vinegar and hot peppers and served chilled.

## SOUPS

Chinese soups are thick or thin. Thick soup is usually thickened with a cornstarch paste and filled with meat and vegetables — pork, beef, bean curd, bamboo shoots and black mushrooms. Thin soup consists of broth and shredded meat and vegetables, and tends to be much lighter.

月日母鷄湯
8. Chicken Soup:
*Chicken pieces are sautéed, then cooked until tender in broth with bamboo shoots and black fungi.*

三片湯
9. Assorted Meat and Black-Mushroom Soup, or Sliced Three Kinds of Meat Soup:
*Spinach leaves and sliced ingredients, such as chicken, ham and black mushrooms, are cooked in a broth. In the traditional version of this dish, tender shoots of snow peas are used rather than spinach.*

蘿白絲鯽魚湯
10. Shredded Radish and Fish Soup:
*A bream-like fish is fried, then cooked in broth with shredded Chinese white radish. After prolonged cooking, the soup turns white. Some restaurants, to shorten the cooking time, use milk to whiten the soup. A vinegar-and-shredded-ginger sauce is served on the side. Sprinkle a teaspoon of sauce over the soup before eating.*

## 鷄片湯
**11. Chicken Slices Soup:**
Chicken slices are cooked in a broth with ham and black mushrooms.

## 金錢口蘑湯
**12. Stuffed Mushroom Soup:**
Black mushroom caps are stuffed with ground chicken, then steamed and served in a broth with ham and Chinese greens.

## 肉圓湯
**13. Pork-Ball Soup:**
Ground pork balls are served in a clear broth with vegetables, and sometimes with transparent bean thread noodles.

## 連鍋湯
**14. Including Pot Soup:**
A pork hock is cooked until tender in a broth with ginger and Szechwan peppercorns. It is sliced thinly and served in a casserole pot with the broth and chunks of Chinese white radish. A spicy soy-and-Szechwan-peppercorn dip is served on the side.

## 酸菜尤魚湯
**15. Pickles-and-Cuttlefish Soup:**
Sour pickled mustard greens are sliced and cooked with bamboo shoots and dried cuttlefish in broth.

## 尤魚鷄湯
**16. Cuttlefish-and-Chicken Soup:**
Chicken and dried cuttlefish are cooked in broth to create a briny-tasting soup.

豌 豆 肚 條 湯

17. Shredded Pig's Stomach and Pea Soup:
Cooked pig's stomach is shredded and served in a broth with green peas.

一 品 豆 腐 湯

18. First Rate Bean-Curd Soup:
This is a broth served with a bean-curd pudding. Ground chicken is mashed with bean curd, poured into a bowl, topped with shredded ham and black mushrooms and steamed. The pudding is then transferred into a bowl of hot broth and served in one piece. Slice the pudding before eating it.

川 竹 蓀 湯

19. Tips of Bamboo Shoot Soup:
The tips of bamboo shoots, abundant in Szechwan but seldom exported, are sliced and cooked in broth with sliced ham, chicken and tender shoots of the snow pea.

肝 糕 湯

20. Liver-Pudding Soup:
Pig's liver is ground up, mixed with eggs and steamed in a bowl until it forms a pudding. It is served in one piece in a bowl of broth garnished with shredded ham. This soup is a Szechwan specialty, but it is not always available in restaurants. Slice the pudding before eating it.

鷄 茸 豆 花 湯

21. Minced Chicken and Egg-White Soup:
Ground chicken is sautéed with egg whites, then served over steaming hot bean curds. Shredded ham is sometimes used as a garnish.

口蘑竹蓀湯
### 22. Mushroom and Tips of Bamboo Shoot Soup:
*This soup is seldom available outside Szechwan because the two key ingredients, dried mushrooms and bamboo-shoot tips are seldom exported. Fresh bamboo-shoot tips and dried mushrooms are cooked in a broth with slices of ham and chicken. The tender shoots of the snow pea or spinach leaves are added right before serving.*

口蘑鍋粑湯
### 23. Dried Mushrooms and Sizzling Rice Soup:
*This is two dishes in one: Szechwan mushrooms cooked with vegetables in a thick broth, and pieces of rice crusts that have been deep-fried. At the table, the waiter pours the mushrooms over the piping-hot rice, which sizzles. This dish should be eaten immediately or the rice crusts will become soggy.*

## MAIN DISHES—BEAN CURDS

Bean curd or tofu dishes are popular in Szechwan. Szechwan cooks like to braise bean-curd cubes in spicy or pungent sauces. Made from soybeans, bean curd provides protein and calcium and is delicious and delicate.

麻婆豆腐
### 24. *Ma Po* Tofu, or Pock-Faced Lady's Bean Curds, or Braised Bean Curds with Minced Beef:
*Legend has it that this dish was made famous by a female Szechwan cook. It consists of tender pieces of bean curd that have been braised with minced pork and chili sauce.*

家常豆腐

**25. Family Style Bean Curds, or Fried Bean Curd with Meat, Home Style:**
*Triangular pieces of bean curd are fried, then sautéed with minced pork and brown bean sauce. Although the traditional version is not spicy, some restaurants serve this dish laced with chili sauce.*

鍋貼豆腐

**26. Pot-Sticking Bean Curds:**
*Mashed bean curds are mixed with minced dried shrimp, ham and black mushrooms. The mixture is steamed in a bowl, cut into slices, dipped in batter and fried to a golden brown.*

麻辣豆腐

**27. Mah Lah Bean Curds, or Aromatic Hot Bean Curds:**
*Rarely available in restaurants, these deep-fried bean-curd cubes are braised with pork, brown-bean sauce, bamboo shoots and a fragrant mixture of mashed green onions, sesame oil and Szechwan peppercorns.*

熊掌豆腐

**28. Bear's Paw Bean Curds:**
*Fried bean-curd pieces are braised in a brown sauce with ham, bamboo shoots, chicken meat and black mushrooms. No bear's paw is served in this dish.*

## MAIN DISHES — BEEF

The Szechwanese traditionally do not use much beef in cooking, so original beef dishes are few. Beef, however, can be substituted for pork in many of the pork dishes.

### 乾煸牛肉絲

**29. Dry-Sautéed Shredded Beef, or Beef with Chilies:**
*Shredded beef is marinated, fried and sautéed with a slightly sweet sauce and shredded celery, carrots, green onions and dried chilies. Some restaurants fry the beef until it is crunchy and chewy, then sauté it with the vegetables.*

### 魚香牛肉絲

**30. Fish-Fragrant Shredded Beef, or Beef in Chili, Sour-and-Garlic Sauce:**
*Shredded beef is quick-fried, then sautéed in a spicy vinegary sauce and served with sautéed spinach. In the traditional version of this dish, shredded celery, carrots and black fungi are used instead of spinach.*

### 陳皮牛肉

**31. Beef with Tangerine Peels:**
*The traditional version consists of beef slices that have been braised until chewy with chilies, soy sauce and dried tangerine peels. Most restaurants prefer to serve the beef sautéed rather than braised. Thinly sliced beef is marinated, quick-fried, then sautéed with reconstituted tangerine peel and dried red chilies.*

重慶牛肉

32. Chungking Beef:
*This dish, invented in recent years, is marinated beef slices quick-fried and sautéed with garlic, ginger, red chilies and crushed Szechwan peppercorns. It is served piping hot.*

## MAIN DISHES—CASSEROLES

A Chinese casserole pot, made of clay or carbon steel, is placed directly on the stove for cooking. When properly made, a casserole dish is always brought to a boil before serving. Transferred to the table, it is then uncovered and served bubbling. In some restaurants, it is called a hot pot.

紅燜牛腩砂鍋

33. Red-Braised Beef Casserole, or Braised Beef in Casserole:
*Pieces of beef brisket are stewed tender in a full-flavored sauce of soy and brown-bean sauces, then served bubbling in a casserole. Often dried red chilies are added.*

紅燜鷄翼砂鍋

34. Red-Braised Chicken-Wings Casserole, or Braised Chicken Wings in Casserole:
*Chicken wings are stewed in soy and brown-bean sauces and served bubbling in a casserole.*

雲南汽鍋鷄

35. Yunnan Steamed-Chicken Casserole:
*The cooks of Yunnan, a province neighboring Szechwan, use*

a special kind of casserole pot. It is made of red clay and has an air funnel in the middle. Chicken pieces and broth are placed in the casserole, covered and steamed. Because the special Yunnan casserole pot is needed to make this dish, it is rarely available in restaurants.

## 四生菊花鍋
### 36. Szechwan Chrysanthemum Hot Pot:
A Mongolian-style brass fondue pot is filled with hot broth, and garnished with a fresh chrysanthemum flower for fragrance. Raw ingredients are served on small dishes around the fondue: fish, chicken, giblets, pig's kidney, bean thread noodles, Chinese cabbage, spinach and tender shoots of the snow pea. Deep-fried peanuts, which require no cooking, are served on the side. Cook each morsel of food in the bubbling broth, then dip it in a mixture of soy and hot chili sauces before eating.

## 毛肚火鍋
### 37. Organs Hot Pot:
An assortment of organs—cow's stomach, liver, kidney, brain—is sliced and served with beef, strips of beef bone marrow and Chinese cabbage in a casserole of seasoned liquid. A scrambled-egg dip is served on the side. To eat, remove food from the bubbling casserole, dip it in the scrambled eggs, then in soy sauce mixed with chili sauce. Advance notice is required for this dish.

## MAIN DISHES—CHICKEN AND EGGS

辣 子 鶏 丁

**38. Peppering (Diced) Chicken:**
*Chicken cubes are marinated, quick-fried and sautéed with hot peppers or red dried chilies and fresh or canned water chestnuts. (The canned chestnuts are as crunchy as the fresh but not as tasty.)*

乾 椒 子 鶏

**39. Dried Chilies with Diced Chicken:**
*Diced chicken is quick-fried, then sautéed with dried chilies, soy sauce and chili oil.*

油 淋 鶏

**40. Fried Chicken with Sweet-Vinegar Sauce or Fried Chicken with Special Sauce:**
*Marinated pieces of chicken, on the bone, are fried until crispy, cut and served with shredded green onions and a sweet-vinegar sauce. The chicken is ordered whole or in halves.*

魚 香 鶏 丁

**41. Fish-Fragrant Shredded Chicken, or Diced Chicken in Chili, Sour-and-Garlic Sauce:**
*Marinated cubes or slivers of chicken are sautéed with ginger, garlic and a spicy-vinegar sauce. Some restaurants serve the chicken with sautéed spinach. Traditionally, shredded celery, snow peas and black fungi accompany the spicy chicken.*

青椒雞絲

42. Diced or Shredded Chicken with Green Peppers:
Shredded green peppers are sautéed with green onions and shredded marinated chicken meat.

宮保雞丁

43. *Kung Pao* Chicken, or Diced Chicken with Red Peppers and Peanuts:
Marinated chicken cubes are sautéed with fried peanuts, diced hot peppers and sweet bean sauce.

雞絲鍋粑

44. Chicken Over Sizzling Rice, or Crispy Rice with Chicken:
This is two dishes in one. First, diced chicken is sautéed with vegetables and a thick sauce. Then pieces of rice crust are deep-fried. At the table, the waiter pours the chicken over the piping-hot crusts, which sizzle. This dish should be eaten immediately or the crusts will become soggy.

川椒雞

45. Szechwan Peppercorn Chicken:
This new dish consists of marinated chicken cubes sautéed with Szechwan peppercorns. Spinach leaves, fried until crunchy in oil, are used as garnishes.

紅油雞

46. Red-Oil Chicken:
Poached diced chicken meat is served with peanuts, diced pressed bean curds and a spicy sesame-seed sauce.

口蘑鷄

**47. Mushrooms and Chicken Slices:**
*Marinated chicken slices are sautéed with dried mushrooms. In many restaurants, canned button mushrooms are used.*

成都子鷄

**48. Chengdu Chicken:**
*Named after the captial of Szechwan, this dish is rarely available in restaurants. Pieces of chicken, on the bone, are braised with garlic, chili sauce, peppers, Szechwan peppercorns and bits of celery.*

黃燜鷄翼或塊

**49. Yellow Braised Chicken Wings or Pieces:**
*Marinated pieces of chicken, still on the bone, are fried, then braised in broth, soy sauce and bamboo shoots.*

粉蒸鷄

**50. Rice Powder Steamed Chicken:**
*Deboned marinated chicken slices are dredged in a pulverized mixture of roasted long-grain rice, Szechwan peppercorns and five spices, then steamed and served hot. The crumbly rice gives an interesting texture to the supple chicken.*

陳皮鷄

**51. Tangerine-Peel Chicken:**
*Chicken meat is sliced, marinated, quick-fried and sautéed with reconstituted tangerine peels, green onions and hot chilies.*

貫耳全鷄

**52. Stuffed Chicken:**
A whole deboned chicken is stuffed with cooked minced pork, preserved vegetables, dried shrimp and ham; then it is rubbed with spices, wrapped with caul and fried. It is served cut up and garnished with more preserved vegetables.

水晶南瓜

**53. Chicken in Pumpkin:**
A hollowed-out pumpkin is stuffed with chicken pieces that have been dredged in a mixture of powdered long-grain rice and Szechwan peppercorns. The pumpkin is steamed, then served whole. Sometimes sautéed Chinese greens are used as garnishes. Advance notice is required.

鍋貼鷄片

**54. Pot-Sticking Chicken:**
Chicken meat is layered with pork, bamboo shoots and ham, smeared with a batter and pan-fried. Vinegar and ketchup are served as dips on the side.

魚香雙脆

**55. Fish-Fragrant Double Crunch:**
Sliced pig's stomach and chicken giblets are sautéed with red chilies, black mushrooms, bamboo shoots and a spicy vinegary sauce.

白油四件

**56. Sautéed Four Pieces:**
Two chicken livers and two giblets are sliced and sautéed with bamboo shoots and black fungi and served sprinkled with Szechwan peppercorn powder.

魚香四件

57. Fish-Fragrant Four Pieces:
*Two chicken livers and two giblets are sliced and sautéed with red chilies, bamboo shoots, black mushrooms and a spicy, tangy sauce.*

墨魚燉鷄

58. Chicken with Octopus:
*Chicken pieces, still on the bone, are braised with octopus until both are soft and tender.*

魚香烘蛋

59. Fish-Fragrant Omelet, or Fried Egg with Chili, Sour-and-Garlic Sauce:
*A thick omelet is pan-fried, then cut into bite-sized pieces and served with sautéed pork, black fungi and a spicy vinegar sauce.*

白油烘蛋

60. Fried Omelet:
*A thick omelet is cut into slices and deep-fried until crunchy.*

## MAIN DISHES — DUCK

### 香 酥 鴨

**61. Fragrant Crispy Duck or Special Fried Duck:**
*A duck is rubbed with spices such as five spices and Szechwan peppercorns, then steamed and deep-fried until the skin is crispy. You can order a whole duck or a half duck. Advance ordering may be required because of the elaborate preparation.*

### 樟 茶 鴨

**62. Szechwan Smoked Duck or Smoked Fried Duck:**
*A duck is rubbed with salt and spices such as cloves and Szechwan peppercorns. Traditionally, it is then smoked, steamed and deep-fried. The smoking, which is a special procedure, is skipped in most restaurants, but this omission does not usually detract from the overall effect. The skin should be crispy and the meat flavored with Szechwan peppercorns. You can order a whole duck or a half duck.*

### 子 薑 鴨 塊

**63. Young Ginger and Duck:**
*Duck pieces, still on the bone, are sautéed with sweet pickled pink ginger, garlic, chilies and salty bean sauce.*

### 醬 爆 鴨 塊

**64. Duck Pieces in Sweet Sauce:**
*Fried duck pieces, on the bone, are braised with bamboo shoots and sweet-bean or* hoi sin *sauce.*

鍋 貼 鴨

**65. Pot-Sticking Duck:**
*In this Yunnan dish, duck meat is layered with pork and salty vegetables, smeared with batter, then pan-fried to a golden brown. A salt-and-pepper dip is served on the side.*

溜 鴨 肝

**66. Sautéed Duck's Livers:**
*Sliced duck's livers are sautéed with chilies, bamboo shoots and black mushrooms.*

鮮 菇 燴 鴨 腰

**67. Mushrooms and Duck Testicles:**
*Crunchy duck testicles are sautéed with sliced mushrooms, ham and bamboo shoots. This dish is only available in specialty restaurants and requires advance notice.*

## MAIN DISHES — EXOTIC INGREDIENTS

These extraordinary seafood dishes require elaborate preparation because principal ingredients, such as shark's fins or sea cucumber, are dehydrated and must be reconstituted through repeated soaking. Considered delicacies, shark's fins and sea cucumbers must be soaked, slow cooked, then braised. Cooked until soft, shark's fins have a rich, pleasing flavor. Sea cucumbers, spongy and gelatinous after cooking, are prized for their texture. Because these dishes are uncommon and require special cooking, they are reserved for special occasions and tend to be expensive. Some may need to be ordered in advance.

## 什錦海參

**68. Sea Cucumbers with Assorted Ingredients, or Sea Cucumbers with Mixed Meats:**
*Soft and spongy sea cucumbers are braised with a variety of ingredients, such as ham, bamboo shoots, black mushrooms, and dried shrimp.*

## 酸辣海參

**69. Hot-and-Sour Sea Cucumbers:**
*Spongy sea-cucumber slices are braised with meat and mushrooms in a hot tangy sauce.*

## 海參鍋粑

**70. Sea Cucumbers with Sizzling Rice, or Crispy Rice with Sea Cucumbers:**
*This is actually two dishes in one. First, sea cucumbers are sautéed with assorted meats and vegetables. Then rice crusts are deep-fried. At the table, the waiter pours the sautéed sea cucumber over the hot rice crusts, which sizzle. Rice crusts that don't sizzle have been improperly prepared. This dish should be eaten right away or the rice crusts will become soggy.*

## 魚唇鍋粑

**71. Fish Lips with Sizzling Rice:**
*This dish is prepared the same as the sea cucumbers above except reconstituted slivers of fish lips are used instead of sea cucumbers.*

## 魚肚海參

**72. Fish Bladder Braised with Sea Cucumbers, or Braised Beche-de-Mer with Fish Maw:**
*The swim bladder of a large fish, dehydrated and sold in*

*large sheets, is reconstituted, shredded and braised with sea cucumbers until soft and gelatinous. This dish has an intriguing spongy texture and contrasting colors; the bladder is white and the sea cucumbers are black.*

## 鷄汁魚肚
### 73. Chicken-Flavored Fish Bladder:
*Spongy slices of fish bladder are braised in a thick sauce with an assortment of ingredients such as dried scallops, bamboo shoots and black mushrooms.*

## 家常田鷄
### 74. Family Style Frog Legs:
*Marinated frog legs are sautéed with garlic, ginger and hot chili sauce.*

## 乾燒魚翅
### 75. Dry-Braised Shark's Fin:
*This is a rather thick stew made of shark's fin.*

## 爛鷄魚翅
### 76. Shark's Fin Soup with Finely Chopped Chicken Meat:
*This is a thick stew made with shredded chicken meat and shark's fin.*

## 三絲魚翅
### 77. Shark's Fin Soup with Three Kinds of Meat:
*In this stew, julienned chicken, pork and ham complement the soft, noodle-like shark's fin.*

# MAIN DISHES — FISH

The Szechwanese seafood repertoire is small. In the interior and far from the ocean, Szechwan does not have much fresh seafood. Although some fresh-water fish, such as carp, is available, seafood is usually brought in frozen. To disguise the lack of freshness in frozen fish, Szechwan cooks use pungent seasonings, such as brown-bean and chili sauces. Most fish is served with the head and bone intact, because the Chinese believe that the least-handled fish retains the most flavor.

## 乾燒魚

**78. Dry-Braised Fish, or Braised Fish in Chili Sauce:**
*A whole fish, such as bream, is fried, then braised in a hot and pungent sauce of ginger, garlic, dried chilies and soy, brown-bean and chili sauces.*

## 乾燒魚塊

**79. Dry-Braised Fish Slices, or Braised Fish Pieces in Chili Sauce:**
*This dish is prepared the same as Dry-Braised Fish, except that fish slices are used instead of whole fish. If you want the slices boned, be specific with the restaurant staff.*

## 四川豆瓣魚

**80. Szechwan Brown-Bean Sauce with Fish, or Hot Chili Fish:**
*A whole fish, usually carp, is fried, then braised in a pungent sauce of garlic, ginger, green onions, brown-bean and chili sauces.*

## 鬆子魚
**81. Fish with Pine Nuts:**
*In this elaborate dish, a whole fish, such as rock cod, is fried, then topped with a tomato sauce garnished with peas, black mushrooms and pine nuts. Advance notice may be required for this dish.*

## 大蒜鯰或鮎魚
**82. Garlic Fish:**
*A whole fish, usually weighing about one pound, is braised in a spicy and sour sauce.*

## 豆腐鯽魚
**83. Fish with Bean Curds:**
*A small fish, such as bream, is fried, then braised in a spicy sauce with chunks of bean curd.*

## 貴州八寶魚
**84. *Kwei Chow* Eight Precious Fish:**
*A fish, such as carp, is cut up, fried and braised in a spicy sauce with sea cucumbers, black mushrooms, shrimp, pig's stomach, chicken and kidney slices.*

## 乾煸小魚
**85. Dry-Sautéed Small Fish:**
*Small dried fish, like anchovies, are sautéed with soy sauce, sugar and vinegar until dry and brittle.*

## 辣豆瓣鯉魚
**86. Hot Bean-Sauce Fish:**
*A carp or similar fish is fried, then braised with red chili sauce, shredded mushrooms and marinated pork slices.*

脆 皮 桂 魚

**87. Crispy Fish:**
A whole fish is dipped in flour, fried and served with a sweet-and-sour tomato-based sauce. Traditionally, Chinese mandarin fish is used for this recipe.

魚 香 魚 塊

**88. Fish-Fragrant Fish Slices:**
In this newly invented dish, a large fish steak, such as halibut, is pan-fried, then served with a spicy vinegary sauce.

粉 蒸 鯽 魚

**89. Rice-Powder Steamed Fish:**
A whole fish, such as bream, is smeared with powdered rice that has been roasted with spices and steamed. The crumbly rice offers an unusual textural contrast to the tender fish meat. This dish is seldom available in restaurants.

乾 煸 鱔 背

**90. Sautéed Eel:**
Slices of deboned large eel are fried, then sautéed with red chilies, celery and salty bean sauce.

鍋 貼 魚

**91. Pot-Sticking Fish:**
Marinated fish slices are layered with meat and preserved vegetables, dipped in batter, then pan-fried.

## MAIN DISHES — PORK

魚香肉絲

**92. Fish-Fragrant Pork or Pork with Chili, Sour-and-Garlic Sauce:**
*Shredded pork is sautéed in a spicy vinegar sauce and served with sautéed spinach. Traditionally, shredded celery, carrots and black fungi are used instead of spinach.*

回鍋肉

**93. Twice-Cooked Pork, or Sliced Pork with Garlic, Pepper and Cabbage:**
*Thin slices of poached marbled pork are sautéed with chunks of pepper and cabbage, minced garlic, and* hoi sin *and chili sauces. This mélange of meat and vegetables is spicy and slightly sweet.*

榨菜肉絲

**94. Preserved Kohlrabi with Shredded Pork, or Pork with Szechwan Pickles:**
*Preserved kohlrabi is shredded and sautéed with shredded marinated pork. Sometimes julienned bamboo shoots are also added. The preserved kohlrabi is pungent, crunchy and salty.*

魚香茄子

**95. Fish-Fragrant Eggplants, or Shredded Pork with Eggplant and Chili, Sour-and-Garlic Sauce:**
*Chunks of peeled eggplant are fried and sautéed with garlic, ginger, minced pork and a spicy vinegar sauce. This dish is*

*particularly good when made with sweet and slender Oriental eggplant.*

# 魚香茄子餅

**96. Fish-Fragrant Stuffed Eggplants:**
Ground pork is sandwiched between Oriental eggplant slices, deep-fried, then braised in a spicy, vinegary sauce.

# 螞蟻上樹

**97. Ants Up a Tree, or Minced Pork with Bean Thread Noodles:**
Minced pork is braised in a spicy sauce with strands of deep-fried bean thread noodles. This dish is noted for its contrasting textures — the slipperiness of the noodles set against the firmness of the pork.

# 辣子肉丁

**98. Chilies with Pork:**
Marinated pork cubes are sautéed with water chestnuts, hot chilies and brown-bean sauce.

# 醬爆肉

**99. Pork Sautéed with Sauce:**
Sliced pork is fried until chewy, then sautéed with mustard greens, garlic and sweet bean sauce.

# 肉絲鍋粑

**100. Shredded Pork with Sizzling or Crispy Rice:**
*This is two dishes in one. First, shredded pork is sautéed with vegetables in a thick sauce. Then rice crusts are deep-fried. At the table, the waiter pours the sautéed pork over the hot rice crusts, which sizzle. Rice crusts that don't sizzle have been improperly prepared. This dish should be eaten right away or the rice crusts will become soggy.*

## 什 錦 鍋 粑

**101. Assorted Meat with Sizzling or Crispy Rice:**
*This dish is prepared the same as Shredded Pork except that pork, shrimp, giblets and chicken are served as the topping.*

## 粉 蒸 肉

**102. Rice-Powder Steamed Pork, or Steamed Pork Szechwan Style:**
*Thick pork slices are marinated, dredged in a roasted mixture of powdered long-grain rice, Szechwan peppercorns and five spices, then steamed. The rice mixture provides an unusual crumbly texture. The pork inside is tender.*

## 粉 蒸 排 骨

**103. Rice-Powder Steamed Spareribs, or Steamed Spareribs Szechwan Style:**
*These spareribs are prepared like Steamed Pork, above.*

## 生 爆 鹽 煎 肉

**104. Sautéed Pork:**
*Thinly sliced pork is sautéed with sweet bean sauce, hot peppers and garlic. This is a sour and spicy dish.*

## 泡 菜 肉 未

**105. Szechwan Pickles and Minced Pork:**
*Ground pork is sautéed with red chilies, garlic and chopped homemade Szechwan pickles. The pork is spicy, the pickles tart and crunchy. Szechwan pickles have to be made on the premises, so restaurants that don't make them don't serve them.*

釀青椒

106. Stuffed Peppers:
*Small green peppers (usually jalapenos) are stuffed with a mixture of ground pork, ham and dried shrimp; they are fried and served with a sauce.*

珍珠肉丸

107. Pearl Balls:
*Meatballs made of ground pork are dredged in glutinous rice and steamed. Eat them with soy and hot chili sauces.*

東坡肉

108. Tung Po Pork:
*Named after a well-known Tang-dynasty gourmet poet, this is pork belly that has been slow-cooked in salt and wine.*

火爆猪肝

109. Sautéed Pig's Liver:
*Sliced pig's liver is sautéed in a garlicky sauce with bamboo shoots and black fungi. The finished dish is sprinkled with Szechwan peppercorn powder.*

魚香腰花

110. Kidneys with Fish-Fragrance, or Spicy Kidneys, or Kidneys with Chili, Sour-and-Garlic Sauce:
*Thin pig's kidney slices are sautéed with water chestnuts, black fungi, carrots and sometimes celery in a spicy vinegar sauce.*

麻辣腰花

111. Mah Lah Kidneys, or Hot and Tingling Kidneys:
*Poached kidney slices are tossed with cucumbers, green*

onions and a soy-and-Szechwan-peppercorn dressing. Sometimes this dish is made with slippery Tientsin bean sheets instead of cucumbers.

紅 油 腰 花

112. Red-Oil Kidneys:
*Poached kidney slices are tossed with cucumber slices, Tientsin bean sheets and a spicy dressing of red chili oil and sesame-seed paste.*

椒 鹽 蹄 膀

113. Peppery-Salt Pork Hock:
*A whole pork hock is stewed until tender, dipped in a batter, fried and served in bite-sized pieces. A salt-and-pepper dip is served on the side. Advance notice is required for this dish.*

燒 雲 腿

114. Barbecued Yunnan Ham:
*Chunks of Yunnan ham are roasted, dipped in batter, fried and then sliced thin. The slices are sandwiched between slices of bread, then steamed. This highly unusual dish is seldom available in restaurants.*

## MAIN DISHES—SHELLFISH

### 乾燒明蝦
**115. Fried Shrimp with Tomato Sauce, or Fried Prawns with Chili Sauce:**
*Medium shrimp are fried in the shell, then braised in a hot, garlicky tomato sauce. Some restaurants have imported Tsing Tao jumbo prawns; they are expensive but delicious.*

### 宮保蝦仁
**116. Kung Pao Shrimp, or Shrimp with Red Pepper and Peanuts:**
*Shelled medium shrimp are sautéed in a spicy tomato sauce with garlic, chili sauce and fried peanuts.*

### 魚香蝦仁
**117. Fish-Fragrant Shrimp, or Shrimp with Szechwan Sauce:**
*Shelled medium shrimp are sautéed with ginger and garlic in a spicy vinegary sauce.*

### 蝦仁鍋粑
**118. Shrimp over Sizzling Rice, or Crispy Rice with Shrimp:**
*This is two dishes in one. First, small shelled shrimp are sautéed with diced vegetables in a transparent sauce. Then pieces of rice crust are deep-fried. At the table, the waiter pours the shrimp over the hot rice crusts to produce a sizzling sound. Rice crusts that don't sizzle have not been fried at the right temperature. This dish should be eaten immediately or the rice crusts will become soggy.*

茄 汁 蝦 仁 鍋 粑

119. Shrimp and Tomato Sauce over Sizzling Rice, or Crispy Rice with Shrimp Tomato Sauce:
*This is prepared the same way as Shrimp over Sizzling Rice except that the shrimp are sautéed in a tangy tomato-based sauce.*

三 鮮 鍋 粑

120. Three Seafoods over Sizzling or Crispy Rice:
*This is prepared the same way as Shrimp over Sizzling Rice except that crab meat, shrimp and scallops are used.*

豆 瓣 帶 子

121. Scallops in Hot Bean Sauce:
*Quick-frozen medium scallops are marinated, quick-fried and sautéed in a spicy brown-bean sauce.*

魚 香 帶 子

122. Scallops with Fish-Fragrance:
*Quick-frozen medium scallops are marinated, quick-fried and sautéed with garlic and ginger in a spicy vinegar sauce.*

魚 香 酥 蟹

123. Fish-Fragrant Crab or Fried Crab with Szechwan Sauce:
*Crab pieces, in the shell, are dipped in flour, fried, then sautéed in a spicy vinegar sauce with garlic and ginger.*

魚 香 魷 魚

124. Fish-Fragrant Cuttlefish:
*Dehydrated brown cuttlefish slices are reconstituted by soaking, then sautéed in a spicy vinegar sauce. Cuttlefish have a chewy texture and a briny taste.*

金鈎魷魚

**125. Shredded Cuttlefish, or Cuttlefish with Chilies:**
*An assortment of shredded ingredients, such as dried cuttlefish, pork, and black mushrooms, is sautéed with bean sprouts, chives and red dried chilies.*

宮保魷魚

**126. *Kung Pao* Cuttlefish:**
*Small slices of cuttlefish are sautéed with red dried chilies and a spicy sauce.*

韭菜魷魚

**127. Sautéed Cuttlefish:**
*Shredded reconstituted dried cuttlefish, pork, bean sprouts and pungent yellow chives are sautéed together.*

魚香鮮魷

**128. Fish-Fragrant Squid or Squid in Chili-and-Garlic Sauce:**
*Slices of white squid are sautéed with garlic and ginger in a spicy vinegary sauce.*

## MAIN DISHES—VEGETABLES

Most Szechwan vegetable dishes are rich and spicy. If you want something lighter and not piquant, try a non-Szechwan dish of sautéed seasonal Chinese greens, such as *bok choy* or *gai lan*. These make refreshing side dishes for a Szechwan meal.

成都素燴

**129. Chengdu Assorted Vegetarian Dish, or Deluxe Vegetable Szechwan Style:**
*This is a dish of greens cooked with mushrooms and pieces of bean curd. Chinese greens such as* bok choy *or* choy sum *are sautéed with black mushrooms and bean curd or processed gluten.*

魚香茄子

**130. Fish-Fragrant Eggplant, or Shredded Pork with Eggplant and Chili, Sour-and-Garlic Sauce:**
*Chunks of peeled eggplant are sautéed in a spicy vinegary sauce with minced pork, garlic and ginger. The minced pork can be omitted if desired. You can also substitute black mushrooms for pork. This dish is especially good when the sweet long Oriental eggplant is used.*

椒油茄子

**131. Peppercorn Oil Eggplant:**
*Chunks of eggplant are fried and marinated in a soy-and-Szechwan-peppercorn-oil sauce.*

糖 醋 白 菜

**132. Sweet-Vinegar White Cabbage:**
*Strips of Chinese cabbage are braised with a sweet and tangy sauce of sugar, vinegar, Szechwan peppercorns and dried red chilies. This dish is served hot or cold.*

糖 醋 黃 瓜

**133. Sweet-Vinegar Cucumbers:**
*Cucumber chunks are pickled in a spicy sauce of sugar, ginger, soy sauce, green onions and dried red chilies. They are served chilled.*

乾 煸 四 季 豆

**134. Dry-Sautéed Green Beans:**
*Green or French beans are cut and sautéed with minced dried shrimp, preserved kohlrabi, chilies and minced pork.*

素 三 鮮

**135. Sautéed Three Vegetables, or Fried Snow Pea Pods with Chinese Mushrooms and Bamboo Shoots:**
*Seasonal Chinese vegetables, such as* bok choy *or snow peas, are sautéed with bamboo shoots and canned or black mushrooms.*

清 炒 時 菜

**136. Sautéed Seasonal Greens:**
*A variety of vegetables, such as* bok choy, *Chinese broccoli* (gai lan) *or* choy sum *may be used. They are sautéed in oil with salt and pepper. Although this dish is of Cantonese origin, it makes a wonderful vegetable accompaniment to a Szechwan meal.*

金鈎白菜

**137. Dried Shrimp and Cabbage:**
*Chinese white cabbage is sautéed until wilted with briny-smelling dried shrimp.*

乾燒菜心

**138. Dry-Sautéed *Choy Sum*, or Fried *Choy Sum* Style:**
*Choy sum, a southern vegetable like spinach, is sautéed with dried shrimp and green onions.*

乾燒冬筍

**139. Dry-Sautéed Bamboo Shoots, or Fried Bamboo Shoots Szechwan Style:**
*Bamboo shoots are sliced and braised with dried shrimp and green onions. This dish is refreshing when made with fresh bamboo shoots. Unfortunately, they are not readily available outside of Asia. Canned bamboo shoots are a poor substitute for the real thing.*

乾燒芥菜心

**140. Dry-Sautéed Mustard Greens:**
*Tender hearts of the slightly bitter mustard green are sautéed with dried shrimp and soy sauce.*

鳳尾青筍

**141. Green Bamboo Shoots:**
*Chunks of green bamboo shoots are cooked in broth and milk. This dish is seldom available because of the difficulty of procuring green bamboo shoots.*

口蘑蠶豆

**142. Mushrooms and Broad Beans:**
*Green broad beans are braised until soft with mushrooms, usually canned.*

麻辣黃瓜

**143. *Mah Lah* Cucumbers:**
*Cucumber chunks are marinated in salt, garlic and chili oil to create a hot and sour side dish that is served chilled or at room temperature.*

---

## SNACKS OR SIDE DISHES

---

Except for the Red-Oil Won Tons, these are noodle dishes with toppings. Any one makes a simple meal for one, but if you are in a group, you can order one or several as side dishes for your meal.

榨菜肉絲湯麵

**144. Kohlrabi and Shredded Pork over Noodles in Soup, or Szechwan Vegetable and Shredded-Pork Noodle Soup:**
*Spicy Szechwan preserved kohlrabi is shredded and sautéed with strips of pork, then served over thin noodles and broth. The salty, crunchy kohlrabi and chewy pork make a tasty topping for the plain noodles.*

擔擔麵

**145. *Dan Dan* Noodles, or Street Vendor's Noodles:**
*This is one of Szechwan's best-known dishes. Thin noodles*

*are topped with a variety of minced ingredients: garlic, peanuts, green onions, dried shrimp and preserved kohlrabi. The noodles are served with a little broth and a spicy peanut-butter sauce. Mix the topping with the noodles before eating.*

## 紅油牛筋麵

**146. Red-Cooked Beef Ligaments over Noodles, or Braised Spicy Beef Muscles with Noodles in Soup:**
*Beef ligaments are stewed until tender with dried red chilies and soy sauce, then served over thin noodles and broth. The ligaments, soft and gelatinous, provide a textural contrast to the firm noodles.*

## 紅燒牛肉麵

**147. Red-Cooked Beef over Noodles, or Braised Spicy Beef with Noodles in Soup:**
*This is a spicy beef stew cooked with red chilies, soy sauce and brown-bean sauce, and served over noodles and broth.*

## 四川芥菜牛肉麵

**148. Szechwan Beef and Celery over Noodles in Soup, or Noodle Soup with Beef and Celery:**
*A spicy beef stew is cooked with celery and served over thin noodles and broth.*

## 紅油抄手

**149. Red-Oil Won Tons, or Won Tons with Spicy Sauce:**
*These won tons are enlivened with a rich and spicy sauce. Pork-filled dumplings are boiled, drained and served with a spicy sauce of chili sauce and sesame paste or peanut butter.*

## DESSERTS

Szechwan desserts are often made with red-bean paste, sesame seeds, glutinous rice or combinations of these ingredients. For non-Chinese, they may require some getting used to. Fresh fruits provide the best finale to a Szechwan meal.

## 炸羊尾
### 150. Deep-Fried Lamb's Tail:
Red mung-bean paste, extremely sweet and rich, is shaped into small balls, dipped in an egg-white batter, then deep-fried. It is served dusted with white sugar. This dish is not widely available in restaurants.

## 芝麻包子
### 151. Sesame-Seeds Wrapped Buns:
Sesame seeds, crushed and mixed with sugar and fat, are wrapped in dough, rolled in crushed rice and steamed. This dish is not widely available in restaurants.

## 水果拼盤
### 152. Fresh Fruits:
A complimentary plate of oranges is sometimes served at the end of a Chinese meal. Better restaurants will, if requested, put together a fruit platter made up of seasonal fruits.

# CHAPTER NINE

# A Cantonese Dim Sum Menu

Cantonese dim sum is a popular cuisine among the Chinese. In a country of good food, dim sum, with its visual appeal and its inimitable atmosphere, can excite or rejuvenate even the most jaded diner.

Literally translated, "dim sum" means "to touch the heart." The meal is also known as "yum char" which means "to have tea accompanied by a few appetizers." Dim sum is actually a lunch consisting of an array of dainty and delicious Cantonese snacks served in an intriguing way: they are displayed on tea trolleys pushed around the dining area by dim sum waitresses, who call out the dish names in Cantonese. To order, you look at the dishes on the trolleys that pass by your table and indicate to the dim sum waitress the dishes you want.

This makes dim sum difficult to order for non-Chinese and first-timers. Go for your first dim sum with someone who has been before, or, better still, read this chapter before you go. So that you can identify the dishes by name, we have included the Cantonese pronunciations of dishes in quotation marks. If you have difficulty with the Cantonese, most waitresses should be able to tell you the English names of the dishes. Look them up in this menu to find out their contents. We have also included fairly detailed physical descriptions of the snacks.

Dim sum usually begins at 9:00 AM and winds down at about 3:00 PM. The ideal time to go is at around 11:00 AM or after 1:30 PM on a weekday. When you arrive at the restaurant, go to the reception desk, tell the manager how many of you are eating, and take a numbered card. Then wait until your number is called.

When you get a table, tell your waiter what kind of tea you want. Hot tea is the right drink for dim sum because the snacks are rich and somewhat greasy, and tea is an effective grease-cutter. (For details on tea, see page 26.) Allow the tea to steep for five minutes before pouring. If you need more water, just remove the teapot lid; this will signal the waiter.

When your waiter brings the tea, he will also bring a chili and yellow mustard dip, which is spicy and goes well with most savory dishes. Soy sauce is also a popular dip with many of the dishes.

Dim sum snacks are served on different kinds of trolleys, usually in covered bowls, in steamers or on small plates. Some dishes are served from specially heated trolleys. To order, wait for a dim sum waitress to come near, then signal to her to push her trolley close to your table. Find out what the dishes are, and ask the waitress to remove the lids so you can see the contents, if you want. The usual custom at dim sum is to wait for the waitress to come to you, not to take matters into your own hands by walking around the dining area in search of food. After putting your order on the table, the waitress will mark your bill for the waiter to tally up later.

Dim sum is better with a large group, say five or six people. This way you can sample a greater variety of dishes. When ordering, you may want to have large and small dishes. Most small dim sum dishes, such as *Ha Gow* (Shrimp Dumplings) and *Siu Mai* (Pork and Shrimp Dumplings), have three or four little items per serving; you may want to order two of them. The larger dishes, such as *Ngor Mai Guy* (Glutinous Rice Tamale with Chicken) and *Larp Chuen Guy Farn* (Chinese Sausage and Chicken over Rice), are more filling. They usually have one large item per serving, which can be shared among several people.

For easy recognition, the dim sum dishes are categorized by the different types of trolley on which they are served. The categories appear in this order: Steamer Trolley, Pan-Fried Dishes Trolley, Baked Dishes Trolley, Sautéed Dishes Trolley, Deep-Fried Dishes Trolley, Rice Casserole Trolley, Stuffed Rice Rolls Trolley, Blanched Dishes Trolley, Stewed Dishes Trolley and Dessert Trolley.

## STEAMER TROLLEY

There are two kinds of steamer trolley: little steamer and big steamer. The little steamer trolleys are piled high with stacks of little saucer-sized bamboo or stainless-steel steamers. In the steamers are a great variety of dishes, such as dumplings and stuffed rolls. The big steamer trolley has only one large round bamboo steamer on it. In this steamer are various kinds of steamed buns or "joan," glutinous rice tamales. The little steamer trolley dishes, numbers 1 to 30, are listed first.

蝦餃

### 1. "Ha Gow" — Shrimp Dumplings:
*Four to a steamer, these are tiny cresent-shaped dumplings made with a light translucent dough and a filling of minced shrimp, fatty pork and bamboo shoots. For special occasions, some restaurants will wrap these dumplings to resemble tiny rabbits or goldfish.*

# 燒 賣

**2. "Siu Mai" — Pork and Shrimp Dumplings:**
*These tiny muffin-shaped dumplings, made with won ton skins, are stuffed with minced marbled pork, shrimp, bamboo shoots and black mushrooms. The dumpling top is usually dotted with an orange-colored mixture or minced carrots. There are four dumplings per steamer.*

# 鵪 鶉 蛋 燒 賣

**3. "Um Chun Dahn Siu Mai" — Pork-and-Shrimp Dumplings with Quail Eggs:**
*In these dumplings, half a hard-boiled quail egg is added to the minced pork and shrimp stuffing. The dumplings are served upside down with the quail egg showing through the won ton skin. There are four dumplings per steamer.*

# 牛 肉 燒 賣

**4. "Ngow Yuk Siu Mai" — Beef Dumplings:**
*These dumplings are stuffed with ground beef. There are four dumplings per serving.*

# 北 菇 燒 賣

**5. "Buk Goo Siu Mai" — Pork-and-Shrimp Dumplings with Black Mushrooms:**
*In these dumplings whole black mushrooms cover the dumpling tops. Minced pork and shrimp are used in the stuffing.*

# 猪 潤 燒 賣

**6. "Gee Yuen Siu Mai" — Pork-and-Shrimp Dumplings with Pork Liver:**
*Minced pork and shrimp dumplings are served with a piece of pork liver. There are four dumplings per serving.*

粉果

7. "Fun Gwar" — Minced Pork and Dried Shrimp Dumplings:
*Three to a steamer, these white dumplings are shaped like a half moon. Light and bland, the dough is stuffed with minced pork, dried shrimp, bamboo shoots and Chinese parsley.*

潮州粉果

8. "Tsiu Tsow Fun Gwar" — *Chiu Chow* Minced Pork Dumplings:
*These are white, oval-shaped dumplings. White and bland, the thin dough is stuffed with minced pork, peanut and vegetable filling. There are three dumplings per serving.*

魚翅餃

9. "Yue Tze Gow" — Shark's Fin Dumplings:
*These are yellow oval-shaped dumplings with creases on the top. The dumplings are made with thin squares of won ton skin and are stuffed with minced shrimp, pork, carrot and Chinese parsley. Some traditional restaurants still add softened shark's fin to the filling. There are three dumplings per serving.*

鳳冠餃

10. "Fung Quoon Gow" — White Pork Dumplings:
*These white oval-shaped dumplings have creases at the top. A wheat-starch dough is rolled out thinly, cut into rounds, stuffed with minced pork, shrimp and vegetables, then wrapped and steamed. There are usually three dumplings per serving.*

## 灌湯餃

**11. "Quoon Tong Gow" — Broth Dumplings:**
*These are large yellow crescent-shaped dumplings with a soupy filling of minced pork, shrimp, crab meat and vegetables. There are two dumplings per serving and they are served in steamers on greased stainless-steel lifters. Lift the dumpling by the lifter and transfer it to your bowl before eating. A vinegar and shredded-ginger sauce is served on the side.*

## 韭菜包

**12. "Gow Choy Bow" — Chives Dumplings:**
*These are small round white dumplings filled with chives and minced pork. There are usually two dumplings per serving.*

## 豉汁排骨

**13. "See Jup Pai Qwat" — Spareribs with Black-Bean Sauce:**
*Small pieces of spareribs, still on the bone, are steamed with a black-bean sauce. They are served on small plates.*

## 梅子排骨

**14. "Mui Tze Pai Qwat" — Spareribs with Sour Plums:**
*Small pieces of spareribs are marinated and steamed with reddish-colored, tangy preserved sour plums. Some restaurants, use ketchup, unfortunately, instead of plums. The spareribs, still on the bone, are served on small plates.*

## 山竹牛肉

**15. "San Juk Ngow Yuk" — Steamed Beef Balls:**
*Seasoned ground beef is mixed with minced ginger and dried tangerine peels, shaped into large meatballs and steamed on strips of bean-curd skin. There are two meatballs per serving. Break up the meatballs with chopsticks before eating.*

## 蝦丸

**16. "Ha Yuen" — Steamed Shrimp Balls:**
Shrimp is mixed with minced water chestnut and fatty pork, shaped into small balls and steamed on small plates. There are two balls per serving. The shrimp balls are pinkish in color.

## 鷄絲或三絲粉卷

**17. "Guy See Fun Guen" or "Sarm See Fun Guen" — Shredded-Chicken Rice Rolls or Three Shredded Meats Rice Rolls:**
Shredded pork, chicken, shrimp and bamboo shoots are stuffed into canneloni-like rice noodles and steamed on small plates. The rolls have a slippery texture, and there are two rolls per serving.

## 鮮竹卷

**18. "Seen Juk Guen" — Bean-Curd Rolls:**
Pieces of bean-curd skin are stuffed with minced pork, shrimp and vegetables, rolled, deep-fried, then steamed on small plates with a sauce. There are two rolls per serving.

## 香茜瑤柱餃

**19. "Heung Sai You Chee Gow" — Parsley and Dried Scallop Dumplings:**
These crescent-shaped dumplings are made with a white wheat-starch dough and stuffed with minced pork, shredded dried scallops and Chinese parsley.

## 鳳爪

**20. "Fung Tsow" — Steamed Chicken's Feet:**
Whole declawed chicken's feet are cut, deep-fried and stewed in black-bean sauce. They are steamed on small plates. There are three to four pieces per serving.

鴨掌

21. "Arp Jeung" — Steamed Duck's Feet:
*Whole duck's feet, stewed tender in oyster sauce, are steamed on small plates.*

牛柏葉

22. "Ngow Ba Yip" — Steamed Omasun or Beef Stomach:
*Omasun, the white third stomach of the cow, is sliced, cooked until tender and steamed with black-bean sauce on small plates.*

牛肚

23. "Ngow Toe" — Steamed Tripe:
*Sliced honeycomb tripe is cooked until tender in a seasoned liquid and steamed on small plates. A small chili dip is served on the side.*

牛孖筋

24. "Ngow Ma Gun" — Steamed Beef Ligaments:
*Chunks of beef ligament, stewed until tender in a flavorful sauce, are steamed on small plates.*

芋頭糕

25. "Woo Tao Go" — Taro-Root Pudding:
*Mashed cooked taro roots are mixed with minced dry-cured pork, dried shrimp and green onion, then steamed into a large pudding and cut into squares. The pudding is purple-gray in color. To eat, break up with chopsticks and dip pieces in soy sauce.*

## 牛骨髓

**26. "Ngow Qwat Shiu" — Steamed Beef-Bone Marrow:**
*Strips of beef-bone marrow, cooked until tender in a flavorful sauce, are steamed on small plates.*

## 鶏扎

**27. "Guy Tsart" — Chicken Bundles:**
*Strips of marinated chicken, bamboo shoots, fish maw and barbecued pork are tied into small bundles with strips of dough and steamed on small plates. There are two bundles per serving.*

## 鴨脚扎

**28. "Arp Gurk Tsart" — Duck's Feet Bundles:**
*A duck's foot is tied into a small bundle together with slices of black mushroom and bamboo shoot, then steamed. Sometimes sliced liver or sea cucumbers are included in the bundle. There are two bundles per serving.*

## 鶏包仔

**29. "Guy Bow Tsai" — Steamed Small Chicken Buns:**
*These are small buns with a sweet dough and a minced chicken filling. There are two buns per serving.*

## 南乳猪手

**30. "Narm Yue Gee Sow" — Stewed Pig's Feet:**
*Pig's feet are cut into chunks, stewed with red preserved bean curds and steamed on small plates.*

The following dishes are served from the big steamer trolley. With steamed buns, there are usually two per serving.

## 叉 燒 包

**31. "Cha Siu Bow" — Steamed Barbecued Pork Buns:**
*These are white, fist-sized buns with a sweet dough and a diced barbecued pork filling. Break up a bun and dip in soy sauce before eating.*

## 鷄 包

**32. "Guy Bow" — Steamed Chicken Buns:**
*These buns are filled with chicken and black mushrooms.*

## 豆 沙 包

**33. "Dow Sa Bow" — Red-Bean Paste Buns:**
*These buns are filled with a sweet red-bean paste. A red dot on the top of this bun signifies that it is sweet, not savory.*

## 蔴 蓉 包

**34. "Ma Yung Bow" — Lotus-Seed Buns:**
*These buns are filled with a sweet sesame-seed paste and a lotus-seed paste. A red dot on the top of this bun signifies that it is sweet, not savory. When only lotus-seed paste is used as filling, the buns are called "Leen Yung Bow."*

## 腊 腸 卷

**35. "Larp Cheung Guen" — Steamed Chinese Sausage Rolls:**
*These are white rolls stuffed with pieces of sweet Chinese sausage. You can see the sausage sticking out at both ends. There are two rolls per serving.*

糯 米 卷

36. "Ngor Mai Guen" — Glutinous Rice Rolls:
*This is a white bread roll stuffed with a sautéed glutinous rice and minced Chinese-sausage filling, then steamed. There is one roll per serving. Sometimes the roll is served as a round bun. It is then called "Ngor Mai Bow."*

裹 蒸 粽

37. "Gwar Jing Joan" — Glutinous Rice Tamale or Pudding:
*This is a large pyramid-shaped glutinous-rice tamale stuffed with a mixture of salted pork, barbecued pork, split peas, black mushrooms and salty duck egg yolk. The tamale is wrapped in bamboo leaves, tied with string and steamed. The waitress unwraps the leaves and drizzles the rice with soy sauce. There is one tamale per serving.*

糯 米 鷄

38. "Ngor Mai Guy" — Glutinous Rice Tamale with Chicken:
*This is a square lotus-leaf package made of glutinous rice, stuffed with minced chicken, pork and vegetables. The package is steamed and served at room temperature. The waitress cuts open the leaves and drizzles the rice with soy-based sauce. There is one tamale per serving.*

鹹 肉 粽

39. "Harm Yuk Joan" — Salty Pork and Glutinous Rice Tamale, or Sweet Rice Wrap with Pork:
*Glutinous rice, stuffed with salted pork, is wrapped in bamboo leaves, then boiled. Unwrap the leaves and sprinkle rice with soy sauce to eat.*

## PAN-FRIED DISHES TROLLEY

The pan-fried trolley has two shelves. The lower shelf, which is actually a frying surface, is about waist level. The higher shelf, which is several feet above, is stacked with different dim sum items. When an order comes in, the waitress transfers the items to the frying surface and pan-fries the items to a golden brown.

蘿蔔糕

### 40. "Law Bark Go" — Chinese Radish Pudding Slices or Turnip Cake:
*Shredded pungent white Chinese radishes are mixed in a batter with minced Chinese sausages and green onions, then steamed in a cake pan. The cooled pudding is sliced and pan-fried. Sprinkle with soy sauce before eating. There are two slices per serving.*

鍋貼

### 41. "War Tip" — Pan-Fried Northern Chinese Perogies:
*Though northern Chinese, these perogies are often served at dim sum. They are crescent-shaped, with folds on one side of the dumplings. A flour-and-water dough is rolled out thin, cut into small rounds and stuffed with a minced pork and vegetable filling. The dumplings are folded and pan-fried until crunchy at the bottom; the top remains soft and pliable. There are three dumplings per order. Worcestershire sauce is usually served on the side.*

釀青椒

### 42. "Yeung La Jeel" — Stuffed Green Peppers:
*Green bell peppers are stuffed with ground fish meat, and*

*pan-fried. A black-bean sauce is sometimes drizzled over the cooked peppers. There are three peppers per serving.*

## 釀豆腐

**43. "Yeung Dow Foo" — Stuffed Bean Curds:**
*Triangular pieces of bean curd are hollowed out, stuffed with seasoned ground fish meat, then fried. A black-bean sauce is drizzled over the fried bean curds. There are two or three pieces of bean curd per serving.*

## 釀矮瓜

**44. "Yeung Ngai Gwa" — Stuffed Eggplant Slices:**
*Seasoned ground fish meat is sandwiched between two eggplant slices, pan-fried, then served with a black-bean sauce. There are two per serving.*

## 煎鮮竹卷

**45. "Jeen Seen Juk Guen: — Pan-Fried Bean-Curd Rolls:**
*Pieces of bean-curd skin are stuffed and rolled with shredded pork and vegetables. They are then pan-fried until golden brown. The rolls are egg-colored.*

## 腸粉

**46. "Cheung Fun" — Pan-Fried Speckled Rice Rolls:**
*These are long white rice noodles speckled with green onions and dried shrimp. They are pan-fried until slightly brown and served with soy sauce, sesame seeds,* hoi sin *and chili sauces. The rice noodles are crunchy and slippery.*

## 炒銀針粉

**47. "Chow Ngun Jum Fun" — Pan-Fried Needle-Like Rice Noodles:**
*These inch-long round rice noodles have pointed ends. They are sautéed with shredded pork and vegetables. Sometimes*

they are already fried, and are served in small glass bowls; sometimes they are heaped on the heated surface of the trolley. The waitress pan-fries and ladles out individual portions as she pushes the trolley along.

## 炒米粉
### 48. "Chow Mai Fun" — Pan-Fried Vermicelli-Sized Rice Noodles:
The noodles are pan-fried with shredded pork and vegetables on the heated surface of the trolley and served in small portions.

# BAKED DISHES TROLLEY

Baked goods on the Baked Dishes Trolley are served uncovered, on medium-sized plates, usually two to a serving. The dishes are baked in the kitchen and served warm or at room temperature.

## 焗叉燒包
### 49. "Goak Cha Siu Bow" — Baked Barbecued Pork Buns:
These baked round buns have a slightly sweet barbecued pork filling. The buns are brown with shiny glazed tops.

## 叉燒酥
### 50. "Cha Siu So" — Barbecued Pork Pies:
Made with shortening and flour, these half-moon-shaped pies with crumbly crusts are filled with shredded barbecued pork. The pies are baked until golden brown.

咖喱角

**51. "Gar Lei Gork" — Curry Beef Puffs:**
These are half-moon-shaped small pies made with a puff pastry and stuffed with a curry-flavored minced-beef filling. The pies are baked until golden brown. The pastry is flaky but very rich.

鷄撻

**52. "Guy Tard" — Chicken Tarts:**
These small pies have a crumbly crust and are filled with chicken and black mushrooms. The pies are baked until golden brown.

叉燒撻

**53. "Cha Siu Tard" — Barbecued Pork Tart:**
These are similar to the Chicken Tarts, above, except a slightly sweet barbecued pork filling is used.

## SAUTÉED DISHES TROLLEY

The sautéed dishes trolley has a frying pan or small wok heated by a hot plate.

豉椒蜆

**54. "See Jill Heen" — Black-Bean Clams:**
Clams, still in the shell, are sautéed in black-bean sauce. They are ladled from the wok onto small plates.

炒東風螺

55. "Chow Dong Fung Law" — Sautéed Snails:
*Shelled snails are sautéed in black-bean sauce or oyster sauce. They are served on small plates.*

---

## DEEP-FRIED DISHES TROLLEY

---

These dishes are deep-fried in the kitchen and served slightly warm or at room temperature, on medium-sized plates. They are usually displayed without covers on the trolley.

春卷

56. "Chuen Guen" — Spring Rolls:
*Long rolls are stuffed with shredded pork and vegetables, then fried until crispy. There are two rolls per serving. To prepare your order, the waitress cuts the rolls into sections and then asks you whether you want Worcestershire sauce sprinkled over the rolls.*

芋角

57. "Woo Gork" — Taro-Root Dumplings:
*These long oval dumplings are reddish-brown and have a lacey appearance. Mashed taro root and flour are mixed together and pressed into small round shapes, then stuffed with minced pork and vegetable filling, folded and deep-fried. The filling is lightly flavored with five spices. Cut the dumplings in half before eating.*

# 蝦多士

**58. "Ha Dor See" — Shrimp Toasts:**
*Pieces of bread are smeared with a raw shrimp paste, cut into small triangles, then deep-fried to a golden brown. The toasts are sometimes topped with sesame seeds or sprigs of Chinese parsley. There are three toasts per serving.*

# 炸蝦丸

**59. "Jar Ha Yuen" — Fried Shrimp Balls:**
*Shrimp, water chestnuts and fatty pork are minced, shaped into balls and deep-fried.*

# 鹹水角

**60. "Harm Shiu Gork" — Salty Water Dumplings:**
*These are half-moon-shaped dumplings with a glutinous-rice-flour dough and a filling of minced pork and vegetables. The filling is lightly flavored with five-spices powder. The dumplings, deep-fried to a golden brown, are crunchy on the outside and slightly sticky.*

# 炸雲吞

**61. "Jar Wun Tun" — Deep-Fried Won Tons:**
*Ravioli-like dumplings are stuffed with minced pork and deep-fried to a golden brown. A sweet-and-sour dip is served on the side or over the won tons.*

# 蝦盒

**62. "Ha Hup" — Shrimp Rounds:**
*Minced pork and shrimp are sandwiched between two small pieces of thin round dough, sealed and deep-fried until golden brown.*

## 鮻魚球

**63. "Lang Yue Kow" — Fried Fish Balls:**
Carp meat is ground up, shaped into small balls and deep-fried. They are served over shredded lettuce, sometimes with tiny preserved salty clams. There are usually four fish balls per serving.

## 紙包鷄

**64. "Tze Bow Guy" — Paper-Wrapped Chicken:**
Boned, bite-sized pieces of marinated chicken meat are layered with bamboo shoots and green onions, and wrapped either in small pieces of parchment paper or in edible wafers. The packages are deep-fried to a golden brown. The edible wafer is crunchy and light. If parchment paper is used, unwrap before eating.

## 炸鮮魷

**65. "Jar Seen Yow" — Fried Squid:**
Squid slices are dipped in seasoned flour and deep-fried. They are usually served with a vinegar dip on the side.

## 煎粉果

**66. "Jeen Fun Gwar" — Fried Minced Pork and Dried Shrimp Dumplings:**
These are half-moon-shaped dumplings stuffed with minced pork, dried shrimp, shrimp and vegetables. The flour-and-water dough is rolled out thinly, cut into small rounds and stuffed with the filling. The dumplings are folded, then fried until golden brown. There are usually three dumplings per serving. They are served with a bowl of broth on the side. Dip dumplings in broth before eating.

釀蟹拑

**67. "Yeung Hi Keem"** — **Stuffed Crab Claws:**
*Crab claws are wrapped with a shrimp-meat mixture and deep-fried. There are two claws per serving. Some restaurants serve this dish with a* hoi sin *dip.*

炒糯米飯

**68. "Chow Ngor Mai Farn"** — **Sautéed Glutinous Rice:**
*Although this dish is sautéed, it is usually found on the Deep-Fried Dishes Trolley. Round sticky glutinous rice is sautéed with minced Chinese sausages, diced vegetables and soy sauce, then served in a small glass bowl.*

---

# RICE CASSEROLE TROLLEY

---

The Rice Casserole Trolley is filled with casseroles of rice, which are served with different toppings. The casseroles, deep round ceramic containers, are four inches high with a three-inch diameter. Steamed rice is placed at the bottom of the casserole and the topping is placed on top. Rice casseroles are usually covered, to keep them warm. To eat: transfer topping to a separate plate, spoon rice into your rice bowl and then take small portions of the topping with your rice.

腊腸鷄飯

**69. "Larp Chuen Guy Farn"** — **Chinese Sausage and Chicken over Rice:**
*A piece of Chinese sausage and marinated pieces of chicken, still on the bone, are steamed over a casserole of rice.*

## 排 骨 飯

70. "Pai Qwat Farn" — Spareribs over Rice:
*Marinated pieces of spareribs, still on the bone, are steamed over a casserole of rice.*

## 葡 國 雞 飯

71. "Po Gork Guy Farn" — Macao or Portuguese Chicken over Rice:
*Chicken pieces, onions, carrots and potatoes are cooked in a curry-coconut sauce, and baked over rice in a casserole.*

---

# STUFFED RICE ROLLS TROLLEY

---

Stuffed rice rolls are served on medium-sized plates and covered to keep them warm. The waitress will drizzle your rolls with a soy-based sauce. Stuffed rice rolls look like stuffed canneloni, except that they are white and have a limp, slippery texture. Break them up into sections with chopsticks before eating. There are two rolls per serving.

## 牛 肉 腸 粉

72. "Ngow Yuk Cheung Fun" — Beef-Stuffed Rice Rolls:
*White rice noodles are stuffed with marinated minced beef, then steamed.*

## 叉 燒 腸 粉

73. "Cha Siu Cheung Fun" — Barbecued Pork-Stuffed Rice Rolls:
*White rice noodles are stuffed with shredded barbecued pork, then steamed.*

# 蝦腸粉

**74. "Ha Cheung Fun" — Shrimp-Stuffed Rice Rolls:**
White rice noodles are stuffed with marinated shrimp, then steamed.

---

## BLANCHED DISHES TROLLEY

---

This trolley has one or two basins of heated water, used to blanch ingredients. The different ingredients are stacked on a shelf over the basins. When an order comes in, the waitress blanches the ingredients in the heated water, transfers them to a plate and drizzles them with a sauce.

# 菜心或芥蘭

**75. "Choy Sum" or "Gai Lan" — Chinese Greens:**
This is always a good choice, as vegetable dishes are seldom available at a dim sum. Long stalks of choy sum or gai lan are blanched and served with a soy-based sauce.

# 白灼牛肚

**76. "Ngow Toe" — Blanched Honeycomb Tripe:**
Slices of honeycomb tripe are blanched and served with a black-bean dip. The tripe is beige and chewy. It has a honeycomb pattern on one side.

# 白灼牛栢葉

**77. "Ngow Ba Yip" — Blanched Omasun:**
Omasun, the cow's third stomach, is sliced, blanched and served with a black-bean sauce. Omasun is white and chewy.

白灼魷魚

78. "Yow Yue" — Blanched Cuttlefish:
*Dried cuttlefish is reconstituted, then sliced. It has a chewy texture. For dim sum, it is blanched and served with soy and green-onion dip.*

白灼猪潤

79. "Gee Yuen" — Blanched Pork Liver:
*Sliced pork liver is blanched and served with a soy-based sauce.*

白灼猪腰

80. "Gee Yeel" — Blanched Pork Kidney:
*Sliced pork kidney is blanched and served with a soy-based sauce.*

韭菜花猪紅

81. "Gow Choy Far Gee Hung" — Blanched Pig's Blood with Chives:
*Pig's blood is steamed, then cut into cubes. It is then mixed with chives, blanched and served with a soy-based sauce. Pig's blood cubes have a curd-like texture and are very rich.*

## STEWED DISHES TROLLEY

This trolley usually has three heated compartments, each with a different stewed dish. When an order comes in the waitress ladles out the hot contents into small bowls.

牛什

82. "Ngow Jarp" — Assorted Beef Organs:
*Sliced beef tripe, omasun, lung and spleen are sliced and stewed until tender in a savory sauce. Sometimes Chinese white radishes are added. A chili dip is served on the side.*

牛腩

83. "Ngow Narm" — Stewed Beef Brisket:
*Chunks of beef brisket are stewed until tender in a savory sauce with Chinese radishes. They are served hot in small glass bowls. This dish goes well with steamed rice. (Order the rice from the waiter.)*

咖喱牛腩

84. "Gar Lei Ngow Narm" — Curry Beef Brisket:
*Chunks of beef brisket are stewed until tender in a curry sauce. Steamed rice is sometimes served with this dish.*

猪皮蘿蔔

85. "Gee Pay Law Bak" — Pork Rinds and Chinese Radishes:
*Reconstituted dried pork rinds are sliced, then cooked until tender and spongy with Chinese radishes.*

猪 脚 羌

86. "Gee Gurk Gurn" — Pig's Feet with Ginger:
*Chunks of pig's feet are stewed until tender in dark soy sauce with ginger roots.*

皮 蛋 瘦 肉 粥

87. "Pei Dahn Sow Yuk Joke" — Preserved Black Duck Egg and Pork *Congee:*
*Chunks of preserved black duck eggs and salted pork are served in a bowl of hot* congee. *This dish is served steaming hot by the bowl.*

咖 喱 鱿 鱼

88. "Gar Lei Yow Yue" — Curry Cuttlefish:
*Dried cuttlefish slices are reconstituted, then stewed in a curry sauce.*

# DESSERT TROLLEY

Dim Sum desserts are usually served chilled or at room temperature. They may be displayed on regular trolleys or in glassed-in trolleys to prevent the dishes from drying out.

## 馬拉糕

**89. "Ma Lai Go"** — Steamed Sponge Cake:
*Served in a three-inch square, this is a steamed cake made with eggs, flour and brown sugar. The cake, spongy and light brown, is light and sweet but somewhat bland.*

## 馬蹄糕

**90. "Ma Tai Go"** — Water-Chestnut Pudding Slices:
*Minced water chestnuts are mixed in a batter with water-chestnut flour, poured into a cake tin and steamed. The pudding, sweet and greenish-yellow, is sliced and served at room temperature. Sometimes the slices are pan-fried. The pudding is sweet, slightly crunchy but bland. There are two slices per serving.*

## 煎年糕

**91. "Jeen Neen Go"** — Pan-Fried Glutinous Rice Pudding:
*Glutinous rice flour, brown sugar and shortening are mixed into a batter, poured into a cake tin and steamed. The pudding, dark brown with a sticky consistency, is sliced and pan-fried. There are two slices per serving.*

開口笑或笑口棗

**92. "Hoi How Sieu" — Fried Round Cookies:**
*Eggs, flour and sugar are made into a batter, shaped into small balls, rolled in sesame seeds and deep-fried. The cookies are about two inches in diameter. Sometimes they are one inch in diameter, and called "Sieu How Joe."*

馬仔

**93. "Ma Jai" — Chinese Crispies:**
*This dessert looks like Rice Krispies squares. An egg-and-flour dough is rolled out thin, shredded and deep-fried. The crunchy strips are coated in syrup and sesame seeds, pressed into a large square mold, cooled and cut into squares.*

蛋撻

**94. "Dahn Tard" — Custard Tart:**
*Small tarts made of flaky pastry are filled with egg custard, then baked until golden brown. The pastry is light and the filling soft and sweet. Served warm, this dish has two tarts per serving.*

煎堆

**95. "Jeen Doi" — Fried Sesame Balls:**
*These are deep-fried glutinous rice balls with a sesame-seed coating. The balls are stuffed with red-bean or lotus-seed paste, wrapped into balls, rolled in sesame seeds and fried until golden brown. The dough is sticky and crunchy and the filling sweet. There are two or three balls per serving.*

糯米糍

**96. "Ngor Mai Tze" — Glutinous Rice Coconut Balls:**
*Small rounds of dough made with glutinous rice flour are filled with coconut and chopped nuts, steamed and rolled in*

*coconut flakes. Marachino cherries are often used to garnish the balls. Coconut balls are soft and stick to the teeth.*

沙翁

97. "Sar Yung" — Deep Fried Puffs:
*Eggs and flour are mixed into a batter, shaped into balls, deep-fried and dusted with white sugar.*

芝蔴糊

98. "Tze Ma Woo" — Black Sesame-Seed Soup:
*Black sesame seeds are ground and cooked into a thick, black fragrant soup with sugar and water. This dish is usually served hot in a rice bowl from a heated trolley.*

三色啫喱

99. "Sam Sic Jair Lei" — Tricolored Jelly:
*Three kinds of gelatin, each with a different flavor and color, are chilled one on top of the other and served cut into small oblong pieces. At dim sum, many kinds of layered gelatin or gelatin with fruit are available, each with a different color, flavor or fruit added to it.*

豆腐花

100. "Dow Foo Far" — Soybean Curds:
*Soybean milk is cooked, then coagulated to a soft curd. It is served hot or cold in a rice bowl and topped with brown sugar or sugared water. Mix well before eating.*

蛋撒

101. "Dahn Sarn" — Fried Glazed Cookies:
*An egg-and-flour dough is rolled out thin, cut into thin strips and deep-fried until golden brown. The crunchy strips are then glazed with syrup.*

## 椰 汁 糕

**102. "Yeh Jup Go" — Coconut Jelly:**
Coconut milk, gelatin and beaten egg whites are folded together and chilled into a jelly, which is then cut into squares. The jelly is white, has a strong coconut flavor and melts in your mouth.

## 紅 豆 糕

**103. "Hung Dow Go" — Red Mung-Bean Pudding Slices:**
Red mung beans are cooked with sugar and water, thickened and chilled in a cake tin, then sliced. There are two slices per serving.

## 豆 沙 粽

**104. "Dow Sar Joan" — Glutinous Rice Tamale with Red-Bean Paste Filling:**
Glutinous rice, stuffed with sweet red-bean paste, is wrapped in bamboo leaves, boiled and served warm. The waitress unwraps the bamboo leaves, which are not edible. Break the tamale up with chopsticks before eating.

## 千 層 糕

**105. "Tseen Chun Go" — Thousand Layer Cake:**
This steamed white multilayered cake is stuffed and steamed with shortening and shredded candied fruits. It is cut in diamond-shaped pieces.

## 皮 蛋 酥

**106. "Pei Dahn So" — Preserved Duck Egg Pies:**
A flour-and-shortening pastry is rolled out thick, cut into small rounds and stuffed with a mixture of lotus-seed paste, shredded pickled pink ginger and preserved black duck eggs. It is wrapped to form small round buns and baked to a

*golden brown. The pie has a crumbly crust and a slightly salty filling. There are two pies per serving.*

# 梘水粽

**107. "Garn Sui Joan"** — Translucent Glutinous Rice Tamale, or Sweet Rice Wrap:
*Glutinous rice, specially treated in a lye solution so that the rice becomes translucent, is wrapped in bamboo leaves, boiled and served hot. To eat, unwrap leaves, which are inedible, and sprinkle rice with white sugar. There is one tamale per serving. Break up into pieces before eating.*

# 九層糕

**108. "Gow Chun Go"** — Nine Layer Cake:
*This cake is made with two kinds of batter. One is white and made with milk; the other is pink and made with a red-colored rice mixture. The layers are steamed one at a time then placed one on top of the other. Then the cake is cooled and cut into squares.*

# 蓮蓉水晶餅

**109. "Leen Yung Sioy Jing Bang"** — Transparent Cake:
*A translucent glutinous rice dough is cut into rounds and stuffed with lotus-seed paste and a salty duck egg yolk. The cake is wrapped, then pressed into a cookie mold. A pattern is stamped on the top, then the cake is steamed.*

# 西米卷筒糕

**110. "Sai Mai Guen Tone Go"** — Tapioca Rolled Cake:
*Tapioca is layered and steamed with an egg-white batter and red-bean paste. The cake is then rolled up, chilled and sliced.*

## 蔗汁糕

**111. "Jare Jup Go" — Sugar-Cane Pudding:**
Sugar-cane juice and water-chestnut flour are cooked to a thick paste, chilled in a mold and cut into thick slices. The pudding is grayish-beige and there are two slices per serving.

## 蓮蓉酥盒

**112. "Leen Yung So Hup" — Lotus-Seed Paste Stuffed Fried Pies:**
These half-moon-shaped pies are made with a flaky pastry and a coconut and peanut stuffing. The wrapped pies are deep-fried until golden brown and served at room temperature.

## 豆沙百合酥

**113. "Dow Sa Bak Hup So" — Red-Bean Paste Stuffed Fried Pies:**
Small round pieces of flaky pastry are stuffed with sweet red-bean paste or with lotus-seed paste, wrapped into round or crescent-shaped buns, cut in a crisscross pattern on top and deep-fried. Because of the cuts, the fried pie opens up like a flower. Some restaurants add food coloring to the pastry to make it more colorful. The pies are cut to resemble certain flowers, such as chrysanthemums or lotus flowers.

## 白糖糕

**114. "Bak Tong Go" — White Sugared Pudding Slices:**
Rice flour, sugar and baking powder are mixed to form a soft dough. Sugar water, egg whites and wheat starch are added and the dough is allowed to rise to a spongy mass. Then it is steamed, cooled and cut into thick pieces. The slices are sweet, sticky, spongy and slightly sour in taste.

## 糯米糖藕

**115. "Ngor Mai Tong Ngow" — Glutinous Rice Stuffed Lotus Root:**
A large lotus root is stuffed with glutinous rice and steamed.

The root is then cut into thick slices and served with a clear syrup. Lotus root is crunchy but bland. There are two slices per serving.

## 蒸蛋糕

**116. "Jing Dahn Go" — Steamed Cake:**
An egg, sugar and flour batter is poured into a cake tin, steamed, and garnished with chunks of salty duck egg yolk and Chinese parsley sprigs.

## 八寶糯米飯

**117. "Bak Bo Ngor Mai Farn" — Stuffed Glutinous Rice Molds:**
Glutinous rice, garnished with candied fruits and stuffed with red-bean paste, is steamed in rice bowls. There is one mold per serving. To eat, break up the mold.

## 豆沙班戟卷

**118. "Dow Sar Barn Gig Guen" — Red-Bean Paste Stuffed Pancake:**
A thin pancake is wrapped into a roll with a sweet red-bean paste stuffing. There are two rolls per serving.

## 布丁

**119. "Bo Deen" — Strawberry, Mango or Chocolate Milk Pudding:**
This is a chilled milk pudding, served in a small glass bowl. It is flavored with strawberry, mango or chocolate and garnished with fresh fruits.

## 鮮奶馬荳糕

**120. "Ma Dow Go" — Yellow Split-Pea Pudding:**
This is a two-inch cube of white gelatin speckled with yellow split peas. Served chilled, it is sweet but bland.

# GLOSSARY

**Abalone:** *There are three kinds—fresh, canned and dried. Fresh abalone, about five inches in diameter, is usually fresh-frozen in the shell. It has a firm, supple texture. Abalone is cooked in a seasoned broth before it is canned. Dried abalone, which comes from Japan, is considered a delicacy and is expensive.*

**Angled or ridged squash:** *This long thin cucumber-like ridged squash has a white interior and a dark-green skin which has to be peeled. It tastes like zucchini.*

**Anhwei (or Anhui):** *A province in Eastern China*

**Baby corn:** *This is a miniature corn sold fresh or canned. The whole ear is edible.*

**Bamboo leaves:** *These long, dried, faded-green leaves are used to wrap Chinese tamales. They give a herbal flavor to the food wrapped in them.*

**Bamboo shoots:** *The large round tips of enormous bamboo trees are sold either fresh or canned. Canned bamboo shoots are peeled and cut in chunks. They are crunchy but have little flavor and are most commonly used in restaurants. Fresh bamboo shoots have a tasty milky flavor. They are about five inches long with a three-inch diameter. They are covered by overlapping brown leaves, which have to be removed.*

**Bean sauce or brown bean sauce:** *This is a brown salty bottled bean sauce made with fermented soybeans. Each different regional cuisine has its own variety of bean sauce. It is used to flavor stews and braised dishes.*

**Bean curd:** *Made from coagulated soybean milk, bean curd is usually sold fresh, cut in three-inch squares. Bean curd has a smooth, slightly beany taste and a high protein and calcium content.*

**Bean-curd skins:** *Made from soybean milk, these come dehydrated in yellow sheets or in sticks. Bean curd sheets are also available frozen.*

**Bean sprouts:** *These are the sprouts of either mung beans or soybeans. See green mung beans and soybean sprouts.*

**Bean-thread noodles:** *Made from green mung beans, these are dried thin white noodles. They are soaked, softened and added to soups, or deep-fried into crunchy noodles. They are also called cellophane noodles or bean vermicelli.*

# GLOSSARY

**Bear's paws:** *A stewed dish using just the paws of a bear, served in Imperial times to please the emperors. This dish is still served, but only for very special banquets.*

**Beef bone marrow:** *Prized for its texture, the marrow extracted from beef bones comes in soft silky strips.*

**Bird's nest:** *Two different dishes are called by this name. The first, which looks like a bird's nest, is a deep-fried shoestring potato basket or a taro-root basket with a sautéed filling. This dish is also sometimes called a phoenix nest. The second dish is made with an ingredient that actually comes from a bird's nest—hardened bird's saliva. This is an expensive dehydrated ingredient, which requires elaborate preparation: it is cleaned and slow-cooked, and is usually served in a thick soup. It tastes like noodles and is believed to enhance health.*

**Bitter melon:** *A pale-green cucumber-like squash with bumpy skin, the melon has a bitter taste and is believed to cool the body.*

**Black beans:** *Fermented black soybeans have a pungent aroma and salty taste. Sold dried or bottled in liquid, they are used to flavor food.*

**Black fungus or fungi:** *See* fungi.

**Black moss:** *Black hair-like dried moss, which is softened in water, is used in vegetarian dishes.*

**Black mushrooms:** *Dried large black mushrooms have a strong mushroom taste and a supple texture. Only the caps are eaten.*

**Black sesame seeds:** *Black-colored sesame seeds are used mostly in desserts.*

**Bok choy:** *This succulent vegetable has white stems and jade-green leaves.*

**Broad or fava beans:** *There are two kinds: green broad beans, which are usually sold frozen, and brown broad beans, which are sold dried. The first are sautéed; the second are soaked and slow-cooked.*

**Camel's hump:** *A stewed dish using only the hump of a camel, this specialty was served in Imperial times to please the emperors. It is still served, but only for very rare and special banquets.*

**Canton (or Guangzhou or Kwangchow):** *A southern seaport, capital of Kwangtung (Guangdong) province.*

**Cassia bark:** *see* Cinnamon bark.

**Cassia flowers:** *Called* gwai far *in Chinese, these are small yellow flowers that grow in clusters on tree branches. They are native to south China and have a beautiful scent. The flowers are used to flavor sweets.*

**Caul:** *A webbed thin piece of animal fat; it is used to wrap ingredients to make rolls.*

**Chang choy:** *See* choy sum.

**Chekiang:** *A province in east coastal China; its capital is Hangchow (Hangzhou).*

**Chengdu (or Chengtu):** *The capital of Szechwan, in central China.*

**Cheung fun:** *These long slippery rice noodles are speckled with dried shrimp and green onions.*

**Chiang qua:** *A light brown bottled pickle, which is salty and crunchy, it is used in sautéed dishes and as a side dish.*

**Chicken testicles:** *These are yellowish, small, kidney-shaped and have a marbled pattern. They are believed to have an aphrodisiac effect.*

**Chili sauce:** *This is a spicy dip. Cantonese chili sauce is an orange-colored fine paste. The other regional cuisines have a grainier chili paste, made with chili flakes and brown bean sauce.*

**Chi hau sauce:** *A savory sauce used to flavor Cantonese meat dishes, it is slightly sweet and has a hint of* hoi sin *sauce.*

**Chin jew:** *See* Szechwan peppercorn.

**Chinese box thorn:** *This vegetable has a thorny stem and small oval green leaves. The leaves are picked and cooked. They taste like watercress and smell like herbs.*

**Chinese cabbage (or Tientsin cabbage or** *siu choy***):** *This is a long white vegetable with white or light green overlapping leaves. It is sweeter and more watery than Western cabbage.*

**Chinese clover:** *A delicate clover prized by the Shanghainese, it tastes like watercress.*

**Chinese ginger powder:** *It is made with a special kind of ginger powder and white-pepper powder.*

**Chinese greens:** *This usually means either* choy sum *or* gai lan.

**Chinese ham:** *This dry-cured ham is salty and chewy.*

**Chinese parsley:** *A pungent, wild-tasting herb, it is also called cilantro or fresh coriander.*

# GLOSSARY

**Chinese radish or white radish:** *Also called daikon or Chinese turnip, this is a white, tube-shaped root vegetable. It can be eaten raw or cooked and has a pungent flavor, like cabbage.*

**Chinese sausage:** *There are two kinds. One is made with pork and is colored red. The other is made with pork and liver and is brown. Chinese sausages are chewy and slightly sweet.*

**Chiu Chow:** *A seafaring people who live in South China, in and around Swatow (Shantou), a seaport about 170 miles east of Canton.*

**Chives:** *Chinese chives are flat-bladed and more pungent than Western chives. Yellow chives are grown in darkness and are very pungent; the less pungent jade-green chives taste more like Western chives.*

**Chop suey:** *A Chinese-American dish of sautéed vegetables, it usually consists of sliced carrot, broccoli, bok choy, onions and green peppers.*

**Chow fun:** *A dish of sautéed flat rice noodles, it usually comes with shredded meat and vegetables.*

**Chow mein:** *A dish of sautéed or pan-fried noodles usually topped with a meat or seafood mixture.*

**Choy sum:** *This Chinese vegetable has light green stems and leaves and yellow flowers. The whole vegetable, including the flowers, is edible. Also known as* chang choy.

**Cinnamon bark:** *Similar to a cinnamon stick in appearance and flavor, but it has a thicker and rougher skin. It is broken up and added to seasoned liquids. It has a mixed clove and cinnamon flavor.*

**Conch:** *This is a sea mollusk with supple meat and a large spinal shell.*

**Congee (or conjee):** *A hot smooth porridge made of rice, it is usually served with sliced meat or seafood. It is called* joke *in Chinese.*

**Cuttlefish:** *This is a brown, dried, large squid-like shellfish prized for its chewiness and flavor. It is soaked, sliced, then sautéed or added to soups.*

**Dim Sum:** *Literally translated, the words mean to touch the heart. Dim sum used to mean a between-meals snack. Now, it is often used to describe a Cantonese brunch consisting of a variety of snacks and appetizers, which are pushed around on trolleys by waitresses.*

**Dragon Well tea:** *Also called* lung jang *tea, it is a green fragrant tea. It is also used in some Shanghai dishes.*

**Dried oysters:** *Shelled, dark brown dried oysters which have a chewy texture and slight oyster taste. They are added to stews, or minced, then sautéed.*

**Dried pork ligaments:** *Yellow in color, these have a crunchy, chewy texture after prolonged cooking.*

Dried scallops: *These are dried, orange-colored small scallops which are added to soups, or shredded, then sautéed. They have a salty seafood flavor.*

Dried shrimp: *These are small shrimp that have been salted and dried. They have a strong fishy taste.*

Dried tangerine peels: *Used in stews and to flavor meats, they are soaked and softened for cooking.*

Dry-cured duck or pressed duck: *A whole duck is flattened, salted and dry-cured. It is beige and sold whole or in large pieces. It is usually added to boiling rice for flavor. It is chewy and tastes like ham.*

Dry-cured pork: *Strips of marbled pork belly are salted, dry-cured, tied on strings and hung. They are dark brown in color and quite fatty. This pork is sliced and added to boiling rice for flavor.*

E Mein: *Round deep-fried egg noodles, they have a delicate taste and crinkly texture.*

Eel: *There are two kinds used in Chinese cooking: white or large eel, similar to European eels, and yellow slender eel, which resembles a small snake. The white eel is meaty and served in chunks. The yellow eel is boned first, then sliced or shredded and sautéed with lots of garlic. It has a firm, supple texture.*

Eggs foo yung: *This Chinese-American dish is an omelet stuffed with sautéed bean sprouts and shredded pork.*

Far dew: *See glutinous rice wine.*

Fennel seeds: *Small seeds that taste like anise, they are used to flavor poaching liquids.*

Fish balls: *Usually made from a white fish, such as cod or ling cod, these are small white fish balls with a bouncy texture. They are usually served in soups.*

Fish lips: *Sold dehydrated, fish lips require prolonged cooking. After cooking, they have a soft gelatinous texture.*

Fish maw or bladder: *This is the large dehydrated flotation or swim bladder of a fish. After cooking, it has a spongy texture.*

Fish sauce: *A clear, light brown sauce made from salted fish, it is used to flavor food. Most fish sauces are not made in China, but in Southeast Asia.*

Five spices: *A brown powder used to flavor meat or fish, it consists of star anise, fennel seeds, cinnamon bark, cloves and Szechwan peppercorns.*

**Foo yung:** *Traditionally, this term means that egg whites are used in the dish.*

**Frog fat:** *These are kernels of fat said to be removed from the hibernating frog. They are believed to be health-enhancing.*

**Fun:** *These slippery rice noodles come in three shapes: thin or vermicelli-sized (called* mai fun*), round or spaghetti-sized (called* lai fun*) and flat (called* hor fun*). The flat noodles, when unsliced, are also used to make stuffed rice rolls at dim sum.*

**Fungi:** *There are two kinds: black and white. Black fungi, also called cloud's ears, are black and crunchy. White fungi, also called silver or snow ears, resemble large white flowers. Both kinds of fungi have to be soaked and cleaned before use. They have a crunchy texture.*

**Gai lan:** *This is a jade-green long-stemmed vegetable that vaguely resembles Western broccoli. It is crunchy and has a slight bitter taste.*

**Gain don choy (or Peking winter vegetables):** *These are yellowish preserved vegetables that have a pungent, salty taste.*

**Geoduck:** *Pronounced "gooey duck," this is a giant clam found on the west coast of North America. It has a firm, chewy texture.*

**Ginger:** *This spice is a light brown root with thin, dry skin. Aromatic and hot, ginger is peeled, then minced or shredded.*

**Gingko nuts:** *The fruit from the gingko tree is white, meaty and shaped like an olive. Gingko nuts are used in vegetarian cooking.*

**Gluten or gluten balls:** *These are round balls made from unrisen yeast-bread dough. The dough is washed to remove the flour so that only the stringy gluten is left. The gluten is cut into pieces and deep-fried. Gluten is high in protein and used mostly in vegetarian cooking. Its texture resembles that of meat.*

**Glutinous rice:** *A white, round-grained rice, different from the long-grain variety, it is sticky, sweet and rich. It is used to make Chinese tamales or desserts.*

**Glutinous rice noodles (or neen go):** *Glutinous rice flour and water are combined to make slabs of glutinous rice cake. The slabs are sliced, then soaked and sautéed or cooked in broth. Native to the Shanghai region,* neen go *have a delicious sticky texture.*

**Glutinous rice wine (sweet):** *Glutinous rice is combined with water and an alcohol-producing ingredient, then allowed to ferment. It turns sweet, then slightly sour. The resulting wine and the fermented rice are used to flavor savory and sweet dishes.*

**Glutinous rice wine (or far dew):** *This yellow rice wine is made in Soochow and is used to flavor savory dishes.*

**Golden needles:** *Also called tiger lily buds or gum jum, these are the thin brownish stems and buds of a special kind of lily. Used mostly in vegetarian cooking, they taste like mushrooms.*

**Green mung beans:** *When sprouted, these beans are the "bean sprouts" used in Chinese cooking. They are crunchy and have a light taste. Unsprouted, the green beans are cooked to a paste with sugar and water to make desserts.*

**Green soybeans:** *They come in dark fuzzy pods. The beans inside are light green and chewy. Prized particularly by the Shanghainese, they are usually braised and eaten at room temperature.*

**Gwai far:** *See* cassia flowers.

**Hakka:** *Displaced northerners who migrated to South China in the twelfth or thirteenth century. Hakka means "guest families." They are known for their delicate cuisine.*

**Hangchow (Or Hangzhou):** *The capital of Chekiang province, in East China. It is known for its physical beauty, particularly West Lake, after which many dishes are named, and for its Dragon Well tea.*

**Heen choy:** *This vegetable is an amaranth with green or purple leaves. The leaves are tender and taste like spinach. This is also called Chinese spinach.*

**Heung chung (or salty preserved vegetables):** *These vegetables are the color of mustard greens. They are salted, then chopped and used as a flavoring.*

**Hoi sin sauce:** *A reddish-brown bottled sauce with sweet anise flavor, it is used in cooking and as a dipping sauce.*

**Honan (or Henan):** *A province in northeastern China. Its name means south of the Yellow River.*

**Honeycomb tripe:** *This is a beige-yellow tripe with a honeycomb pattern on one side. It has a chewy texture and gamy taste.*

**Hopei (or Hopeh or Hebei):** *This is a province in northeastern China. The name means north of the Yellow River. Peking, the capital of China, is in this province.*

**Hot bean sauce:** *A spicy, coarse-grained dip made with crushed red chilies, oil and brown bean sauce, it is commonly used in Szechwan cooking.*

**Hot sauce:** *See* chili sauce.

**Hunan:** *A province in south central China known for its spicy cuisine, which is similar to Szechwan's.*

**Hwang River (or Huang or Yellow River):** *A major river in Northern China.*

**Jellyfish:** *Jellyfish is yellow and crunchy. It is sold packed in salt in sheets. After special preparation, it is shredded, tossed in salt and sesame oil and served as a salad.*

**Jinjiang (or Qinjiang):** *A city in Kiangsu province on the east coast, known for its dark rice wine vinegar.*

**Kaoliang:** *This is either sorghum, a grain, or the alcohol made from sorghum. See also* Mao Tai *alcohol.*

**Kiangsu (or Jiangsu):** *A province on the east coast of China.*

**Korfu:** *This is a dense gluten made from bread dough. It is sold in chunks and used in braised vegetarian dishes. It is heavier than gluten balls, which are also used in vegetarian dishes.*

**Kwei Chow (Guizhou):** *A province in Southern Central China.*

**Lah mein:** *These northern noodles are made by hand with flour and water. Boiled, then sautéed or served in broth, they have a soft bouncy texture.*

**Lemon grass:** *This Southeast Asian spice vaguely resembles a stiff stalk of green onion. It has a wonderful lemon scent.*

**Lemon leaves:** *The leaves from the lemon tree are jade-green and have a refreshing lemony flavor.*

**Lily buds (or gum jum):** *See* golden needles.

**Lily bulb petals:** *The petals from the bulb of the lily grow in garlic-like clusters. When broken up and skinned, the petals are white. They are used to make desserts.*

**Lo mein:** *This is a plate of thin won ton noodles that have been boiled, then tossed with a topping. A bowl of broth is served on the side.*

**Lotus leaf:** *The large dried leaf of the lotus flower is soaked, softened, then used to wrap or flavor food. It imparts a straw-like flavor to food.*

**Lotus seed paste:** *Lotus seeds are cooked in sugar water until mushy, then ground to a paste. The paste is used to sweeten desserts.*

**Lotus seeds:** *The olive-sized seeds of the lotus plant are used in desserts. Lotus seeds—*leen tze*—sounds the same in Chinese as "to have many sons." Chinese people use them in food for good luck.*

Lychee: *A succulent fruit grown in South China, it is round, twice as large as a grape and has a leathery red shell. To eat fresh lychees, remove shells, eat the white juicy meat and discard the stones. Lychees are also available in cans.*

Lye: *It is used in minute amounts in commercial Chinese food preparation, to clean or tenderize certain ingredients, such as omasun. Ingredients treated this way are usually thoroughly cleaned after the treatment.*

Mandarin fish: *This fish belongs to the carp family.*

Mandarin pancake: *This is a northern pancake, like a tortilla, made with flour and water. It is used to wrap fillings.*

Mango: *This sweet succulent yellow tropical fruit has a large stone.*

Mao Tai alcohol: *This extremely potent Chinese alcohol is distilled from kaoliang (sorghum).*

Melon seeds: *There are two kinds: small red melon seeds and large black melon seeds. Both are eaten as snacks, or shelled and used as stuffings.*

Molasses: *This thick dark syrup is used as a dip or in desserts.*

Monosodium glutamate (MSG): *A crystallized powder used to add flavor to food, it does intensify flavor, but can leave a chemical aftertaste in the mouth. Some people are allergic to MSG and suffer palpitations, headache, skin tingling and tightening, and thirstiness. The only antidote is to drink lots of water to flush the MSG out of the system. You can ask for food without it. Although most meat or seafood is already marinated with MSG, you can reduce the quantity by requesting that your food be sautéed without it.*

Mui choy: *A brown semidried preserved vegetable, sold in bunches or bags, it has a pungent, salty taste.*

Mung bean sprouts: *See* Green mung beans.

Mustard green: *This pale-green Chinese vegetable with a slightly bitter taste is also called* gai choy.

Omasun: *Sometimes called tripe in Chinese restaurants, this is the third manyplies stomach of the cow.*

Oriental eggplants: *These eggplants are longer, narrower and more delicate than Western eggplants. The skin is usually left on during cooking.*

Oyster sauce: *A thick brown sauce made from oyster extractives used to season food. It is also called oyster-flavored sauce. It has little oyster flavor and is a delicious seasoning.*

Peanut oil: *This oil is extracted from peanuts and is commonly used in Chinese cooking and prized for its peanut aroma.*

Pei pa: *A Chinese mandolin.*

Peking (or Beijing): *The capital of China, situated in northern China.*

Peking winter vegetables: *See* gain don choy.

Peppery salt: *This dip is made of roasted salt and ground pepper.*

Pickled mustard green: *Mustard green is pickled in salt and vinegar. With a tart taste and crunchy texture, it is eaten as a pickle and used in sautéed dishes.*

Pickled pink ginger: *Young ginger, which is pink, is pickled in sugar and vinegar. It is tender and crunchy.*

Pig's blood: *Blood is drained from the pig. The blood is then salted, steamed and cut into cubes. It is poached or added to soups.*

Pork rind: *These are dehydrated pieces of fried pork skin. Soaked, softened and added to braised dishes, they are spongy.*

Preserved bean curd: *Fermented bean curd is pickled in salt, wine and chili powder. It has a taste and texture similar to blue cheese. Bottled commercially, it is eaten as a side dish or used to flavor meat and vegetable dishes.*

Preserved black duck egg: *Erroneously called hundred-year-old egg, this is a duck egg that has been preserved in a brine for several weeks. The egg becomes black in color and has the pungency and texture of blue cheese. To eat, dip in soy sauce. In recent years, there has been a controversy surrounding the chemical composition of the brine, which may not be safe for human consumption.*

Preserved kohlrabi: *See* Szechwan kohlrabi.

Pressed bean curd: *Bean curd is wrapped and weighed down so that most of the moisture is squeezed out. This type of bean curd is chewy and used in sautéed dishes. There are two kinds of pressed bean curd: white pressed bean curd and five-spices brown pressed bean curd.*

Quail: *This game bird is about half the size of a pigeon.*

Quail egg: *About one-quarter the size of a chicken egg, the quail egg has a speckled shell. It tastes like a chicken egg.*

Red bean paste: *Red mung beans are cooked in sugar water, then mashed. They are then ground to a fine paste and used in desserts.*

Red chili oil: *This red spicy oil is made by combining hot oil with chili powder.*

Red-colored rice: *This is rice that is bright-red in color and used as a food coloring in desserts and meat dishes.*

Red mung beans: *These small red beans are used mostly in desserts.*

Red preserved bean curd: *Bean curd fermented in salt, sugar, alcohol and red coloring, it is sweet and crumbly. It is bottled commercially and used to flavor meat dishes.*

Rice crusts: *Pieces of cooked hardened crusts from the bottom of a pot of rice are deep-fried and served with a topping in Peking and Szechwan cuisine.*

Rice flour: *A fine white flour made of rice.*

Rice noodles: *See* fun.

Rock sugar: *Large chunks of yellow crystallized unrefined sugar are used in meat dishes and desserts.*

Salted bamboo shoots: *The long tender shoots of bamboo trees are dried and salted. The shoots are washed, shredded and sautéed. They are salty, chewy and pungent.*

Salted fish: *Fish is salted and hang-dried. Steamed in small pieces, it is extremely salty and has a crumbly texture and a very powerful aroma. In recent years, scientists have gathered evidence that suggests this fish is carcinogenic.*

Salty duck egg: *A duck egg is salted and preserved in charcoal dust. To prepare, the dust is removed and the egg is washed, then hard-boiled.*

Sar char sauce: *This spicy sauce is used by Chiu Chow cooks. It is made of Chinese and Southeast Asian spices and ingredients, and has a pleasant piquant taste.*

Satay: *This is a kabob of Southeast Asian origin.*

Satay sauce: *See* sar char sauce. *Not to be confused with the Southeast Asian peanut sauce.*

Sea cucumber (or beche-de-mer): *A black or gray dried sea slug, it is prized for its gelatinous texture after cooking.*

Seasoned liquid: *Used to poach meats and fish, this liquid usually contains salt, pepper, soy sauce, fennel seeds, star anise, cinnamon bark, cloves and licorice root.*

Seaweed (or nori): *These purplish-black sheets of processed seaweed with a briny taste can be eaten raw or added to soups.*

Sesame oil: *Oil extracted from sesame seeds, it is used mostly as a flavoring and not for frying.*

**Sesame-seed paste:** *This is a ground-up sesame seed paste with the consistency of peanut butter.*

**Sesame seeds:** *Tiny white seeds with an aromatic flavor, they are used in savory and sweet dishes.*

**Shanghai:** *A seaport on the east coast of China.*

**Shanghai bean-curd skin:** *Called bah yeep, these are soft white paper-thin sheets of bean curd. The Shanghainese shred the sheets and sauté them or use them to make stuffed rolls.*

**Shanghai bok choy:** *Resembling bok choy in taste and appearance, this vegetable has light green stems and leaves.*

**Shansi (or Shanxi):** *A province in north China.*

**Shantou:** *See Chiu Chow.*

**Shantung (or Shandong):** *A maritime province in northeastern China.*

**Shaobing:** *A northern rectangular pocket bread topped with sesame seeds, it is stuffed like pita bread.*

**Shaoshing (or Shaoxing):** *A city in the eastern province of Chekiang.*

**Shaoshing wine:** *Glutinous rice wine made in Shaoshing, it is also called yellow wine.*

**Shark's fins:** *These dehydrated fins of the shark are expensive and need elaborate preparation. After cooking, they have a soft, gelatinous texture and are believed to be nutritious.*

**Shensi (or Shenxi or Shaaxi):** *A province in north central China, with Xian as its capital.*

**Shepherd's purse:** *This watercress-like vegetable is eaten by the Shanghainese.*

**Shrimp chips:** *These are deep-fried chips made from shrimp powder and rice flour. They taste like potato chips.*

**Shrimp eggs:** *These are tiny dried eggs of the shrimp. They are salty and fishy-tasting.*

**Shrimp roe:** *Called shrimp brains by the Chinese, this is the orange roe of the shrimp, extracted from shrimp heads.*

**Silkie:** *A small chicken with white feathers and black meat and bones, it is prized for its nutritional value.*

Silver sprouts: *These are green mung bean sprouts with the heads and roots removed.*

Siu choy: *See* Chinese cabbage.

Snow cabbage: *This salted Shanghainese preserved vegetable is sold in bunches or in cans. It is crunchy and salty and faded green.*

Snow pea pods and shoots: *Crunchy and sweet, the entire pod of the snow pea is edible. The shoots or young leaves are usually sautéed. They are tender and have a delicious flavor, like spinach.*

Soochow (or Suzhou): *A city in Kiangsu province on the east coast of China.*

Sour plums: *These pickled small plums are sold in jars. They are slightly red and very sour.*

Soybean sprouts: *Sprouted from soybeans, these are more chewy than the more popular green mung bean sprouts. Soybean sprouts have a yellow nutty head and require a long braising time.*

Soy sauce: *There are two kinds: light and dark. Light soy sauce is light brown and salty. Dark soy sauce is dark brown, thicker and sweeter.*

Soybean milk: *White milk is extracted from ground soybeans. It is heated and made into sweet or savory breakfast soups.*

Star anise: *This is an eight-point star the size of a quarter. This brown spice has a strong licorice flavor.*

Steamed rice: *Commonly served as a staple with Chinese food, this is rice boiled in water until most of the moisture has evaporated. It is then cooked, covered, over low heat for twenty minutes.*

Stem lettuce: *This plant has a long stem with a few leaves at the top. In Shanghainese cooking, the stem is peeled, salted and served as a salad; the leaves are not eaten.*

Stinky bean curd: *This bean curd is fermented in snow-cabbage juice. It is steamed or deep-fried. It tastes like blue cheese.*

Straw mushrooms: *These are oval-shaped crunchy mushrooms with a marbled brown pattern.*

Sugar cane juice: *The sweet juice extracted from crushed sugar cane.*

Swatow: *See* Chiu Chow.

Sweet bean sauce: *A smooth reddish-brown paste used in Szechwan cooking, it is similar to* hoi sin *sauce.*

Sweet dark vinegar: *This dark brown thick vinegar is sold in jars. It has a sweet, tangy flavor and is used to make Cantonese pork and pig's feet stew.*

## GLOSSARY

Szechwan (or Sichuan) *An interior province in southwestern China.*

Szechwan kohlrabi: *Crunchy kohlrabi is preserved in salt and chili powder. It is salty and has a crunchy texture.*

Szechwan peppercorn: *Also called fagara or red peppercorn, this tiny peppercorn has a distinct and heady aroma. It is indigenous to Szechwan.*

Szechwan peppercorn oil: *A green oil flavored with Szechwan peppercorns, it is often used as a flavoring.*

Tamale: *The word is often used for a Mexican dish made of meat stuffed in a corn dough, wrapped in corn husks and steamed. Non-Mexican dishes, made similarly, are also called tamales. Chinese tamales are served at dim sum or as desserts.*

Tarp qwar choy: *This flat leafy bok choy has dark green leaves and white stems.*

Taro root: *A fuzzy brown oval root vegetable the size of a small potato, it has a speckled beige-brown meat, which turns gray when cooked. It tastes like sweet potatoes.*

Teppan (or Tappan): *Japanese in origin, this is a cast-iron oval serving plate. It is heated, and the food served on it sizzles.*

Tientsin bean sheets: *Transparent slippery noodle sheets are made from green mung beans. They are sold fresh or dehydrated. They are served in salads and in braised dishes.*

Tientsin cabbage: *See* Chinese cabbage.

Toi tew: *Dried seaweed which has been processed into long thin flakes. They have a rich briny taste.*

Tripe: *See* honeycomb tripe.

True water chestnut: *This small black nut has two little horns. The white meat inside is extracted and used in cooking.*

Tsingtao (or Ching Tau or Qingdao): *A peninsula in Shantung province in north China, renowned for its prawns and for Tsingtao beer.*

Udon: *This thick Japanese noodle is made of flour and water.*

Vinegar: *In cooking, the Chinese use white rice vinegar or dark wine vinegar from Jinjiang. Very infrequently they use a sweet dark vinegar.*

Water chestnut: *This crunchy round root vegetable with a purplish-black skin is about the size of a chestnut. When fresh, the white crunchy meat has a milky flavor. Canned water chestnuts have little flavor.*

Water-chestnut flour: *This is flour made from water chestnuts which is used as a thickening agent.*

Watercress: *A climbing plant with small tender leaves, it has a delicate herbal taste and is most often cooked in soups.*

Wheat starch: *Flour with the gluten removed, it makes a very delicate and translucent dough used for dumpling skins for many savory dim sum snacks.*

White bait: *This white-colored fish, smaller than an anchovy, has a soft mushy meat.*

White Fungus: *See* fungi.

Wine residue juice (or joh): *This is a brown semi-dried residue left over from making glutinous rice wine. It has a fragrant alcohol taste and is used to flavor many Peking and Shanghai dishes.*

Winter melon: *This is a squash the size of a watermelon with jade-green skin and white meat. The meat is used in soup. It has a soft, delicate texture.*

Won ton noodles: *These are Cantonese yellow noodles usually served in fast-food won ton houses. There are two kinds: thin and flat. The thin version, also called silver thread noodles, are firm and chewy and a definite favorite among the Cantonese. The flat noodles are softer and less chewy.*

Won ton skins: *There are two kinds: white and yellow. The white kind, made of flour and water, is used to make Shanghai won tons. The yellow kind, made of high-gluten flour, is firmer and used to make Cantonese won tons and some dim sum dumplings.*

Won tons: *Folded dumplings resembling ravioli, they are usually stuffed with minced pork and Chinese vegetables. Won tons are served all over China, but each region makes them a little differently.*

Wor mein: *This is a Cantonese noodle dish. A large soup bowl of thin egg noodles in broth is served with a topping. This dish feeds at least four to six people.*

Yangtze River (or Chang Jiang): *A major waterway in China flowing from the Tibetan plateau through central China to the east coast.*

Yellow bean powder: *Ground yellow bean powder used to dust desserts.*

Yellow chives: *See* chives.

Yellow Croaker: *This long yellow salt-water fish has a firm, sweet-tasting meat.*

Yellow mustard: *A pungent spicy mustard dip made from yellow mustard powder, it tastes similar to Western hot mustard.*

Yunnan: *A remote province in southwestern China known for its beautiful climate. Literally translated, the name means "south of the clouds."*

Yunnan ham: *Ham made in Yunnan is considered to be the best in China. It is dry-cured, salty and chewy.*

Yunnan Pot: *This is a red clay pot with an air funnel in the middle. Food and liquid are put in the pot, covered and steamed.*

# ABOUT THE AUTHORS

A psychologist and food writer, Ginger Chang wrote THE GUIDE TO VANCOUVER'S CHINESE RESTAURANTS (1985), and has appeared on numerous radio and TV talk shows in Canada and the U.S. As well, she is a contributor to WESTERN LIVING Magazine and BON APPETIT. Fluent in Cantonese, Shanghainese and Mandarin, Ginger currently lives in Hong Kong, her birthplace, where she writes and does research on Chinese food.

Ginger's husband, Stephen Nathanson, is a lecturer in law from British Columbia. At present, he is teaching at the University of Hong Kong.